THE GREAT ESTATES

THE GREAT ESTATES

GREENWICH, CONNECTICUT

1880-1930

by

The
Junior League
of Greenwich

Published for

THE JUNIOR LEAGUE OF GREENWICH, CONNECTICUT, INC.

---

by

PHOENIX PUBLISHING

Canaan, New Hampshire

The Great Estates, Greenwich, Connecticut, 1880/1930.

  Bibliography: p. 201
  Includes Index.
  1. Dwellings—Connecticut—Greenwich. 2. Greenwich
(Conn.)—Biography. 3. Architecture, Domestic—
Connecticut—Greenwich. 4. Greenwich (Conn.)—Buildings,
structures, etc. 5. Greenwich (Conn.)—Social life and
customs. 6. Upper classes—Connecticut—Greenwich—
History. I. Junior League of Greenwich, Connecticut.
F104.G74   1986   974.6'9   86-12820
ISBN 0-914659-19-7

Printed in the United States of America

In memory of
Alan Burnham,
whose love of architecture
and love of Greenwich
inspired this project.

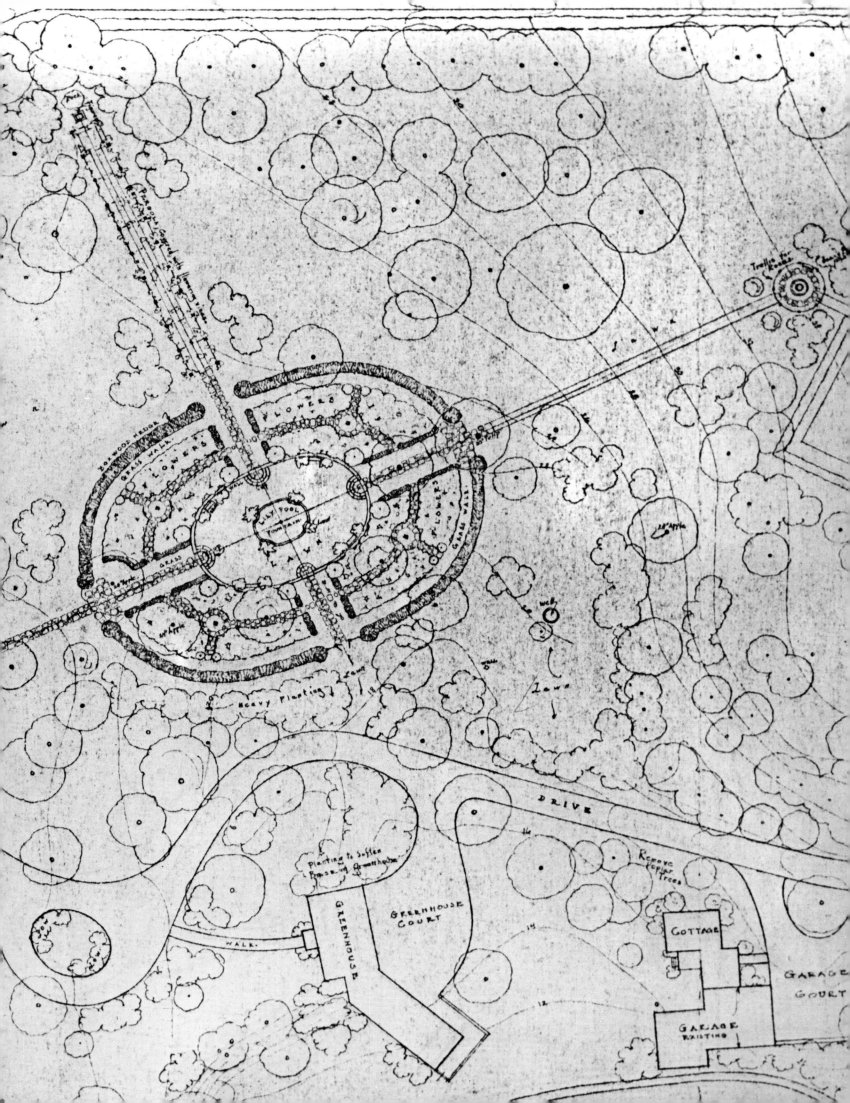

CONTENTS

THE GREAT ESTATES
Junior League Project Staff

Project Chairmen

Kathleen D. Martin 1984-86   Davidde E. Strackbein 1982-84
Diane W. Fox 1981-83

Managing Editor
Kathleen D. Martin

Editor
Regina K. Monteith

Writers

Susan D. Elia

Renee F. Seblatnigg

Val P. Storms

Contributing Writers

Virginia G. Monroe

Kathy H. Richards

Chief Researchers

Nancy Connors
Virginia W. Keller
Kathleen D. Martin
Renee F. Seblatnigg
Mary L. Stowell

Susan D. Elia
Birgitta Longnecker
Kathy H. Richards
Val P. Storms
Davidde E. Strackbein

Researchers

Sara Ann Clark
Marty Cronk
Beatrice Crumbine
Chantal A. Curtis
Dee Herckner
Toni Jackson
Deborah Jones
Deborah Lipner

Mary Huyck
Barbara H. MacDonald
Lynn B. McNulty
Cynthia Petrow
Mollie Rhodes
Linda Ritch
Stacy Roe
Karon Wille

Transcribers

Diana Grunow

Ursula Harvey

Betty N. Street

FOREWORD

THIS BOOK depicts what I would like to call "The Flowering of Greenwich," the changing of a farming community into a quiet genteel town, interested in community improvement and appreciation for its historical past. The period 1880-1930, perhaps the zenith in Greenwich's nearly 350-year history, was the age when the word Greenwich became a synonym for "millionaire."

Greenwich was founded by a few pioneer families from England. With patience and much hard labor they cleared forests and built stone walls to make way for tillable fields and open pastures. Crude dwellings were erected and orchards set out. New families came and more land was cleared until the town encompassed fifty square miles made up of little villages, each with its church, school, general store and post office.

By the late nineteenth century the center of Greenwich was almost entirely residential with wide, unpaved streets shaded by towering elms. Business was confined pretty much to the area of Sherwood Place and on the southwest corner of Putnam and Greenwich avenues. The Mansion House, later the Lenox House, a country inn from the stage coach era, occupied the southeast corner. There were three churches: Christ Church, the Second Congregational Church and the First Methodist Church, all on the same sites they are today. Greenwich Avenue, a mere lane called "the walk to Pipen Point," cut through the farm lands of Merwin and Smith Mead.

This was the picture that met the eyes of those first families of New York business tycoons who came to Greenwich for the summer. Summer visitors were drawn to the beautiful views of the sparkling Sound and interesting drives along the shore with its many little coves, inlets and sandy beaches. They enjoyed drives into the "back country" to explore the quaint villages such as Round Hill and Stanwich. What views from those higher elevations were to be had! No wonder these new people were enchanted with Greenwich. Perhaps it took them back to the days of their youth, when they had been born and raised in rural communities before "making it big" in the world of finance.

At first the "summer people" boarded or perhaps took farmhouses for the season. Gradually summer hotels, most of them really over-grown farmhouses, were established.

By 1880 some of the well-to-do had purchased property and built summer "cottages." These "cottages" marked the beginning of the "Great Estate" era. Their owners gave much to their adopted town: libraries, schools, parks, beaches, and fine new buildings for the established churches. They repaired old roads and laid out new ones. They organized golf clubs, yacht clubs, riding and hunt clubs.

Gone now are the days when one knew everyone in town. Gone are the days of housemen and liveried coachmen and chauffeurs. Gone are the days when the stores and markets of Greenwich were individually owned and when the proprietors took pride in knowing each of their customers well.

All of this passed and that is why we shall be forever grateful to the Junior League of Greenwich for publishing this work so that future generations may learn something of the age of "Greenwich's Great Estates." It will be a lasting account of a Greenwich that was.

William Finch, Jr.
Town Historian

Greenwich, Connecticut
January 2, 1986

PREFACE

THE TRANSFORMATION of Greenwich from a farming community to a genteel town took place over a fifty-year period, beginning about 1880 and ending around 1930. This change generated a unique architectural legacy which is being eroded by time and by continuing development. In an attempt to record and thus to preserve this legacy, the Junior League of Greenwich, Connecticut, Inc., upon the recommendation of its Historical Preservation Study Group, initiated a three-year Great Estates Survey project in 1981. The original purpose of the project was to train a volunteer corps of Junior League members to identify and research the important estates of Greenwich in order to produce a booklet which would provide Greenwich with an architectural and historical record of the great estate building era of 1880 to 1930. The Junior League wanted to complete this project before the continuing loss of primary oral history sources, period photographs, and architectural plans, together with further subdivision of the estates, effaced this important segment of Greenwich history.

The late Alan Burnham, noted architectural historian and preservationist and former executive director of New York City's Landmarks Preservation Commission, proposed in a lecture at Yale University that many of Greenwich's estates needed to be formally recognized as significant examples of American architecture. Being a Greenwich resident, he was enthusiastic about the survey and supplied the project with a preliminary list of estates to be considered for inclusion.

During the initial year of the project, under the chairmanship of Diane Fox, members researched the estates on this list and identified additional properties for possible inclusion. Members received training in historical research techniques from several community advisors. Joseph Zeranski, a Greenwich researcher, trained project members in researching deeds filed in the town hall records; Barbara Bloch, founder and former chairman of the Friends of Greenwich Library Oral History Project, trained members in techniques for compiling and recording oral history; William E. Finch, town historian and past president of the Greenwich Historical Society, furnished substantial historical background to the project; Marion Nicholson and Louise Gudalis, historical librarians at the Greenwich Library, assisted members in using the library's local history materials.

The principal issue confronted by members of the project at the end of the first year was the definition of a "Great Estate." Following consultation with the community advisors listed above, the project members defined a great estate as a Greenwich property which included an important structure built between 1880 and 1930, as well as reflecting significant architectural merit, and possessing extensive grounds.

Following adoption of this definition members of the project, under the chairmanship of Davidde Strackbein, identified each property which satisfied these criteria on the 1930 Grand List of taxable property in Greenwich. The resulting list of architecturally important structures was then compared with Mr. Burnham's preliminary list and a third list developed comprising estates common to both. Each of these properties was then reviewed with William Finch from the standpoint of historical importance.

Following these steps, members prepared a final list of forty-five representative estates. Each property then became the subject of extensive deed and historical research. During this period, Junior League Sustainers Mary Kay Stowell, Ginny Keller, and Val Storms provided advice and guidance. Guest speakers and community members augmented the project's research efforts throughout the year.

During the third year of the project, research continued while preparation of the initial draft of the text began under the direction of the editor, Regina Monteith. Several professional architectural photographers were interviewed, and Gil Amiaga, noted New York architectural photographer, was chosen to undertake the color photography of selected estates. Communication with five Junior Leagues in the United States which had successfully completed historical publications provided members of the project with an opportunity to compare their respective approaches to methodology and publication. At this point it was agreed that the booklet originally contemplated would hardly do the project justice and a more ambitious publication would be required.

The fourth and fifth years of the project were completed under the chairmanship of Kathleen D. Martin. During this period research was completed and the raw data was translated into text. Extensive interviews were held with families associated with the estates. Over five hundred photographs, both period and recent, were acquired. The Greenwich Library Oral History Project and local realtors provided photos from their files, and concerned residents of Greenwich both past and present lent their family albums. Gil Amiaga completed the color photography of selected estates. Additional photography was done by well-known Greenwich photographers, William Hubbell and Christopher Semmes. Charles Bernhard reproduced the majority of the period photographs.

Next a publisher was required to help organize the mass of information which had been compiled. Pyke Johnson, Herbert Schutz, and Warren Cassell, all local residents in the publishing business, helped direct us and book designer Martha Vida lent her expert advice. Publishers were contacted and in November 1985 the League retained Phoenix Publishing to design, edit, and publish the book. The result will provide not only a permanent architectural record of the great estates of Greenwich but also a documented history of a significant portion of the town over a period of five decades.

At this writing, some five years after the inception of the project, the booklet originally envisioned is reaching the final stages of becoming *The Great Estates: Greenwich, Connecticut, 1880-1930*; a 224 page casebound volume of considerable distinction. It represents the culmination of a volunteer effort which included hundreds of hours of research; over three hundred interviews with people from all over the United States; the acquisition of over five hundred photographs; and hundreds of hours of writing and editing.

Members of the project and the Junior League of Greenwich are particularly grateful to the owners of the great estates, both past and present, who contributed information, photographs, and plans to the project, and who shared their memories with researchers and writers. Many other people, too numerous to name, contributed to the project. Without their cooperation and interest, this work could never have been successfully completed.

The Great Estates exemplifies the Junior League's commitment to volunteerism and to service in the Town of Greenwich. The net proceeds of the book will support the community projects of the Junior League of Greenwich, and the original research will be donated to the archives of the Greenwich Historical Society.

Kathleen D. Martin
Davidde E. Strackbein
Diane Fox

Greenwich, Connecticut
February 3, 1986

THE GREAT ESTATES

INTRODUCTION

A Half Century in Perspective

ITHIN THE 350-year history of Greenwich, the age of the Great Estates was remarkably brief, beginning near the end of the nineteenth century and continuing through three decades of the twentieth. But the changes which took place in that span altered the quiet farm town forever, and they are evident today.

With the coming of regular railroad service to the town, New Yorkers discovered coastal Greenwich as a summer resort, and by the 1870s boarding houses and cottages flourished near the shore. These New Yorkers, drawn from many parts of the country, were a varied lot; and among them were new tycoons who were amassing fortunes in areas such as railroads, oil, utilities, and finance and spending with a style that reflected confidence in America's future and in themselves. With their personal fortunes largely untaxed, their sophistication heightened by extensive travel through Europe, the national economy robust, and the mood of the nation optimistic, many of these businessmen began to establish country estates as logical extensions of their prosperity. Some, not satisfied with providing mere comfort, built homes which in time became monuments to their wealth and power. Others, however, constructed simple and informally furnished houses. Whether they were designed as summer homes or as year-round residences, these places became important centers of their family life.

Here in the countryside, far from the restraining scale of the city, the owners exercised great artistic freedom in planning their estates. Although it was a time of architectural innovation in the United States, they sought established architects known for their use of historical precedents in the buildings they designed. The resulting houses were constructed primarily of stone and masonry, with a few in the shingle style. Medieval castles, Italian villas, French châteaus and English manor houses became dominant as the estate builders searched for designs that reflected their tastes and interests. The architects planned the main houses and, in many cases, stables and other outbuildings as well. Occasionally they supervised interior decoration and landscape planning. Architectural elements were adopted but usually adapted to meet modern American needs such as central heating, indoor plumbing, elevators, the ubiquitous pipe organs and, during Prohibition, hidden wine cellars. Spacious grounds frequently included large greenhouse complexes, swimming pools, tennis courts, bowling greens, and shooting ranges, as well as fine stables. Sizable household and grounds staffs were required to maintain these properties, and frequently European superintendents, butlers, and governesses were hired abroad and brought to Greenwich.

World War I was only a temporary intrusion into the way of life on these estates. In the twenties new estates rose, even as a few of the older properties were divided and their houses razed.

1

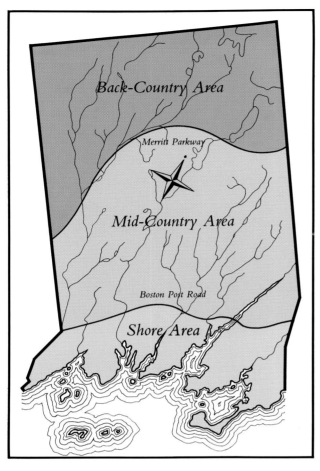

Map of Greenwich showing boundaries of the three estate areas.

But time was running out on this golden age. The new income tax diluted personal wealth, and the 1929 stock market crash destroyed many fortunes. The optimism and boldness of an earlier generation faded into the reality of the Great Depression, and — although few noted it — the era of great estate building was over. Still, the houses that had been built in prosperity were generally maintained until World War II. At that time drastic staffing shortages caused many owners to sell their houses or to close them for the duration. But the war's end did not bring a return to the old way of life. Without the ready supply of trained personnel the old scale of living became obsolete. In the growing suburban real estate market, some families sold parcels of land for residential developments. Others, unable to find buyers for the now too-large houses, saw their mansions destroyed so that the land could be divided. Considering the drastic changes which Greenwich underwent in the postwar decades, it is surprising that 33 of the 46 houses discussed in this volume still stand, and that most remain as residences. A precious few of them have their acreage intact.

This book recalls the extraordinary era when these estates were being built. It is divided into three parts, reflecting the geographic sections of Greenwich: the shore area nearest Long Island Sound; mid country, the band lying east to west above the Post Road; and the back country, the northernmost tier. The heading of each estate contains the name of the owner regarded as its founder, as well as that of the architect, when known. The dates refer to design or construction and where appropriate, significant renovations.

I

THE SHORE ESTATES

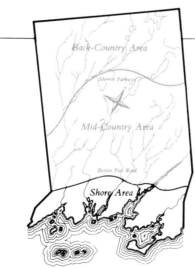

Indian Harbor as it looks today. William Hubbell photo.

Principal Owner: E. C. Benedict
Architect: Carrère and Hastings
Construction Date: 1895

T MIGHT BE SAID that the history of Indian Harbor began with the birth of Elias Cornelius Benedict (1834-1920). The son of a Presbyterian minister, he was born in Somers, New York. Through his extraordinary energy, Benedict rose from genteel poverty to enormous wealth. He joined the New York Stock Exchange when he was twenty-nine and created his own brokerage firm, from which he did not retire until he was eighty-three. During his long lifetime, E. C. Benedict built a great fortune, a great mansion, and the Benedict Building of Greenwich Hospital. He sailed more than 450,000 miles on his own yachts from the coast of Maine to the heart of the Amazon River. He was a member of six yacht clubs, including Seawanhaka Corinthian, where in 1906 he succeeded William Vanderbilt as commodore.

Benedict was mentioned as a candidate for governor of Connecticut in 1888, and again a few years later, but declined the honor. He became the companion and confidant of many of the great men of his day. His friendship with Grover Cleveland occasionally caused discomfort when ambitious men tried to use his influence for political appointments. Benedict solved such problems by going to sea. "There is a right way and a wrong way to go about seeking public office," he said. "And the right way is not through me." It was aboard his two-hundred-foot steam yacht, the *Oneida*, moored in Greenwich Harbor, that the secret operation to remove the malignancy on President Cleveland's jaw took place. E. C. Benedict knew the vagaries of the financial world too well to risk a panic by letting the public know about the president's illness.

What remains today as Commodore Benedict's most impressive legacy is his palatial dwelling at Indian Harbor. Built on a rocky peninsula just east of Greenwich Harbor, this Italian Renaissance villa is a landmark for sailors and the gem of the Greenwich shoreline. In 1895 Benedict commissioned the New York firm of Carrère and Hastings to design his estate on the promontory that had once held Boss Tweed's infamous "Americus Club." Following Tweed's demise, the huge Indian Harbor Hotel occupied the site, but Benedict had the hotel torn down. Alan Burnham, the late architect and historian, noted that this was the unusual case of a large public building being removed for a private residence.

Combined with the singular beauty of the site, the ingenuous blend of nature and architecture makes Indian Harbor unique. Surrounded by water on all but the north side, the three-story mansion is bulwarked by seawalls and vine-covered terraces. The whitewashed stucco walls rise gracefully from their rugged base to be capped by a terra-cotta tiled roof. Wisteria twists around a pergola that drops away in four measured steps from the west face of the building, following the easy slope of the land and connecting with a smaller house, carrying the eye back to the mainland.

The interior of the villa originally contained nearly thirty spacious rooms, each with exceptional views. To the north was the elegant entrance through the park; to the west, the harbor; and on the south and east, the endless expanse of Long Island Sound. When a later owner remodeled the residence and removed the entire upper story, little impact was made on the overall magnificence. For it has never been the mansion alone that ranked Indian Harbor as one of the greatest of American country estates. It was Carrère and Hastings's custom to design the landscaping and the outbuildings as part of their work, and it is their concept of Indian Harbor as a whole that is remarkable. Benedict's eighty acres included several cottages, a farm, an icehouse, carpenter's and painter's shops, a gashouse with a floating dock, a coalhouse, and a water tower with a windmill. Yet none of these buildings was evident as one approached from the charming entrance lodge.

The great staircase leading to the porte-cochere.

Looking aft aboard the "Oneida."

View from the southwest before remodeling.

The macadam drive wound away from the granite lodge through the woods to a second gate. This gate was of wrought iron, opening from two stone pavilions inset with oval windows. From here a straight avenue of maples led to the graveled entrance court and regal porte-cochere. The oval drive was surrounded by rhododendrons and filled with flower gardens. The centerpiece of the formal garden was the complex of conservatories which included two towering palm houses and working greenhouses. Beds of perennials outlined by a boxwood hedge rose above the terraces in the southwest angle of the house, and an imposing sundial marked the end of the southern axis. The terrace, which ran 150 feet along the south wall, ended in broad steps leading to a bathing beach at the southwest and to a landing dock on the southeast.

Beyond the dock on the eastern shore was the capacious boathouse — once the dining room of the old club. Behind was the tennis court and the stables with their red-roofed clock tower. Farther on were the kitchen gardens, the greenhouse, and the garage. A small lake reclaimed from tidal flats was stocked with smallmouth black bass in the Commodore's day. About three full acres here were created from marshland and so cleverly planted they seemed to have been there always. It was typical of Carrère and Hastings's genius to choose only trees and shrubs that would complement the existing plants and also survive the harsh coastal climate. No rare species were introduced, and only the hardiest evergreens were used to conceal the juncture of rock and masonry. Exotic flowers — roses, carnations, palms — bloomed in conservatories.

Extravagant entertainments were frequent at Indian Harbor, but the most splendid was the wedding in May 1900 of the second of the Commodore's three daughters, Helen, to Thomas Hastings, a member of the firm that designed the estate. More than half of the 800 guests were met at a special train from Grand Central Station by 145 carriages. Nearly two hours passed before the last carriage reached Indian Harbor from the Second Congregational Church for the reception. Among those who feasted on imported caviars and champagne were former president Cleveland, his wife and members of his cabinet, Mr. and Mrs. Andrew Carnegie, Charles Dana Gibson, Stanford White, and Charles F. McKim.

Guest house, pergola, and main house from the harbor before remodeling.

Essentially the same view after remodeling.

Twenty years later, the Commodore's funeral was held in equal if more solemn state. The casket was hidden from view at the far end of the drawing room by blankets of roses and masses of floral tributes. Thirty members of the New York City Mendelssohn Club sang the anthems, and six of the then forty employees on the estate—those who had been longest in the Commodore's service—acted as pallbearers. Among the mourners were R. A. C. Smith whose Greenwich home, Miralta, is also one of the great estates.

E. C. Benedict enjoyed his life at Indian Harbor with appropriate enthusiasm. A true gentleman, an excellent businessman and sportsman, he was known fondly as the greatest of old salts, an "ancient mariner," whose favorite drink was said to be salt spray served with a West Indian hurricane. During the last year of his life—which was also the occasion of his first illness—he had his bed carried to the great sea porch on the south veranda of his villa where he watched the ships sail up and down the Sound. No doubt he wished them the wind at their sterns.

Quarry Farm

The main house and broad lawns of Quarry Farm. Gil Amiaga photo.

Principal Owners: Henry Walker and Nancy Reynolds Bagley
Original Architect (1929): Frank Forster
Architect for Renovations (1933): Parsons and Wait

T IS DIFFICULT to know what shape the land that is Quarry Farm took at the time of its earliest settlement. Since the seventeenth century the waterfront site has been valued for its bluestone outcropping, and years of quarry operations have pushed the cliff face back from the beach to where it now rises to a height of nearly one hundred feet.

Deed research for the property known as Quarry Farm shows that since the seventeenth century the land has been held by a succession of owners whose names are familiar in Greenwich history — Ferris, Lyon, Bush, Grigg — and that one of these owners built a house there, on the line that separated Byram from Horseneck, as central Greenwich was known, probably in the 1680s. Some form of stonework must have been undertaken since before 1760 when the will of Justus Bush listed a "stone drill" among the bequests. It was the enterprise of the Voorhis family which is best remembered, however.

From the time Peter Voorhis purchased property in 1852 until early in the twentieth century, the Voorhis Quarry was a thriving operation. Stone blasted from the face of the cliff was cut and sledded to the quarry's dock on Byram Cove, where it was loaded for shipment on one of Voorhis's large sailing schooners. On the quarry property there was a seventeenth-century house called Quarry Cottage, a countinghouse or office, and a small, heavy-doored stone dynamite house for storing blasting materials.

Tradition tells us that stone for the Brooklyn Bridge footings and the Statue of Liberty's pedestal are from this or the Ritch Quarry nearby (where Byram Park is now), and there is no doubt that countless New York buildings of that era owe their strength to Greenwich bluestone. With the growing importance of concrete as a building material, this business ceased to be lucrative, and the quarry closed. Partially dressed stones lay where they had fallen, and the wooden schooners were left at their moorings to rot and even-

tually sink. In 1918 nine acres were sold to artist and architect Paul Chalfin, who lived in the antique Quarry Cottage and used the countinghouse for a studio. During his ownership several motion pictures were shot on location, and moviegoers across the country saw the quarry's cliffs as background for Pearl White's *The Perils of Pauline* and other films. Since the scooped-out site seemed an ideal shape for an amphitheater, Chalfin tried to use it for dramatic and musical productions, but the acoustics were never satisfactory. The land, which was bordered on the east by Tom's Brook, was finally left to grow wild.

But in the 1930s Greenwich history changed for the better with the arrival of Mrs. Nancy Susan Reynolds (1910-1985), heiress to the R. J. Reynolds Tobacco Company fortune. In the fifty-one years she lived in the town she was benefactress to many civic causes, including the library's oral history project. Then the wife of Henry Walker Bagley, she had been a student at Rosemary Hall and was familiar with Greenwich. The house the Bagleys purchased had been built no more than three years earlier for Frederic E. Schluter, a New York bond broker with Minsch, Monell, and Company, and his wife on land purchased from the Belle Haven Land Company and Greenwich attorney Wilbur Wright. The French Normandy-style château had been designed by Frank Forster, an architect recognized for excellence in the field of domestic architecture. It sat on the western edge of Belle Haven on a hillside that sloped down to Tom's Brook and the old quarry. A six-foot-high stone wall enclosed the property's five acres, but steep slate roofs and tall brick chimneys of the house could be seen beyond it.

Although the stone residence was still quite new and in excellent condition when the Bagleys arrived, they remodeled it extensively. Rather than return to the original designer, they engaged Charles R. Wait of the Boston architectural firm of Parsons and Wait. Most dramatically, a spiral staircase was installed which

The main house and gardens in 1940.

One of Quarry Farm's two garages. Gil Amiaga photo.

swirled from the basement to the third floor. Throughout the house fine woodwork was added, much of which was antique and imported from Europe for the project. The living room was enhanced by eighteenth-century paneling, and parquet floors were added in several rooms. There were such features as an organ room on the ground floor and, upstairs, a cold storage room for furs. Nine months after the renovations were begun, the house was finally ready for its new owners. In time the rooms were filled with antiques and beautiful furnishings. Rembrandt's *Portrait of an Old Man* (1667) hung in the living room for many years, and an oval Aubusson rug was designed and woven especially for the elliptical library. Later renovations would include the addition of a bowling alley in the basement.

Nancy Reynolds Bagley had spent much of her girlhood in North Carolina on her family's wooded estate. She grew up with a love of nature, and as her four children were born she wished to give them a similar experience. Since she had come from what she called a "farming family," she wanted a farm of some sort. Belle Haven's restrictions prevented farming and the keeping of farm animals; but the Bagleys' land bordered on the abandoned quarry which was in Byram, and Byram land-use regulations were less confining. In 1936 the Bagleys bought the quarry acres from Paul Chalfin and built a stone wall along the Ritch Avenue border of the property, thus enclosing it as one estate, with a Belle Haven address and entrance.

It took exceptional imaginations to dream that anything wonderful could be made from the neglected piece of land. The Belle Haven Land Company had used the property for storage of heavy equipment. Worse, the area had been an ash dump for years and was awash at high tide. Its isolation at the head of Byram Cove had made it a perfect landing site for at least one confirmed rum-running operation, but except for such nefarious activities the land had been abandoned for years.

Fortunately, the Bagleys had the help of Michael O'Donnell, their estate superintendent, and Quarry Farm was begun under his supervision. Tom's Brook, which flowed into the head of Byram Cove, was dammed to form a pond, and two thousand yards of fill were brought in to raise the surrounding land above tide level. Finally, the area was seeded with hay grass to create eleven acres of pasture land for the farm's cows and horses. A stable was built with tack room and box stalls for the two riding horses and the pony that the Bagleys usually kept.

The estate, which had grown to fifty acres, became a true working farm in miniature, although its owners characterized it as a "play farm" rather like Marie Antoinette's Grand Trianon at Versailles. Vegetable farming was begun, and apple, peach, and cherry trees were planted. A small dairy was built where milk from the three resident cows was pasteurized and placed in bottles embossed with the name "Quarry Farm."

Despite its elegance, Quarry Farm was a working farm.

Quarry Cottage in 1940.

Hogs were butchered on the premises, and hams were brined by the cooks in the manner they had learned in the South. The farm needed a smokehouse, so the Bagleys studied the one at George Washington's home at Mount Vernon and converted the Dynamite House to suit this need. Following the Mount Vernon model, they added ventilation and used sweet woods to smoke meat.

Chickens and turkeys supplied eggs and meat, and an apiary provided honey which was pasteurized on the farm. An octagonal aviary housed tropical birds, and many kinds of small animals were also kept there. The only limits that seemed to prevail were those of the owners' creativity. The buildings were constructed after the style of the manor house to give the appearance of a Normandy farm estate. When the farm was in full operation a staff of about fifteen was required.

The estate's gardens were designed by Henry J. Marquardt and were managed as carefully as the farm. A house was built for Mike O'Donnell with a greenhouse attached. This hothouse operation, managed by Jack Robertson from 1948 to 1978, became famous for the beautiful displays it produced for Quarry Farm's gardens.

During World War II many adjustments were made to life on the little farm. The main house was closed to conserve heating fuel, and the family moved into the old Quarry Cottage. The farming operations took on new importance in the war effort, and no

estate farm surpassed Quarry Farm in food production except Henry Fisher's much larger Sabine Farm.

Tucked away at the end of its little cove, Quarry Farm must have seemed a pastoral haven far from harsh reality. But in the 1950s the real world invaded the estate with the coming of the Connecticut Turnpike. Eleven acres of pasture and orchards had to be sold for the state's right-of-way, and thereafter the roar of trucks would intrude on the farm's privacy.

In 1970 the former Mrs. Bagley, now divorced, resumed the name Reynolds. The children had grown, and the farming operations had ceased. Although the farm buildings were useless, the setting was still beautiful, and Mrs. Reynolds sought new uses for them. She renovated these structures and sold them as private homes, so that the compound remained an estate of a different sort, a private community. It was the fate of many of Greenwich's estates to be carved into smaller plots, but Quarry Farm was one of the few whose division was planned by the owner who had lovingly created it. In 1972 she moved from the main house into the O'Donnells' former home, making adaptations to suit her life-style, and she sold the main house.

Nancy Susan Reynolds died in January 1985. Her kindness and generosity are legendary in Greenwich. And her little farm is just a sweet memory in a corner of the town which she left more beautiful than she found it.

The Frueauff Estate

The terraces and great mullioned windows of the south facade face Long Island Sound. Gil Amiaga photo.

Principal Owner: Charles A. Frueauff
Architect: Edgar Self
Construction Date: 1929

HEN GEORGE ELDER bought Mead's Point in 1928, he acquired one of the loveliest natural settings on the Greenwich shorefront. The property slopes gently to the water and even boasts two sandy strips of beach in a waterfront known mostly for its rockiness. Once part of the Charles Mead farm, it had been sold in 1888 to a William Wood who built a house of forgotten proportions known as Malvern.

It must have been obvious that this site demanded more than a modest dwelling. Around the point at Indian Harbor stood Commodore Benedict's famous villa; and just off the shore of Mead's Point was the stony grandeur of Horse Island. This was no neighborhood for the architecturally modest, and Elder apparently set out to maintain the standard. He sought the services of architect Edgar Self, a Greenwich resident whose practice was in New York, and in June 1929 plans were drawn for a Tudor mansion.

Modeled after Compton Wynyates in Warwickshire, England, the brick-and-stone house is an adaptation rather than a copy. (Elder was a partner in the brokerage firm of Warwick and Company, and it is tempting to wonder if the idea of a "Warwickshire house" were more than a coincidence of names.) The main resemblance between the two houses comes from the half-timbering in the gables, the sharply pitched roofs with clustered chimneys, and the use of banks of windows of different sizes to give a feeling of openness. Facing directly south, the house seems to sit close to the ground, raised from the lawn only by its low stone terraces. This design, combined with the varied setbacks of its bays and facade, avoids the feeling of enormousness generally conveyed by such a large house. The sense of lightness in a house of such grand dimensions is remarkable, and the late architectural historian Alan Burnham credited the design's success to its asymmetrical nature which allowed the architect a certain "freedom" with his plan. "It is this quality,"

said Burnham, "plus the light and air provided by the great mullioned windows, which make us realize how readily Tudor architecture could have led us directly into the creation of the contemporary house." Perhaps it was this realization which led both the designer and the owner to choose the Tudor style for their project.

The house was built of stone quarried locally and of bricks especially made to imitate the small size and colors of those of Compton Wynyates. The red-hued bricks were laid in English bond and carefully placed so that their color variations created two-toned diamond patterns on the walls. Self also took inspiration from the entrance bay design of Compton Wynyates in his plan. The front portal, on the north side of the Mead's Point house, consists of a two-story bay, its crenellations suggesting the sort of fortifications still evident in country houses during Tudor times. A Tudor arch in the stone protrusion is embellished with heraldic ornaments and other sandstone carvings. This opening leads to the main entrance itself—some eight feet within the porchlike enclosure—with a heavily paneled wooden door pierced by a single mullioned window. This is the only piece of the design that comes close to being an actual copy of its English model. It is clear that this ceremonial approach to the house was not be be used casually. Just to the west the service wing turns away from the house at an obtuse angle, and here a small many-sided stair tower extrudes from the wall, and its doorway—intended as the "boys' entrance"—would have known the comings and goings of the Elders' children.

But the Elder family would never be a part of the life of this house. Construction was begun in 1929; then the stock market crashed and the Elders' marriage was dissolved. Edgar Self, apparently left with responsibility for the project, was fortunate to find a buyer in Charles A. Frueauff (1879-1950), for whom the house was finally completed.

15

The living room in the early 1930s.

In 1930 Frueauff was fifty-one years old and a successful New York lawyer. Born in Columbia, Pennsylvania, he attended the University of Michigan. He practiced law in Denver, Colorado, for five years before moving to New York. In 1910 he had founded the firm of Frueauff, Burns, Roch and Farrell, specializing in oil producing and refining corporations. He is best remembered as general counsel for Cities Service Company, with which his career was closely linked. It is not known if Frueauff and his wife, the former Hazel Crawley (d. 1944), had any Greenwich connections, but they were probably seeking a country retreat from their New York residence.

How much if any of the interior was completed at the time of the sale is conjecture. Apparently progress was not always smooth, and at one point the construction workers filed suit against the old and the new owners, the architect, and the contracting firm of Richards and Jessup. But the house was completed essentially as it is today.

The theme announced at the entry is repeated throughout the interior design; exterior stone carving is echoed in wood-paneled walls and tracery on the plaster ceilings. Mr. and Mrs. Forest Toates, daughter and son-in-law of architect Self, recalled that some of the interior's decorative elements were imported from England, but many were produced here under the strict supervision of the architect. Mr. Toates described his father-in-law's search for wood-carvers who could produce heraldic beasts from his designs. Finding these artisans in New York, Self worked with them, instructing them as they worked on how the figures should appear. These animals, erect and holding shields, surmount the newel posts of the house's grand stairway.

The banks of small-paned windows, so attractive from without, do much to brighten the interior, framing views of sweeping lawn and open water and making them part of the handsome rooms. And here and there the Elizabethan theme is continued with shields and coats of arms of stained glass incorporated into the casement windows.

A large entrance hall is the center of the first floor. From here radiate hallways leading to the other rooms. One leads to a living room with a sun porch beyond. Another passes the paneled dining room with its adjoining six-sided breakfast room and gives access to the service wing: kitchen, pantry, and cold-storage room and — for the servants — a dining room and a sitting room. The second floor contained a total of fourteen bedrooms in the main and service wings, and the attic floor above held another three sleeping rooms.

The lower level of the service wing housed laundry and needed utilities, such as an enormous boiler room to heat the house's thirty rooms. Under the main section of the house there was also a room-sized vault for safekeeping, and a portion of the basement was a replica of an old English tavern that included a wine vault for entertaining guests.

A greenhouse, a bathhouse at water's edge, and a garage near the driveway completed the estate's buildings. The eleven acres surrounding the mansion received the same meticulous planning as the house itself. The year after the house was completed the Frueauffs engaged landscape architect Armand R. Tibbitts to design a formal garden for them. Tibbitts, a Wisconsin native, had come to Greenwich in the early 1920s to design the naturalistic setting for the new subdivision of Milbrook. His work included gardens

Entry and great mullioned window.

The library bay and south terrace.

The bathhouse with the beach beyond.

for many residences throughout the Northeast as well as extensive landscaping on the campus of Hobart College. A fellow of the American Society of Landscape Architects, Tibbitts was well known for his design of Jackson and Perkins rose gardens which were a popular feature of the New York Flower Shows.

To complement the Frueauff house, he planned a formal English garden, its north–south axis extending directly from the front door. A lily pool with fountain was placed amid concentric ovals of stone walls and boxwood hedges. Stone paths radiated in four directions, each with a different focal point: to the east was the open water, to the north a rose trellis, to the south the house's front entrance, and to the west a one-hundred-foot-long pergola covered with flowering vines. In a corner of the property tall hedges screened extensive vegetable and cutting gardens. Today no traces of the pool and walkways exist, so it is difficult to say how well the plan was carried out, but the owners did create an "arboreal museum" on the grounds. Over seventy trees were imported from many parts of the world and planted on the site, each one carefully labeled and nurtured in its new home. On the eastern side of the property was a greenhouse, and a nearby cottage housed the estate gardener and his family.

The Frueauffs furnished the house in appropriately fine style, filling the rooms with Jacobean antiques and valuable works of art. In the twenty years they lived there their weekend home became known as one of Greenwich's premier showplaces. After Hazel Frueauff died in 1944, her husband kept the house staffed, although he seldom used it during the remaining six years of his life. Since the couple had no children, their will provided that most of their money be placed in a foundation which they established for charitable purposes. But the Mead's Point estate with all its furnishings was placed on the market.

Eventually parcels of the Frueauffs' eleven acres were sold off, and the garage was converted to a separate residence. But the house remains, handsome and serene, behind a stone wall at the end of a quiet lane.

Whitney Castle

Whitney Castle in the 1930s.

Principal Owner: J. Kennedy Tod
Architect: Hunt & Hunt, Architects
Construction Date: 1889

SOME two thousand years ago the Siwanoy Indians named it Monakewaygo meaning "the place of white sands." Today Greenwich Point is a favorite playground for thousands of people who crowd its remarkable beaches and wooded picnic areas, occasionally jamming the narrow, winding roads to the point of gridlock. But at the beginning of the twentieth century this graceful spit of land was the private estate of J. Kennedy Tod (1852-1925). He called it Innis Arden.

Many thought it curious that the small Scot should buy the 147 acres where colonists had made the first settlement in Greenwich two and a half centuries earlier. In 1889 there was still a great deal of waterfront land available, and people wondered why anyone would want property with such difficult access. At that time the point was an island, cut off from the mainland at high tide, approachable only at low water, and then, by means of a sandbar. However, the land offered Tod what he treasured most — privacy — and the opportunity to observe and protect nature. Within this sanctuary he created an extraordinary wildlife preserve as well as a fantastic mansion.

J. Kennedy Tod was born in Glasgow in 1852. With a generous gift from his father he emigrated to this country and in 1879 joined the New York City investment banking firm of J. S. Kennedy and Company, and reorganized the company under his own name when Kennedy retired. The business was involved primarily with the financing and development of railroads, particularly the Great Northern and the Canadian Pacific. In 1882 Tod married Marie Howard Potter of New York City and shortly thereafter, moved to Sound Beach as Old Greenwich was called then. For many years he was the sole commuter from the station there to the metropolis visible from his own point.

Tod's first problem after buying the land was to find a way to bring in building material. The causeway was built because heavy stone could not be carted across sand, and today the Sound washes across this narrow isthmus only during the largest storms. Thirty stonemasons were brought from Italy to build the retaining walls, the foundations, and the miles of drywall that line the cove and the roads. These men lived in small houses on the estate for many years. The Tods themselves lived in one of the cottages while the mansion was under construction, as they did again during World War I when heating fuel was scarce. It was during this second period that the main house was electrified — at enormous expense inasmuch as the underground cable had to be laid more than a mile from the gatehouse to the mansion.

The great shingled dwelling that slowly arose above the freshwater lake at the island's center was as free-form as the land itself. According to the architect and historian Alan Burnham, Hunt and Hunt created here "a house which literally grew out of its site," climbing "from water level to its rather high entrance plateau - a skillful solution, and made in a remarkably smooth transition." The house nestled into the side of a hill so steep that four of the five stories were on ground level at some point. When finished, wings shot out from every direction, and the mansion held thirty-nine rooms, each — including the kitchen — crafted in heavily carved oak or mahogany. Floors were either parquet or marble-tiled, and the casement windows held leaded glass and exquisite hardware. The gabled roof was eyebrowed and turreted like an illustration from *Grimm's Fairy Tales*; capacious porches embraced every side. Built with great care and without concern for cost, Innis Arden seemed magnificent to some, while to others it was an architectural monstrosity.

The original entrance was on the lake front where one climbed six steps into the gameroom and took an elevator, hand-operated at first, to the living room above. Here was a handsome library and a twenty-five-foot square gallery in which priceless paintings were on display. The dining room, paneled in Honduras mahogany, was on the floor above,

23

The main house from the lake.

The dining room during the Tod era.

A group of accessory buildings on the shore.

where, according to legend, Tod rode his horse onto the parquet floor and had his breakfast from the saddle. In later years when the mansion was turned into veterans' apartments, children rode their tricycles across the same tiles on rainy days.

The dining room combined with the living room made a gigantic space where conservatory windows gave a dazzling view of Long Island Sound. Fourteen-foot-high ceilings and life-sized statues emphasized the extravagant dimensions. The decor was Victorian, ornate but austere, with dark wood paneling and heavy beams throughout. A seventy-five-foot hallway led from the living room to the master bedroom, which overhung the lake four stories below. In later years an entrance was made at the living room, and a drive of beautifully dressed stone curved majestically up the hill to meet it.

The mansion housed a staff of thirteen and a chauffeur, a caretaker, gardeners and a gatekeeper lived in the various outbuildings. There was a beachhouse, a barn, a boathouse, and a carriagehouse. The carriagehouse was equipped with a set of chimes imported from Scotland that operated by weights, on the same principle as a grandfather clock. These chimes played Scottish tunes such as "Annie Laurie" and could be heard for great distances. The stone gatehouse held a family of ten, and it was usually one of the gatekeeper's children who would open the enormous wrought-iron gates. The gates were another late addition, reluctantly installed when the Tods discovered that their property was being vandalized. Beach fires got out of control, birds and small animals were shot, even bushes were pulled up. The caretaker was assigned to patrol the beaches and became the nemesis of local children and — during Prohibition — of rumrunners.

Although the Tods had no children of their own, their house was often filled with relatives and guests, many of whom arrived by yacht. A long pier ran from the boathouse to a dock on the cove where the depth was always sufficient for boats with a deep draft. For a short time Tod owned a forty-foot steam yacht, but he preferred the canoes and small sailboats tied up at the landing beside the porte-cochere.

For guests who did not care to fish or boat, there was a skeet range — no hunting was ever permitted. There was also a nine-hole golf course, reminiscent of St. Andrews with its salt-swept greens and fairways. And there was wildlife, flocks of swans and pelicans on the lake as well as a pair of black bears. Tod kept

J. Kennedy Tod and friend.

these exotic pets in cages beside the chimes building, but sometimes they were taken to the village in the mule cart where they delighted everyone with their antics.

Mr. and Mrs. Tod were generous with their property as long as it was carefully used. Many local families had the privilege of swimming from the beach—the longest natural stretch of sand on the Connecticut shore. While children and adults were swimming nearby, fishermen, whose ancestors had worked these same beds for generations, were permitted to dig for oysters and clams.

Despite the fact that the Tods were neither churchgoers nor parents, the First Congregational Church and the public school benefited from their support. The Sound Beach Fire Department—a particular favorite with Mr. Tod—was given its furnishings and truck and Tod served on its board of trustees for many years.

The institution that received the greatest attention from the Tods was the Columbia-Presbyterian Hospital in New York City. It has been suggested that they became interested in the hospital through Elizabeth Olney, a nurse and Mrs. Tod's niece, and possibly because Tod, being a Scot, was raised a Presbyterian. Whatever the introduction, Innis Arden was host to numerous doctors and nurses every sum-

mer, and several small screened-in cottages were built on the west end of the point for their yearly vacations. At Mrs. Tod's death in 1939, fourteen years after her husband's, the entire estate was left to the hospital for use as a convalescent home. Unfortunately, Columbia-Presbyterian had already purchased a site on King Street in Greenwich for this purpose and could not justify the upkeep of such a large estate.

After World War II and with a good deal of bickering, the Town of Greenwich bought the point from the estate as a park for its burgeoning population. The mansion was leased to returning veterans at a nominal rent and was converted into thirteen apartments. From 1945 until it was demolished in 1961, the magnificent quarters were home to an estimated thirty families, all of whom acquired great respect for a man they never knew, a man whose charm and energies were apparent in the exquisite taste and imagination that surrounded them.

When the wrecker's ball arrived, it required four times the estimated number of hours to break the great house apart. J. Kennedy Tod built to last and fortunately some of his efforts remain. The gatehouse, the beachhouse, and the chimes building still stand, as does the garage-boathouse which is now the Old Greenwich Yacht Club. Remnants of the gardens can be seen behind the barn, and the stone steps, walls, and foundations of the mansion are a source of wonder and nostalgia for a past glory. Some people still refer to it as Tod's Point and, if they happen to write the name, usually misspell it. However, Mr. Tod himself said that "if one *d* is good enough for God, it's good enough for me."

Kincraig

Kincraig as it appears today from Long Island Sound. William Hubbell photo.

Principal Owner: Harriet Lauder Greenway
Architect: Unknown
Construction Date: 1898

THE GREENWAY ESTATE, known as Kincraig, dates back to 1893 when John Hamilton Gourlie, one of the original settlers of Belle Haven, purchased the first parcel of land from Ephraim, Spencer, Thomas, and Amos Mead. The property was located on Long Island Sound at the mouth of the Mianus River.

Gourlie, a native of New York City, was with the firm of Johnson and Higgins, insurance brokers and adjusters. Five years after he purchased his Mead's Point property, he built the first and largest part of the mansion which remains today. However, his health began to deteriorate at about that time, and in 1900 he left the United States to travel abroad. When he returned, he announced to his four children that he had married his nurse in London. Because "The marriage was said to be disliked by the children," the *New York Times* wrote, friends tried but failed to have the Greenwich Probate Court appoint a conservator to manage his financial affairs.

In 1904 "the eccentric millionaire" died in his early fifties, leaving no will. As if to prove his eccentricity, his obituary in the *New York Times* ends with the observation that "Mr. Gourlie's two cottages at Belle Haven have been closed for two years because the millionaire declared he was wealthy enough without renting them." His son and three daughters were subsequently given title to his property.

The next year Harriet Lauder Greenway (1879-1959) entered the picture. Gourlie's heirs sold her his fifty-seven-and-a-half-acre property with its house. She added to it with further purchases of land in 1909, 1910, and 1921, and at its peak the estate encompassed over one hundred acres including shoreline both on the Sound and northeastward along the Mianus River. The Greenways and their children enjoyed it thereafter for more than three-quarters of a century.

Harriet Greenway was a member of the Lauder family, well known in Greenwich and Pittsburgh where her father, George Lauder, had been the co-founder with Andrew Carnegie of the Carnegie Steel Company (now U.S. Steel). Thus, she could afford to create such an estate, to make improvements and additions at will, and to maintain the life-style it made possible. Her husband, Dr. James Greenway, was a well-known physician who left the staff of New York Hospital in 1915 to found the Department of Health at Yale, where he remained until his retirement in 1935. Until that time the family used the Mead's Point home only as a summer house, but as there was no longer any need to live in New Haven, it was winterized and became their year-round residence.

In 1912 the Greenways had added two wings to Gourlie's original building, thereby creating the magnificent Neo-French Renaissance mansion that remains today. Built of stone and clapboard with a slate roof, it is sophisticated and elegant and, though made of American materials, has the formality of a French manor house. The tree-lined driveway leads past a stucco and gray clapboard gatehouse which echoes the style of the main building. At the entrance of that great house, two massive round stone towers covered with ivy flank the front door, and two projecting stone gargoyles with slender necks appear to peruse the visitor. A large paneled entry hall leads straight from the door through the center of the house and out to the true focus of the place—the magnificent panorama of water and sky seen from the porches. Facing Long Island Sound, this most spectacular side of the house overlooks formal gardens, sweeping lawns, and steps leading down to the beach. Seen from the water the peaked slate roofs, the flared eaves, the charming dormer windows with pointed arches, and the many balconies are reminiscent of the grand French châteaus.

The main entrance to the estate house.

The east facade facing Long Island Sound.

Looking east to the Sound.

There are twenty-five rooms in the house, fourteen of them bedrooms, which required a staff of at least eight people to cook, launder, do the housekeeping, and otherwise serve the Greenway family. The first floor has a formal atmosphere with its wide staircase and carved banisters, large fireplaces, paneled dining room, and embossed ceilings. The serving kitchen is off the dining room, while the immense main kitchen is on a lower level. A dumbwaiter carried the food and dishes between floors. Behind the dining room in one of the wings added by the Greenways there is a squash court. Other main-floor rooms include a large living room, a library with exceptionally fine paneling, an oval study, and a sizable solarium with a fountain.

The second floor contains a master suite and six more bedrooms; the third has four family bedrooms and a wing with maids' rooms. The brightly papered bedrooms, many of which have fireplaces and sleeping porches, created an atmosphere of country living, for that is what it was then. Some of the Greenway children remember playing games and hiding in the uppermost attic. A trapdoor there leads to the rooftop, and from this spot they watched many Fourth of July celebrations.

This estate, as was true for many others in Greenwich during this period, was a working farm. Vegetables were grown for the whole family, and the orchards produced abundant fruit. Chickens, pigs, dogs, and ponies abounded. A pet pig belonging to one of the children was named Gloria Gump Gump. There are a number of outbuildings, the most notable of which is the former stable, now a garage, built primarily of stone and forming a horseshoe shape around a courtyard. A central clock tower crowns its entrance. A gatehouse, two poultry sheds, a hay barn with a silo, a greenhouse, a manure shed, and an octagonal stone beachhouse are also on the property.

Kincraig was a spectacular setting for the Greenways' many interests and activities, and they enjoyed their life there immensely. Horseback riding through the many trails on the grounds was a popular pastime. Many hours were spent playing on the tennis court. The beautiful beach was fine for picnics, as no doubt were several of the small islands they owned offshore, and family sailboats were moored in the Sound. The children liked to give plays on the porches for the enjoyment of family members, and these sometimes became quite elaborate productions. The Greenways' daughter even had her own little two-bedroom playhouse in which she learned to cook. Summers

The entrance gate and gatehouse.

Ivy-covered stone towers flank the main entrance.

spent in such a green and sun-drenched spot have an almost storybook quality about them today.

Gardening was one of Harriet Greenway's strong interests, and the magnificent beech trees which she planted many years ago still grace the property. A superintendent of the grounds managed the greenhouse and directed as many as six full-time gardeners. The lovely gardens were the setting for family weddings and many parties.

Time, however, does not stand still, and with its passage the estate has not remained intact. Harriet Greenway gave land first to their daughter Anna, then to the Indian Field School. Property was lost to the railroad and to the Connecticut Turnpike. When Mrs. Greenway died, she left the rest of the property to their three sons and daughter.

Dr. Greenway continued to live in the house with their son Lauder, a patron of the arts who has made his name almost synonymous with culture. Perhaps Lauder Greenway's most abiding interest was the Metropolitan Opera, which he served in various capacities for almost forty years. His mother had filled the stately house with noted opera singers such as Madame Emma Eames, Martinelli, and de Luca; he, in turn, invited great operatic performers there to dine but not to perform. "I want them to get the fresh air

of the country in their lungs," *The Nutmegger* has quoted him as saying.

Dr. Greenway died in 1976 — six months before his hundredth birthday; Lauder died in 1981 at Kincraig, where he was born in 1904. The house with its remaining fifty acres was sold two years later for $7.5 million.

The Greenway family will be remembered in Greenwich for their generosity in giving Island Beach (Little Captain Island) to the town and for donating its first ferryboat as well. The minutes of the Town Meeting of October 24, 1918, report that Island Beach is "to be held by the Town of Greenwich in perpetuity as a Recreational Park and Bathing Beach for the use and benefit of the citizens of Greenwich."

The Horse Island estate house, long a sailors' landfall from Long Island Sound. William Hubbell photo.

Principal Owner: George H. Townsend
Original Architect (1921): Frank P. Whiting
Architect for Renovations (1923): Frank P. Whiting

S MANY ESTATE OWNERS sought versions of medieval castles for their homes, so did the builder of Horse Island house. But this estate appears a more genuine version than most with its surrounding moat actually the waters of Long Island Sound.

The illusion is especially strong from the land-side approach: entry is over a causeway where one might expect to see a castle drawbridge, and as the visitor arrives the height of the house looms colossally ahead. But it is the back of Horse Island which is most often seen, as it is a familiar landfall for sailors in Captain Harbor and the Sound beyond.

To those who knew the land in earlier times, such a house might seem a pretentious use for it. Years ago the island could be reached only via a land bridge at low tide, but horses wandered across it for grazing. Local legend says that one horse refused to return to the mainland pasture and took up permanent residence there, thus giving the island its name.

For many generations, the Mead family owned and farmed Mead's Point, and Horse Island was assumed to be part of their property. In the eighteenth century this title was challenged by a local resident named Reynolds, and a long court fight ensued, but the Mead ownership was assured. Too rocky to cultivate, and lying five hundred feet offshore, the eight acres would have been of little use to a farmer. In 1888 Charles Mead sold the island, and it passed through various ownerships until 1920, when the land and causeway rights were purchased by James P. Cahill (1873-1955), president of J. P. Cahill and Company, a New York brokerage firm. Cahill commissioned Frank P. Whiting to design the first house the island had known.

This architect had spent his early training in architectural practice in the offices of Ernest Flagg at the time the firm was designing such landmark buildings as St. Luke's Hospital and the Singer Building in New York. At that time Whiting may have established a working relationship with the Clark family, owners of the Singer Company, because he was later commissioned by them to do other architectural assignments. Although Whiting probably did many residential designs, his most famous work is the Baseball Hall of Fame in Cooperstown, New York.

In 1925 Frank P. Whiting would say of Horse Island that the house was "never designed; it just naturally grew out of the peculiarities of the site." The varied roof heights and the manner in which the house rises from three different foundation levels almost give truth to Whiting's claim; but in fact the designer carefully nurtured its growth, and in two separate stages.

He designed a graceful Tudor-style house on the island's crest for Cahill, and he was proud enough of his plan to exhibit it at the Architectural League of New York. Granite quarried from the site to provide the basement was then dressed to build the thick stone walls. A contemporary magazine article reported that many of the island's chestnut trees supplied wood for the stylish half-timbering that was becoming popular during that era.

A heavy front door opened to a foyer with an oak and glass-paned inner door. From here visitors entered a spacious hall from which the main rooms opened. Most of the decorative wood was white oak. Doors were made with handsomely carved panels and fine custom-made hardware, and stairs to the upper floor had balusters and handrails of carved oak with simple rosettes inscribed atop the newel posts.

The living room was "high English style" with a stone fireplace and tall peaked ceiling braced by beautifully shaped oak beams. Paneling along the fireplace wall disguised a secret stairway which led to a minstrel's gallery above. This room as well as the sun porch opened to stone terraces overlooking the shore. In addition the dining room had a breakfast porch for summer meals.

31

The rear facade from a different perspective. Gil Amiaga photo.

Staff quarters flank the garage entrance.

The transitional tower and its fanciful weather vane.

On the second floor there were four large bedrooms, each with its own bath, three of them facing the open water. The third floor held another four bedrooms, probably intended for staff. A garage with chauffeur's quarters and a billiard room completed the amenities for country living during that period.

How long Cahill occupied the island is uncertain, but in March 1923 Whiting acted as agent in advertising the property for sale. The purchaser was George H. Townsend (1884-1957), a rising entrepreneur whose main interests included fast cars and powerboats.

Townsend was born and raised in New Haven, where his father was a judge of the U. S. Court of Appeals and a law professor at Yale. As a Yale undergraduate in the early 1900s young Townsend pursued his fondness for cars. He was a founder of the Yale Automobile Club and a frequent participant in road races. After graduating in 1908 he was briefly in automobile manufacturing in California, but in 1912 he launched his first great business venture with Harrison Boyce.

Boyce, inventor of a thermometer for automotive cooling systems, needed capital to mass-produce his invention. Together they formed the Motometer Company, and Townsend became its president. Motometers were aggressively marketed throughout the burgeoning automobile industry for use on car radiators, and during World War I the company adapted its design for use on army and navy airplanes and industrial machines. During the 1920s there was a demand for new techniques to place the gauges on dashboards rather than on radiator caps, and Townsend cornered the market by buying a company that produced dashboard panels.

During this period George Townsend and his wife, the former Caroline T. Dederer, acquired the Cahill home, although they realized that it would hardly hold their family of seven lively children. Retaining the house's original architect, Townsend added an easterly wing to triple the size of the home and to change it from stylish house to the fantasy castle that is there today. The old and new sections were linked by a tall square tower crowned with an ornate wind vane bearing the signature of the island: the copper figure of a horse as a creature of both land and sea, with wings of a dragon and tail of a fish. This turret contained a hideaway room, no more than eight by eight feet, with a tiny fireplace. This was Townsend's aerie, with no children allowed, where he could enjoy eagle's-eye views of water and yet unspoiled land. From Horse Island the shores of Greenwich still appeared undeveloped except for the other great estates which could be seen nearby: Innis Arden, Walhall, Indian Harbor, and, later, Frueauff.

Some of the house's renovation involved redesigning the existing wing, such as remaking the former dining room into a living room, since the Townsends found the original room too somber for their taste. With such a large family new bedrooms had to be added, and the number, including servants' rooms, rose from eight to thirteen. The Townsends had planned a master suite for themselves that would include bedroom, dressing room, and office; but seeing the space laid out, they decided to leave one large room open so that they could see land and water views through the casement windows.

While the new addition was in keeping with the house's Elizabethan style, the interior decoration was emphatically Italianate. Decorative tile imported from Italy, Italian-style furniture, and antique wall hangings contributed to the palazzo mood. Where genuinely old materials were not available, illusion was created, and walls were even smoked to appear old.

The most spectacular of the newer rooms was the dining room. Reached by a short flight of steps through a stone wall, it could have been the banquet hall of an Italian palazzo. Romantic lighting was provided by branched wall sconces that bore winged horses with fishlike tails repeating the signature introduced by the house's weather vane. At the far end of the room a lunette by Everett Shinn, recessed over the loggia door, depicted a Venetian revel with a Pierrot and other masked figures. The carnival scene was continued on two decorative panels for doors flanking the fireplace. The fireplace itself was a massive antique of Italian carved stone adorned by the gold-and-polychrome arms of the Townsend family, one of the room's many touches of gilt that included covers for the heating registers. Any somberness suggested by the massive pattern of beams overhead was dispelled by glimpses of sky-blue ceiling between the timbers, and an iron-framed glass door admitted daylight from the plant-filled loggia beyond. A seemingly ancient trestle table was designed and built for the room, complete with "worm holes" to feign age.

During the years that the Townsends owned Horse Island, the dining room was famous as the scene of their Sunday night suppers. "This was the one night of the week when no one was allowed to go out,"

recalled Annie Townsend Wallen, "but we could bring any friends we wanted and there would sometimes be fifty or sixty people for supper." Her sister Mollie Townsend Gibbons added, "Mother never seemed to mind. She was a great cook and loved people."

Both sisters remember happy years growing up on the island with plenty of ways to entertain themselves. Townsend commuted to his New York office aboard his boat *Sazarac* — he eventually owned three boats by that name, ranging in length from fifty-four to seventy-three feet. The children had their own sailboat, named *Cheerio*, which they moored off the island's dock. The family enjoyed skeet shooting, and the island had a shooting house as well as a tennis court. For further entertainment the children often rode at their father's horse farm in Glenville.

A staff of about fifteen, including gardeners, maintained the estate and looked after the children when their parents were traveling. Mrs. Wallen remarked that it was a "carefree" life for the young, with winters in Greenwich and summers at St. Regis Lake in the Adirondacks — and that, growing up during the depression, the Townsend children were not allowed to work lest they take jobs from those who truly needed them.

The island was the scene of two Townsend girls' wedding receptions in the 1930s: Mollie (Mrs. John Gibbons) and Kay, who married Dick Chapman of Round Island, both entertained wedding guests in the estate's waterfront gardens.

At the end of the 1930s the Townsend children had grown, and their parents were divorced. George Townsend lived on at Horse Island for a time with his second wife, Vera Pleshkoya, a former concert harpist, but he sold the house in 1939.

Not all the owners have thought life on Horse Island as carefree as the Townsend girls did. In recent times residents found staffing more difficult, and maintaining a house reached only by a narrow causeway was never simple. A succession of owners dealt with the house's mixed blessings, making alterations to suit their life-styles. In 1985 the house was sold once more, and it is now home to a family with several children as its earliest owners intended it to be.

Walhall

The fountains of Walhall.

Principal Owners: John Jacob and Valeria Knapp Langeloth
Architect: John Duncan
Construction Date: 1912-1914

NE OF THE most beautiful of the shore properties along Long Island Sound is located in Riverside and was first admired by its best-known owner, John Jacob Langeloth, from the water. An avid yachtsman, he knew most of the waters and frontage within easy reach of his New York business offices. Having accumulated great wealth in the metals industry, he set about the task of acquiring this choice place for himself and his wife. He was of German birth but became an American citizen and, though many years her senior, in 1903 married Valeria Knapp. He had risen rapidly in a metals company, Metallgesellschaft, of Frankfort, Germany. In New York he organized and helped to found the American Metal Company, becoming a world-recognized authority in his field. He loved nature and the out-of-doors, and he wanted a country place.

When John Langeloth was finally able to buy the fifty-seven-acre property from Edwin W. Bullinger in 1908, it was no longer a working farm and was considerably run down. Valeria Langeloth described the existing house as a "mid-Victorian monstrosity." However, there were beautiful green lawns; magnificent groves of trees; rocky slopes; and, above all, two miles of curving shoreline with its breathtaking view of the water, Long Island, and in later years even the New York City skyline. In earlier times the area had been well known as a gathering place for many tribes of Indians. In fact, Indian pictures which indicated treaty marks were found by the Langeloths on the rocks of a glen near the center of the estate.

Langeloth made costly changes in the original house. Remodeling and refurnishing the dining room alone cost more than $25,000. However, neither he nor his wife was ever satisfied with the results. Two fires on the property precipitated their decision to demolish the entire structure and to build a new house which would be not only fireproof but more to their taste. John Duncan, the New York architect who was also responsible for the building of Grant's Tomb on Riverside Drive, was engaged to draw plans for the new mansion. It was to be called Walhall, for Langeloth was a devotee of Wagnerian music, and among his favorite passages were those relating to Valhalla, the legendary dwelling place of heroes slain in battle.

Construction of the new mansion was begun in 1912 and finished in 1914. Limestone was quarried at Bedford, Indiana, and floated down the White, Wabash, Ohio, and Mississippi rivers to New Orleans, from there to be shipped through the Gulf of Mexico, north on the Atlantic Ocean to Long Island Sound, and finally unloaded at the Langeloths' concrete yacht landing in Riverside. Meanwhile, Duncan first constructed an outbuilding intended eventually for the superintendent. The Langeloths lived there with their New York servants while the main house was under construction. This building is owned as a private residence today.

Another four-story building was built nearby with root cellar and fruit storage rooms underneath the stables provided for the Kentucky thoroughbred riding horses and Percheron workhorses. The stable area included garages, used eventually for a station wagon and three other automobiles; the Langeloths' cars were kept in steam-heated rooms. The third level was originally planned for miscellaneous storage, but later a dance floor of hard oak was installed and was called the barn ballroom. Many gay evenings were spent there over the years that followed. An orchestra platform was installed, as was a piano, and later, cabaret tables and chairs were added, as well as projection equipment for showing motion pictures.

When Walhall was completed just before World War I began, it was an imposing three-storied Italian Renaissance mansion built of smooth cut limestone, concrete, and steel on Roman classical lines. Its twenty-six rooms had floors of teakwood, hardwood, and marble. Valeria Langeloth wrote in her book, *Utopia in the Hills* (1948), that Duncan had encouraged her in her desire to have nothing but the best. Her husband had the means to provide it, and the couple took great pride in their accomplishment.

When they went to Europe in 1913, they purchased some of the furnishings: rugs, paintings, tapestries, and articles of furniture primarily of the Louis XVI period, many of them museum pieces. In her book Valeria Langeloth noted that "the furnishing of Walhall was a delight to John as it was to me . . . as one carefully selected piece of furniture after another was set in its proper place, the vastness of the house began to shrink. It became a truly livable and lovable home." Unfortunately, John Langeloth was never to move into his beloved Walhall. On the night of August 14, 1914, before the house was completely furnished, he died of a heart attack. A shipment of forty-eight carved limestone jars and vases, carefully chosen to embellish the terraces and grounds, arrived the day after his death.

Valeria Langeloth lived on there for nineteen years with her cousin Elizabeth Knapp for a companion. She filled her active life with social engagements and extensive travel. She raised hundreds of orchids in her own greenhouse. And, most importantly, she created Valeria Home in northern Westchester. She had long dreamed of building a beautiful recreation and convalescent center for "persons of education and refinement" who could not afford vacations. In his will her husband had directed her to establish such a place, and in 1924 she opened the doors of a magnificent Tudor villa set on a thousand acres of rolling, wooded hills near Peekskill.

Nineteen years after her first husband's death, Valeria Langeloth married Frederick T. Bonham, an executive of the *New York Times*, in a double wedding ceremony. At the same time her cousin, Elizabeth Knapp, married Bonham's Tennessee friend, Walter H. Mann. The Bonhams lived in and enjoyed Walhall for almost twenty years thereafter.

From a practical point of view, the estate supplied those who lived there with most of the food they needed. There was a stone building for pigs and Guernsey cattle with a creamery at one end; there were gardeners' cottages, barns, and storerooms filled in winter with farm produce that not only fed the household and staff but also provided ample stocks to share with others. Chickens, ducks, geese, and guinea fowl were raised by the hundreds, and highly bred pheasants as well. A large orchard of apple, peach, pear, and cherry trees produced fruit to spare.

A portion of the walled gardens.

The formal living room.

A long view of the formal gardens.

The grounds of Walhall were spectacular. The house dominated a knoll that slopes abruptly to the water of an inlet on the west and more gently to the south where the view ranges across a low, wooded peninsula and the open Sound. On the east the mansion opened onto a terrace from which, passing a large marble pool where tropical lilies blazed, one reached the formal gardens. The bronze original of a lovely statue called *The Vine* by Harriet W. Frishmuth stood in the center of an avenue of sheared retinisporas; and surmounting a fountain beyond, formal rose and peony gardens were laid out before an entrance portico of limestone composed of white columns and vine-covered trellises. The gardens were bounded by low gray stone walls and filled with the sounds of playing fountains, together with the light of reflecting pools.

To the south of the house landscape architect Noel Chamberlin had designed a green garden or continuous permanent border to enclose a sunken outdoor theater. There on the close-clipped green grass 1,500 guests could be seated to watch musical programs which took place on the stone-paved stage elevated at one side. At one performance of *Iolanthe* the moon was so bright that no electric lighting was necessary. This entire area was surrounded by a rock wall, beyond which broad-leaved evergreens, pink and white dogwoods, and a variety of large native trees provided a picturesque background. Throughout this woodland more than 25,000 daffodils were strewn.

The broad acres of the estate were meticulously kept. Wide expanses of lawn studded with dogwood trees were equipped with underground sprinkler systems, and specimen boxwoods and other rare evergreens also flourished. A forest of trees arranged in a series of *allées*—a replica of Versailles—was of particular interest. Each of the selected specimens, among them elm, pin oak, linden, maple, and beech, had to be planted in a blasted excavation, owing to the presence of solid rock close to the surface. Naturalized narcissus, scattered about on the forest floor, bloomed by the hundreds. In 1936 the Bonhams received a gold medal "for having the most beautiful and best-kept estate near New York," according to the *New York Times*.

A woman endowed with wealth, beauty, and a magnetic personality, a skilled pianist, organist, and charter member of the Metropolitan Opera Association, Valeria Langeloth Bonham entertained thousands of guests in the main house, in the barn ballroom, and throughout the estate with its terraces, gardens,

A view toward the Sound.

beaches, and more than three miles of bridle trails. Many guests drove down the gracefully winding drive bordered by old maples to attend the parties she gave purely for her own pleasure; many more came to large gatherings planned for the benefit of various charities. It must have been a festive scene indeed, as hundreds of paper lanterns flickered fairylike through the trees, private yachts rode at anchor offshore, and professional dancers performed on the front lawn overlooking the Sound. Valeria Bonham told the story of one yacht captain who, intent on listening to one of the open-air concerts in progress, let his boat run aground, there to remain until high tide. Consequently, his guests were invited to come ashore in one of the small boats kept at the dock and proceeded to join in the festivities. The house and gardens were also used as the setting for several early motion pictures, among them David Wark Griffith's *Orphans of the Storm* (1922), which starred Lillian and Dorothy Gish.

In 1952 Valeria Langeloth Bonham died childless at the age of seventy, and two years later the life of Walhall also ended. Frederick Bonham sold the estate, which was then broken up into smaller lots; the main house was torn down. There are those who may remember such details as the thirty-foot domed ceiling over the grand staircase that concealed pipes of an Aeolian organ, or the bath in the master suite with its gold fixtures and Wedgewood inlays in the tiled walls. Today, however, only partial remains of the mansion's balustrades and garden structures are to be found.

Round Island

The main entrance as redesigned in the 1960s. Gil Amiaga photo.

Principal Owner: John D. Chapman
Original Architect (1908): Henry C. Pelton
Architect for Renovations (1924-1934): E. Spencer Guidal

T THE END of the nineteenth century Oliver D. Mead owned Round Island—a wooded island at high tide when the sandy beach linking it with the mainland was awash. It was part of the Mead family farm, and since the early 1800s a small stone warehouse and dock at Bush's Harbor, on the eastern side of the island, had been used for shipping farm produce before better roads made travel to market easier.

Oliver D. Mead (1842-1939) had inherited the family farm and its 120 acres from his older second cousin, Oliver Mead (1800-1887). He was known for his generosity in sharing his waterfront with the people of Greenwich, and Round Island was a favorite picnic and swimming spot. Hoping to preserve this public usage, in 1895 the town agreed to buy the island, plus another six acres on the mainland, from Mead for a town park for $75,000. This was not to be, however. In the previous decade much of Belle Haven (the Nelson Bush farm and that of Augustus Mead) had already been sold for real estate development, and the new summer residents did not like the idea of a public park so near to their exclusive homes. What would surely have been one of the most popular beach areas on the Sound instead became a private enclave adjacent to Field Point Park.

John Davol Chapman (1874-1934) was married to the former Adelaide Foltz (1883-1945), the daughter of a Newcastle, Pennsylvania, banker. The Chapmans must have become acquainted with the Round Island property when they summered at Belle Haven, and in 1908 Chapman purchased a bit over ten acres from the Field Point Land Company, organized by Oliver D. Mead. The Greenwich papers described Chapman, then thirty-four, as a "wealthy New Yorker." The son of a Brooklyn doctor, he had attended Williams College (as did both of his sons in later years) and entered the brokerage business soon after graduating. The year before the purchase of Round Island, Chapman became a special partner in the house of Chisolm and Chapman and a member of the New York Stock Exchange.

The house was designed by Henry C. Pelton, architect of New York City's Riverside Church, but no record remains of how it looked. In 1924 ten years of remodeling was begun that greatly altered the house, creating a fantasy of English country life by the sea. Acting as architect for the project was Edward Spencer Guidal, an Englishman who worked for some years in Greenwich.

Very little is known of the details of Guidal's life, but he greatly influenced Greenwich taste and style. As early as 1908 he was associated with the office of John Russell Pope as an interior designer. It is probable that he became familiar with the town when Pope's firm was designing Merleigh Farm, the Hencken house on North Street. A disagreement with Pope in 1916 caused him to leave the firm and to work on his own. Whether the Chapmans first brought him to work in Greenwich is not known, but he quickly became popular with a circle of wealthy patrons who sought his advice and commissioned him to give an authentic English style to their American homes. He became known for his masterful use of paving stones, brickwork, and carved wood, which he employed in designing and renovating Connecticut residences that could pass as English manor houses. Although he was not a licensed architect, his field experience had taught him to function as one, especially when working with experienced builders.

At Round Island Guidal was teamed with "Pat" Petrizzi, a local builder born near Naples, Italy, who had assembled a crew of craftsmen able to carry out demanding design work. Petrizzi remembered that it was sometimes difficult to work with the capricious designer. "He would never discuss money, and he wouldn't use plans," said Mr. Petrizzi. "He would imagine how he wanted a detail to look and we would do it from his description, or maybe a simple sketch."

View of the main house from the water side. Gil Amiaga photo.

The Lodge.

Garden fountain, part of a later renovation. Gil Amiaga photo.

The team transformed the residence into a manor house in the style of the late Gothic period using limestone and brick and exposed timbers. Tall clustered chimneys rising from a terra-cotta roof gave the structure a romantic silhouette, as did the gothic-windowed porch on the garden end of the second floor. To produce the effect of artful rusticity, Guidal sent his workmen on scavenging trips throughout Rhode Island and Connecticut to buy and disassemble old barns and buildings for their aged beams and weathered wood. Brass and iron hardware, designed by the architect, was manufactured in New York especially for the project.

The redesigned facade featured an arched entry, which opened into the stately entrance hall. From here one reached the music room, with a built-in organ and garden views. Also entered from the hall was the formal living room with its Gothic detailing and mullioned windows. A large stone fireplace with oversized andirons warmed the space, and glass doors decoratively barred with wrought-iron grilles opened to a flagstone terrace and the sloping garden below. Up a few steps from this room was the dining room, the most fanciful room in the house. At the far end of the stone-floored salon a grand fireplace rose almost to the ceiling. Grouped stone pilasters with carved capitals had a Byzantine appearance, and the face of the fireplace was decorated with designs carved in relief in the brick. Overhead Guidal installed old oaken beams in the ceiling, and Petrizzi's artisans enhanced them with delicate Persian painting. Gilded statuary niches were placed here and there in the walls and a heavy iron chandelier was lighted by candles. A stone dining terrace was built just outside. So that al fresco diners would not be overpowered by the spacious grounds, the space was designed as an outdoor room with a fragmentary wall separating this terrace from the one by the living room.

Although each main floor room boasted a view of the water it was not the dominant feature for any of them. Rather it was always focused and seen through window mullions and frames of greenery. From each room one could also see exterior stone window details or brick buttresses so that even in gazing out, the viewer was always mindful of being surrounded by the beautifully detailed walls of the house.

Most of the second floor bedrooms had private tiled bathrooms. In the Guidal-designed renovations they were given different personalities: each was English or Italian or French, with appropriate interior finishes. A breakfast room on this level was linked to the kitchen by a dumbwaiter so that the family could breakfast quietly, while enjoying the view without descending into the more public area of the house. Privacy was also a consideration in the design of the crenellated tower which protruded from the master bedroom's balcony. In it a stairway wound down to a small door which opened onto the lawn, permitting swimmers to go from the bedrooms to the beach without having to appear on the main floor of the house in their swimming attire.

Since the 1930s several owners have altered the interior of the Round Island house. Redecorations have changed the flavor of the interior and have tamed it somewhat. Most representative of this trend is the dining room which now appears more eighteenth century than sixteenth. The stone floor was covered and the ceiling beams were hidden behind conventional plaster. The massive stone fireplace was replaced by a smaller one suited to the now wallpapered room, and a more recent doorway opens directly to the entrance hall. In the former music room the organ, like so many placed in turn-of-the-century houses, was removed, and the space is now a cozy library.

Though the main house has undergone many changes since the 1930s the principal outbuilding, the Lodge, looks much as it did upon completion. This fanciful building sits down the slope from the main house, on the edge of the inner harbor; it was entirely the creation of E. Spencer Guidal.

So charming is this building that one overlooks its intended purpose of housing a five-car garage. The cobbled automobile court was laid with stones discarded from New York City streets during repaving. The Lodge's garage story is stone but with an upper story of exposed timbers infilled with wattle and daub. Access to the second floor living quarters is via a stone stairway and through a charming cone-topped tower which mimics a Kentish oasthouse. From here a narrow passage leads into the large, open living and dining area. Although additions have been made to the building, the original portion of the structure is essentially unaltered. It has been rejuvenated as a separate year-round residence.

From the water Round Island is a marked contrast to the other grand houses of the area. While the homes of Field Point Park sit amid large swathes of open lawn rolling down to the beach, Round Island's mien is more secretive with only hints of the house's charms visible through the trees and only a few

structures clearly seen at the water's edge. Sailors and ferryboat riders have become familiar with them: the original 1827 quayside building where farm goods were once shipped serves as a dockhouse with steps leading down the rock ledge to a small wharf.

A few yards away on the cliff is a stone-and-brick structure built as a pavilion in the Guidal renovations and later enclosed for a guesthouse. But down the stone walk is Round Island's most distinctive small building, the beach pavilion. With buttressed walls and an irregular roofline, this structure appears to be a remnant of a medieval monastery, but stone decorations on the outer walls give the birthdates of the two Chapman sons—John and Richard—and dispel the illusion.  Used brick and Belgian blocks were incorporated into this design in the 1920s along with decorative touches of stone and statuary gathered from the New England countryside and from abroad. A sundial, protectively placed on the inside walls, bears the date 1734 and adds to the feeling of antiquity, but no record of the timepiece's origin remains. The stone walls pierced with wide arches offer transition from the protected walls of the medieval-inspired house to the modern Connecticut waterfront, and it has been the romantic setting for at least one family wedding.

Between beach and manor lie the gardens which have always been an important part of Round Island's beauty. Guidal defined the area with low masonry walls interspersed with tall pillars to create a grand *allée* leading to the beach pavilion. Here and there are arches and tableaus of statuary and brick, including pineapples carved from stone by Petrizzi's expert craftsmen. The Chapmans maintained the garden in formal English style with many flower borders and boxwood hedges. Topiary peacocks lent an amusing note, and vegetable plots were carefully screened by evergreen walls. The landscaping was maintained by a complicated underwater irrigation system fed by a natural spring well.

Although the Chapmans eventually owned other vacation residences, they continued to refer to Round Island as home. John Chapman died in 1934, but his widow maintained the estate until her death in 1945.

Rocklyn

Rocklyn and its commanding view of Long Island Sound.

Principal Owner: Edwin Binney
Original Architect (1895): Unknown
Architect for Reconstruction (1927): George Chappell

I N THE AUTUMN OF 1888, Edwin Binney (1866-1934), whose family would play a leading role in shaping the town of Old Greenwich, explored the rocky stretches of its shore. From Tomac Cove on the Stamford border to the Greenwich Inn at the foot of Sound Beach Avenue, only a tiny oyster-man's watchhouse interrupted his view of Long Island Sound and the distant land beyond. By January 1889 he had purchased a promontory of rock on the shore from Oliver Ford, whose family had farmed the rocky coast for generations. During the spring Binney began to build the first residence on that stretch of the shore, a small, shingled cottage that would be a summer retreat for his New York-bound family. Over the next six years he added more land and two other houses to what was to become a family enclave.

In 1895 the original shore house was moved in-land, and work began on Rocklyn. The Binneys, deter-mined to live in Sound Beach, now known as Old Greenwich, year-round, needed a more substantial home. Though some area residents questioned their choice of a site where there was "nothing to see," the Binneys perched their fieldstone house on the edge of the rocky promontory just feet from the sea. The gambrel-roofed, shingle-style house was approached from the north under a porte-cochere with steep steps leading to a Norman-style stone tower with crenellated ramparts and diamond-shaped leaded windows enclos-ing a circular staircase to the upper stories. The living room and two principal bedrooms above looked out over the Sound. An octagonal dining room with Mrs. Binney's sitting room over it encompassed views all the way around to the beach on the western side of the house. The kitchen wing, with the master bedroom above and the servants' bedrooms on the third floor, looked toward the beach through a wide galleried porch with white wooden columns, later replaced with stone. A terrace led from the side porch to another off the living room, above which a sunroom was even-tually added.

The new Rocklyn was a fitting symbol of the remarkable success Edwin Binney had achieved by his twenty-ninth year. Born in Shrub Oak, New York, on November 24, 1866, he attended school in Peekskill but left school very early to go to work. One of his first jobs was with a carbon-manufacturing company. He tried to continue his education by attending night school in Harlem; but at seventeen he became a travel-ing salesman for a paint company in Springfield, Massachusetts. The following year he opened a branch office in New York. Then, in 1885, at nineteen, he and his cousin organized Binney and Smith Company to manufacture carbon black from natural gas. At about this time he met Alice Stead (1866-1960) who, like his own parents, had emigrated from England. Alice had studied at what is now Hunter College in New York City and was an English teacher in the New York Public Schools. On October 26, 1886, they were mar-ried, and two years later their daughter, Dorothy, was born. By this time the three-year-old Binney and Smith Company was successful enough to allow the Binneys the luxury of a summer cottage, tiny as it was, in Old Greenwich. By 1895, just ten years after its in-ception, the Binney and Smith Company had become one of the largest manufacturers of carbon black in the world, and from one tiny cottage on the shore the estate known as Rocklyn had grown.

Binney and Smith had also begun to diversify. It became a large producer of natural gas and natural gas gasoline. The company introduced colored and in-dustrial crayons and developed a dustless crayon for schoolroom use. Over the next thirty years Binney's experience in the chemical and natural gas industries led him to become president and a director of Sebs Chemical Company, vice-president and a director of the Coltexo Corporation, as well as a director of the Columbian Gasoline Company, the Southern Carbon Company, Piney Oil and Gas Company, Southern Gas Lines, Inc., Western Carbon Company, Mississippi River Fuel Corporation, and Peerless Carbon Black Company.

Rocklyn with Oak Grove Beach before it was acquired by the Binneys in 1916.

Rocklyn and the Binney family about 1900.

Rocklyn after rebuilding, circa 1929.

Despite his increasing corporate responsibilities, Edwin Binney spent a great deal of time with his family. Two more daughters, Helen and Mary, had been born in 1890 and 1892, respectively, and in 1899 a son, Edwin, Jr., nicknamed June, was born. Helen Binney Kitchel remembers how her father "interpreted" the sounds of the wild birds for them and taught them to swim and sail. Boating was a favorite interest of the family from early rowboats to the seventy-two-foot cruiser *Florindia*, built by the family in their backyard in 1917. Bowes & Mower, local naval architects, designed it to government standards in case the Navy might need it for war service! Family picnics and outings were regular events, and a "bad weather playroom" was built in the third-floor attic with two trapezes hanging from the rafters.

The Binney family had also become very involved in the activities of Old Greenwich. In 1900 they worried that Miss Lockwood's one-room schoolhouse, just north of the present Lockwood Avenue, was inadequate. Serving on a committee with H. O. Havemeyer, A. A. Marks, Henry Frost, William Scofield, and other concerned citizens, Edwin Binney worked for the construction of a two-story brick schoolhouse, which forms the core of the present Old Greenwich School. Both the Binneys were active members of the First Congregational Church. They belonged to the Riverside Yacht Club and played golf at Innis Arden, J. Kennedy Tod's estate.

Despite the frenetic building that was changing the appearance of Old Greenwich and its shoreline, life at Rocklyn before World War I continued at a gentle pace. Though the house had been piped for gas during its construction in 1895, this convenience was many years in coming. Kerosene lamps had to serve until electricity came in 1907-1908. D. P. Van Wickell, whose small grocery store was on Shore Road, visited each morning in his horse and buggy taking orders for eggs, flour, bread, and other staples, returning later in the day to deliver them.

Over the years the Binneys had acquired several homes and lots as well as a squash court, a garage, and tennis courts. As each child married, she or he was given a house or lot, so that the area became an enclave of Binneys. In 1916 the acquisition of Oak Grove Beach to the west of Rocklyn completed their dominion over the lane.

During this period the Binneys began to look for other areas to develop. A 1,300-acre pre-Civil War plantation in the pine woods of North Carolina was the focus of their efforts for some time. Later they acquired a winter home in Fort Pierce, Florida, amid 300 acres of citrus groves. Binney was instrumental in opening the harbor at Fort Pierce and built a huge storage plant to prepare and preserve fruit for refrigerated steamers. He became chairman of the board of the Fort Pierce Port Commission, a director of the Fort Pierce Financing and Construction Company, and chairman of the board of the St. Lucie County Bank.

On January 8, 1927, fire broke out at Rocklyn. Though firemen were quickly alerted and neighbors helped douse the flames, the wooden part of the structure was destroyed. Alice Binney, along with architect George Chappell, supervised Rocklyn's rebuilding. A new north wing was added, incorporating basement garages, a new kitchen and dining room on the first floor and three servants' bedrooms above. The old kitchen in the south wing became a library, and the old octagonal dining room became a study. The Norman tower was enclosed by the new wing, so that only a quarter section could be seen from outside. The porte-cochere was not replaced; the open entrance steps were enclosed, and the front door was brought out flush with the new wing. The new second story was built of honey-colored stucco and stone, and the roof was rebuilt in slate—never again would Rocklyn succumb to flames! The roofline was lowered, the third-floor rooms eliminated, and the horizontal line of the porches was emphasized to produce a sleeker house.

The new Rocklyn's interior retained most of its old features while incorporating many improvements. The dark oak wainscoting in the living room and the former dining room, now a study, remained; a pair of oak pocket doors with a stained-glass representation of Rocklyn done about 1915 separated the two rooms. The living room's beamed ceiling was strengthened at this point by encasing massive steel beams; classical columns in dark oak were added to the walls for their support. The fireplace was of rough fieldstone with a bronze plaque of the heads of Edwin and Alice Binney sculpted in high relief hanging above it. The new dining room had a plastered coved ceiling and a tiled corner fireplace; a door to the terrace opened at the opposite corner, and the room shared the incomparable sea views of the living room. To the former kitchen were added a fireplace mantel and bookshelves with egg-and-dart moldings to create a library with access to the long covered porch overlooking the beach.

The second floor now contained five principal bedrooms with spectacular views joined by a wide hall on the inland side of the house and three servants' rooms over the kitchen. Four bathrooms were constructed with the square bisque tiles typical of the 1920s; Edwin, Jr., who had set a world's record while swimming for Yale, had a three-foot-long tile representation of a diver among the wine-and-ocher tiles over his bathtub. The two bedrooms above the living room led out to a glassed-in sun porch and beyond to an open deck built out over the rocks. The house, in plan a squared C, was but one room deep throughout, so that each room sparkled with the reflected light of the Sound.

In 1928 the Binneys' tremendous energies were focused on Old Greenwich; they bought the land between Sound Beach Avenue and Arch Street to create a town park. Edwin Binney deeded the land to the town with the provision that he would be responsible for the landscaping. The area, basically swampland, was filled, and a rock-rimmed lake and an island were created. The project occupied the next four years and helped to carry him through the tragic death of his son, June, at the age of twenty-nine.

On December 17, 1934, just over a year after the dedication of Binney Park, Edwin Binney died of a heart attack near his home in Florida. He was sixty-nine years old.

Alice Binney's commitment to Old Greenwich continued for the remaining twenty-six years of her life. She was a founder and past president of the Greenwich Historical Society. She donated a large sum of money to create the June Binney Memorial Parish Hall, adjacent to the First Congregational Church. She helped finance the purchase of the Natural Park on Harding Road, a part of the Laddin's Rock Farm property, for use by the townspeople. And she was instrumental in obtaining the Hillside Annex to Binney Park. She died at the age of ninety-four in 1960.

Rocklyn and the other Binney homes still stand. They and the parks, the school, and the parish hall are monuments to the energy and vision of Edwin and Alice Stead Binney.

Glen Airlie

Glen Airlie from the Sound side, circa 1910.

Principal Owner: Edgar L. Marston
Architect: Lord, Hull and Hewlett
Construction Date: 1903

N 1901 when Jennie and Edgar Marston came to East Port Chester, which is now known as Byram, they purchased thirteen acres of land from William J. Tingue, founder of Hawthorne Woolen Mills in Glenville and an early developer of Byram. The estate, called Glen Airlie, already contained a house, a cottage, a greenhouse, and a stable, and Marston immediately set out to make improvements on the property. That very year he obtained permission from the state to fill and level portions of the land, and the following summer he undertook construction of a wall along Sound View Avenue (Byram Shore Road) which still stands. Stone for the work was brought to the estate by boat, probably from the quarries on the eastern end of the Byram shore. In the summer of 1902 this kind of activity must have been of great interest to the neighborhood because a humorous mishap—the accidental dunking of an Italian laborer from one of the stone boats—was noteworthy enough to be passed around by the local wags.

Edgar L. Marston (1860-1935) was a founding partner of Blair and Company, investment bankers, which later became Bancamerica-Blair Corporation. He was married to Jennie C. Hunter (1865-1923) whose father, Colonel Robert Hunter, founded Texas and Pacific Coal and Oil, of which Marston later became president.

The improvements were already under way when the stable of the Marstons' summer house burned. Rather than replace the building on its waterfront site, Edgar Marston took the opportunity to develop a more grandiose scheme for his estate. Where the stable had stood, on a rock ledge overlooking the water, he built a lavish new house or "casino," as it was romantically termed. A newspaper article in February 1903 announced that the structure would be 80 by 130 feet and made of stone and wood. It would feature "a palm garden, conservatory, plunge baths, billiard rooms, and music hall." There would be a series

of fifty-four rooms for "the family's entertainment and caprices." In addition the plan included a bath pavilion and an amphitheater. All this was expected to cost $35,000 and to be ready that July!

This sumptuous retreat was designed by Lord, Hull and Hewlett. The architectural firm was led by Austin W. Lord who had worked under McKim, Mead, and White. In 1894 he had formed a partnership with J. Monroe Hewlett and Washington Hull. The architects gave Glen Airlie all the grandeur and sophistication appropriate to a house which would stand next door to Joseph Milbank's magnificent new home, The Towers.

Whether construction progressed on schedule is not known, but the house and outbuildings certainly fulfilled the owners' expectations. In the style of a French manor house, the casino was composed of a series of silo-shaped sections grouped together under curved, sharply peaked roofs. Covered porches encircled most of the house's main floor, their roof sections supported by white columns and following the rounded ends of the house's wings. The center of the house had four stories, and its sharply pitched roof was pierced by gables on the two upper levels. From this core a wing of three stories stretched toward the Sound, its gallery glassed in part to form a garden room.

From the road a driveway curved through the gardens and led to a columned porte-cochere, which was an extension of the front porch. Through the front door one entered a main hall which also gave access to a porch on the shore side of the house. Adjacent to this hall was the music hall. It had wainscoted walls with wallpaper above and a paneled wooden ceiling with carved beams supported by classical columns. Large oriental rugs covered the polished wood floors; and a pipe organ, ever popular in houses of that era, was built into the room. The drawing room was

The main entrance.

The carriagehouse reflected the architectural style of the main house.

dignified with its windowed bay and delicately detailed *boiserie* which included pilasters and carved garlands on the overdoor. The living room resembled a grand hall with coffered ceiling of beautifully carved wooden ribs from which were hung two branched, electrified chandeliers. This room was heated by a handsome marble fireplace and was furnished with a variety of armchairs, occasional tables, and glass-fronted book-cases.

The dining room, large enough to accommodate many guests, was ceilinged with polished wood. This room was served by a large and well-staffed kitchen which was supplemented by generous pantries and a well-stocked wine cellar. A study or smoking room had dark-paneled walls and leather-covered library chairs. As promised, the "family's entertainments and caprices" were remembered in the design of such recreation areas as the billiard room which had ample space for billiard and pool tables.

Robert C. Marston, grandson of the estate's owner, recalls that the operations of the house were overseen by a butler named Henry who was a former slave. The house had such a large number of rooms that another grandson, Edgar J. Marston, remembers being lost there as a child when he was sent to Glen Airlie to escape a diphtheria epidemic.

On the beach, the Marstons had a covelike section of waterfront dammed to create a swimming pool, and nearby a tiny beach pavilion served as a dressing area for bathers. Architecturally this Queen Anne style pavilion was not related to the other structures on the property and probably remained from the Tingue era.

Edgar Marston continued acquiring land for his estate until it totaled forty-three acres in 1906, the largest of the great estates in the Byram area. Across the road from the main house Marston built an imposing carriagehouse. The main and tallest section of the building included a rounded tower mimicking the design of the great house. From here extended, on either side, two-story wings with staff quarters on the upper floors. Although there had been a greenhouse on the property, Marston built a new one near the carriagehouse. This glass structure was 150 feet long. One entire section was devoted to carnations, probably for indoor arrangements. In addition to the propagation area inside, banks of cold frames were placed along the south side of the structure.

As the Marstons's children became adults and returned to the shore to visit with their families, housing for them was provided on the estate. A house originally intended as a gardener's cottage was used by their daughter Jennie after her marriage to Robert J. Adams, an event which took place in Glen Airlie's garden. In 1912 Marston bought a house on the corner of Byram Shore Road and Atlantic Street (now James Street) for his son, Hunter, and his family. This large Queen Anne style shingled cottage had stood on Elbert Briggs's shorefront property nearby until Fred Hirschhorn bought the Briggs land and removed the house to its new inland location. Marston also purchased a neighboring house for his other son, Edgar J. Marston.

In 1920, with Mrs. Marston in failing health, Edgar L. Marston decided to sell Glen Airlie. In 1923 Jennie Hunter Marston died, and a few years later her husband moved to California.

The main foyer and staircase.

View from the drawing room during the Marstons' ownership.

In 1921 Walter Teagle (1878–1962), president of Standard Oil of New Jersey, and his wife came to Greenwich. Rowena Lee Teagle (d. 1968) had been seeking a country house so that the Teagles' son, Walter Teagle, Jr., (1923–1960) would be able to grow up outside of the city. The Teagles announced their intention to purchase the Flagler estate, Northbrook Farm, in January 1921, but the night before the sale was to be closed, the house burned to the ground. Still eager to make their move to the country, they bought the Marston estate on Byram Shore Road five months later. There was irony in the transaction since Edgar L. Marston had tried to sell Texas and Pacific to Standard of New Jersey several years earlier, but Teagle did not like the terms. Apparently the two men had more success negotiating the Byram real estate transaction.

The Teagles put their own identity on the property, first changing the name from Glen Airlie to Lee Shore, probably a play on Mrs. Teagle's maiden name. In the mid-1920s they added a swimming pool wing with doors that opened onto a view of the Sound.

Under Mrs. Teagle's direction the gardens of Lee Shore became renowned. She studied horticulture at Columbia University under Dr. Hugh Findlay, and there met a student of landscape architecture named George Smith whom she hired to help landscape the Lee Shore gardens. He eventually became the estate's steward and remained there in that capacity until the 1960s. Together, Smith and Mrs. Teagle turned the already lovely gardens into a showplace which required the services of twenty gardeners. Every May the grounds were opened to the public, and guests could walk the estate's two miles of paths to enjoy blooming rhododendrons and azaleas and a brilliant collection of perennials and annuals.

Walter Teagle died in 1962 and his wife six years later. After Mrs. Teagle's death the Byram Shore property was sold and subdivided. The sprawling old house was pulled down, leaving only the swimming pool wing, and a new house was built on its site. The gardener's cottage and the carriagehouse now exist as residences, and the little beach pavilion has been relocated to a neighboring property where it is used as a guest cottage. The enormous greenhouse, little used, still stands near the carriagehouse—a reminder of the tremendous gardening operations required to keep the estate looking its best.

The Pryory

Entrance to The Pryory today. Gil Amiaga photo.

Principal Owner: Samuel F. Pryor
Architect: Cross and Cross
Construction Date: 1916

AMUEL FRAZIER PRYOR (1865-1934) was born in Palmyra, Missouri, a few miles west of the Mississippi River, only days after the Civil War ended. The son of a Virginia-born physician, he moved to the larger city of St. Louis as an adult when he went to work for the Wabash Railroad. In 1894 Pryor married the former Ruby Permelia Jacques (1868-1953) of Kansas, and the couple settled in suburban Ferguson, Missouri, where their four children were born—Samuel F., Jr., Jacques, Frederick, and Permelia. While still living in the Midwest, Pryor's career took a variety of turns as he moved from being chief purchasing agent of the Wabash Railroad; to vice-president of Simmons Hardware Company; to president of the Southern Wheel Company, a subsidiary of the American Brake Shoe and Foundry Company.

In 1914 Pryor went east as president of Remington Arms Company in New York at a time when war in Europe would bring large contracts to munitions manufacturers. Before America's entry into World War I rumors circulated that Germans were trying to buy control of American arms factories in order to block supplies to the Allies, but Pryor stoutly denied that such a takeover would be allowed to happen at Remington.

When the Pryors moved east, they went directly to Greenwich and lived for a time on Maple Avenue. They bought twenty acres in Field Point Park on the edge of a hill that sloped down to the water's edge. Although this neighborhood was being developed into a residential park, it had not entirely outgrown its earlier use as farmland. Adjacent to the fine new homes was the old farm built by Zophar Mead in the eighteenth century, and operated by his descendant, Oliver D. Mead.

Pryor called upon the architectural firm of John Walter Cross and Eliot Cross, a partnership of brothers active in the New York area, to design his house. At that time they were involved in construction of the

Eglise de Notre Dame on Morningside Drive, but they were better known for building residences for the upper class. In the decade after the Pryor project was completed they designed one of their greatest remaining buildings, the Barclay Hotel (now the Intercontinental) on East 48th Street in Manhattan.

The house they designed for the Pryor family was a marked contrast to the sophisticated city residences. In its rural setting it most nearly resembled a large cottage transplanted from the Cotswold Hills of England to the Connecticut shore. Brick walls were overplastered in stucco with random bits of brick exposed for an authentically rustic look. From the front entrance the steeply pitched roof was like a cloak of thatch draped over the two upper stories disguising the size of the residence. From this facade only two gables, exposed to their full three-storied height, suggest the house's true mass, but the back view is quite different. Here, where more fenestration was placed to take advantage of morning sun and afternoon breezes, the U-shaped design as well as the size of the house is apparent, and all seven of its tall, stuccoed chimneys are visible.

The front vestibule opens to a stair hall with a nearly free-standing stairway rising through all three main levels of the house and connected with the third-floor hall by a bridge. The stairs were probably designed by the firm of Watt and Sinclair, which is credited with designing the handsome wood paneling used throughout the house. Adjacent to this hall is a two-room ladies' powder suite with wainscoting and a cozy fireplace, and nearby is a "lounge room" for the gentlemen. The entry is at the midpoint of the hallway that extends the width of the house. When stepping across the passage one has a sense of being outdoors again in an extensive loggia walled by the house on three sides with large windows open to the terrace, the lawn, and the sea beyond. On hot summer days the room's cool shadows and tile floors gave relief from

51

Race day at Field Point Driving Park, adjacent to The Pryory, circa 1890.

the heat, and in other seasons open fireplaces at either end of the space added warmth.

The spacious living room, high-ceilinged and formal with many tall windows and a pillared fireplace, was situated at the south end of the house. The paneling here included fluted pilasters with carved rosettes on the capitals, and the tracery on the ceiling was the same pattern used throughout the main floor. At the opposite end of the house the formal dining room was served by a well-equipped kitchen and butler's pantry. Beside the dining room at the house's northeast corner was a smaller breakfast room with windows overlooking fields and the sandy beach that linked Pryor's land with Round Island. On the second and third floors were eleven comfortable bedrooms, but a screened sleeping porch was the dormitory for the Pryor children in both winter and summer. The house was maintained by a butler, several maids, and a cook for most of the years the Pryors lived in Field Point Park.

On the northern edge of the entrance court was a large circular garden with intersecting paths, part of a landscape plan by Mary Rutherford Hay. Beyond this stood a combination gatehouse/garage. Built of the same walling and roofing material as the house, it appeared as likely to contain a Cotswold sheepfold as twentieth-century automobiles. This structure housed the chauffeur and other staff members and complemented the design of the main house.

Shortly after coming to Greenwich, Samuel Pryor retired as Remington's president and became chairman of its executive committee. During the Greenwich years he was a director of the Air Reduction Company, the American Brake Shoe and Foundry Company, the Shell Union Oil Corporation, and the Greenwich Trust Company. He was a partner with Percy Rockefeller and Fred Adams in the Owenoke Corporation, an investment company. Pryor remained active in business until May 1933.

Ruby Jacques Pryor involved herself with civic affairs. She served for many years as a member of the board of directors of the Marian Osborne Home in Rye and was active in the Greenwich Garden Club.

The Pryors spent many years vacationing in Florida, first in Winter Park, and eventually establishing a home in Hobe Sound. After Mr. Pryor's death in 1934, Mrs. Pryor continued to maintain The Pryory. In 1940 she asked her son, Sam, Jr., and his wife to share the twenty-four room house with her. The arrangement worked well in the spacious house, and the senior Mrs. Pryor occupied the entire third floor, which was easily reached by a telephone-equipped elevator.

Samuel F. Pryor, Jr. (1898-1985), a graduate of the Taft School and Yale College, served in the Navy during World War I and then went to work for the American Brake Shoe and Foundry Company, with which his father had been associated. He was married

The stairs from the second floor hall. Gil Amiaga photo.

The rear facade overlooks the Sound. Gil Amiaga photo.

in Pittsburgh in 1926 to Mary Taylor Allderdice (1905-1978), whose father was president of the National Tube Company, which later became a subsidiary of U.S. Steel. In 1940 Pryor joined Pan American Airways and was vice-president of public relations and governmental affairs during the years when the company was becoming a giant in the industry.

It was the second Pryor family's years on Field Point Circle that are best remembered in Greenwich. With their five lively children, Sam and Mary Tay Pryor filled the pastoral-looking estate with activity. Pets of all sorts were welcomed in the house. The tennis courts overlooking the water were a center of activity, and the sloping lawn was often the scene of tag and football games. The pier in front of the house was used for swimming and boating activities, and for a time Pryor moored his amphibious seaplane there. Flying was an important part of the family life. The Pryor children, together with the children of Sam Pryor's close friend Charles A. Lindbergh, were introduced to flying early in life and often practiced takeoffs and landings in the seaplane offshore near the family home.

The Pryors entertained a variety of visitors, including presidents and prizefighters, reflecting Pryor's varied nonbusiness interests, one of which was his vice-chairmanship of the Republican National Committee. In later years, guests would come to see Pryor's famed collection of dolls, which was begun when an associate at Pan Am, Mrs. Ann M. Archibald, willed

him three hundred dolls which she had gathered from all over the world. Pryor set aside a portion of The Pryory's ample basement for the display of the figures, and the famous Pryor Doll Library was begun. With their children grown, Mary Tay and Sam Pryor sold the old family house in 1960 and bought the Mead farmstead next door. They refurbished its ancient barn to house the doll collection, which had grown to some three thousand pieces. In these quarters the library was opened to the public, and Junior League members served as guides and researchers from 1963-1970.

In the years since the Pryor family left, changes have been made at The Pryory, and rooms have been reshaped to suit different families' needs. The roof of thatch has been replaced with more contemporary shingle, and the land has been reduced to two acres as sections of the estate were parceled off and sold. The view from the hilltop is less bucolic, but The Pryory is still known as a fine house which once again shelters an active, growing family.

Miralta

Autumn gold frames the entrance to Miralta. C. Christopher Semmes photo.

Principal Owner: R. A. C. Smith
Architect (1901): Unknown
Architects for Renovations (1910-1913): Oswald C. Hering; Warren and Wetmore

T THE TURN of the century the land that became Field Point Park was yet undeveloped. Sitting high on a promontory of Long Island Sound, it consisted mainly of open fields which had been part of the 120-acre Mead farm. Still owned by Oliver D. Mead, it was the site of Field Point Driving Park, a well-known track for trotting races.

Leaving the raceway and the twenty-two acres of land in the center of the park open, Mead offered lots on the outer edge of the circle for sale, so that a few large houses could be built on generous parcels overlooking the water. Field Point Park eventually became one of Greenwich's most elegant private residential areas. But in December 1901 when Frank L. Froment bought nearly four acres on the circle, the area was still rustic.

Froment (1852-1917), a New Yorker, was a principal of Froment and Company, iron and steel merchants who represented U.S. mills throughout the world. Only days after purchasing the land, he contracted with the Ritch Constructing and Stone Company to build a house, the first on the circle. Construction took one year and cost $30,000.

The three-story house was symmetrical and in the Georgian style. The facade was embellished with Ionic-capped columns and pilasters and featured a portico sheltering a second-floor balcony and the main entrance.

Inside, a broad center hall ran from the front to the rear of the house with a double stairway leading to the floor above. From the main hall one could look upward through two floors of galleries to a large oval stained glass dome. It was planned to add daylight to hallways on all three floors of the house.

After building the house Froment erected stables at the rear of the property. In November 1909 he sold the summer home to entrepreneur R. A. C. Smith. The

following year Smith also bought the lot next door, bringing his holdings to over eight acres.

The new owner, Robert A. C. Smith (1857-1933), was a financier who was well known in shipping and transportation circles. Smith, called "Rac" for his initials, was born in England and spent most of his youth in Cadiz, Spain. After finishing his education in English boarding schools he came to New York, at the age of seventeen, to seek his fortune. He first worked for a company selling railroad supplies in Cuba and Latin American countries. From this he embarked on a series of entrepreneurial projects which eventually brought him wealth and power in business and politics. He helped organize utility and water companies in Havana and, returning to the United States, he embarked on similar projects in Connecticut and in Westchester County. Smith was also founder and president of the Connecticut Railway and Lighting Company (later Connecticut Light and Power Company). Eventually he was said to be associated with at least one hundred companies and corporations including the American Mail Steamship Company, Oakland Bayside Realty Company, American Tobacco Company, and McKesson Robbins.

Smith was probably already a millionaire when he and his wife, the former Alice S. Williams of Brooklyn, came to Greenwich. His younger brother, Alfred Gilbert Smith, had already settled there in a house he named Altaroca. Visiting Europe, Rac Smith had admired the architecture of fine Italian Renaissance villas and determined to create such a house for himself, even in the unlikely setting of the New England coast. One wonders if this dynamic man were naturally drawn to the architecture of an age that had exalted individual achievement. But whatever his reasons, he commissioned Oswald Constantin Hering to design his summer residence.

Trained at Massachusetts Institute of Technology and Ecole des Beaux-Arts in Paris, Hering had been

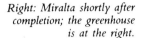

Left: R. A. C. Smith and his wife at a Long Island picnic.

Right: Miralta shortly after completion; the greenhouse is at the right.

in practice in New York for ten years when Smith hired him. In the course of his career he designed many suburban residences and became something of a specialist in concrete and stucco houses, even writing a book on the subject.

For the Miralta renovations he sent to Italy for skilled stonemasons and artists to carry out his plan. An entire village of houses and workshops for the craftsmen was erected on the property. After the project's completion the dwellings were pulled down and most of the workers returned to Italy, although presumably some stayed in Connecticut.

The construction took three years. With the addition of new wings at either end of the house and removal of oversized pillars and pilasters, Hering simplified the facade into the strong horizontal lines of the prototypal fortified Italian house. The shingled roof was replaced with red terra-cotta, and the entire facade was stuccoed.

Preserving the existing interior layout, Hering had every room redesigned with beautifully ornamented *boiserie* and elaborately plastered ceilings utilizing the skills of the Italian artisans. Gold leaf and faux marbre painting was used extensively, and parquet floors were laid, the patterns varying from room to room. A living room and a dining room were added at either end of the main floor expanding the floor plan so that from the spacious entrance hall rooms opened one into another, connected by oversized doorways. This free-flowing design not only welcomed summer breezes, but also was suited to large entertainments. (Most notable of these was a wedding breakfast for five hundred guests when Smith's daughter, Madeline, married Irvin W. Day, only weeks after the house was completed.)

In the court-like entrance hall a marble fireplace, seven feet tall, was carved with a classical bas relief of cherubs. Graceful columns with Ionic capitals framed the entrances to adjacent rooms, and Egyptian-influenced woodwork of the Froment house was overlaid with brilliant Italian stenciling. The ceiling's plaster medallions were adorned with polychrome painting and on the hall's floor lay seven oriental rugs, the largest being twenty-two feet long. This room contained several paintings of religious subjects, but throughout the rest of the house the Smiths seemed to favor scenes of Italy and Spain.

The walls of the formal reception room were draped with antique velvet hangings, and its cornices were painted with heraldic motifs. The adjacent billiard room was elegantly masculine with its red velvet curtains and handsome furnishings. Supporting the wooden fireplace mantel were elongated brackets carved as lions, repeating the design of the iron fireback which was cast in the shape of a lion's face that seemed to change expression as dancing flames cast their shadows on it. Beyond the billiard room a ballroom-sized living room opened to the summer loggia where one could enjoy the lofty views for which Miralta, or "high view," was named.

On the north side of the house was a comfortable library with built-in cabinets faced with stained-glass doors that depicted symbols of printing and bookbinding. This room opened to the spacious dining room, its elegant ceiling patterned with plaster garlands of fruit and flowers and further adorned with hand-painted borders. Panels of the soft gray dining room walls were delicately decorated with griffins and urns.

The second floor contained family and guest bedrooms, seven in all, as well as a sleeping porch. Above, another seven bedrooms were furnished in simple style for the twelve members of the household staff who were usually in residence. In all, the house contained fifteen tiled bathrooms.

Because of the slope of the land the garden, or lowest, level of the house was revealed only at the rear. Here Smith installed an indoor swimming pool. This floor also contained utility spaces and the kitchen,

Family and friends aboard the first "Privateer."

which served the dining room above via a dumb waiter.

In 1913, soon after the house was completed, Smith had further renovations made. One can only conjecture why Hering did not design these alterations, but perhaps Rac Smith's interest in railroads had put him in touch with the firm of Warren and Wetmore who were just completing their involvement in the construction of Grand Central Terminal in collaboration with Charles A. Reed and Alan H. Stem. Whitney Warren and Charles D. Wetmore enjoyed a successful partnership for more than thirty years designing such landmarks as the New York Yacht Club and the Biltmore Hotel.

The addition designed by this firm for Miralta provided a sitting room at the rear of the house at the mezzanine level. In this room was placed a spectacular stained glass window depicting the castle of Chillon on Lake Geneva. A mural on the ceiling of this area supposedly includes the faces of Alice Smith, the couple's two daughters, Margaret and Madeline, and son Bartlett who had died of diphtheria during childhood. An atelier for the seamstress and valet was placed on the level above. At the same time the porches adjacent to the living room and dining room were enclosed with windows, the latter providing a breakfast room overlooking the gardens.

Photographs of the house under R. A. C. Smith's ownership show enormous tubs of blooming plants and topiary trees ornamenting the terraces. These, and the variety of palms and ferns kept in the house, were produced in Miralta's splendid iron-frame greenhouse. This was actually a series of buildings focused on a dome-topped palm house, thirty-five feet tall and nearly thirty-five feet square. Extending north from the palm house was a wing containing "vineries," specialized greenhouses devoted to the indoor cultivation of grapes, and perhaps reflecting the Smiths' epicurean tastes. The complex included cold frames for seedlings and small herb plantings. At the northwest corner was a clothes yard, discreetly walled, so that the sight of the family's laundry drying would not detract from the beauty of the surroundings. To the rear of the palm house was a greenhouse used exclusively for raising roses for which the estate became well-known locally. Miralta's greenhouses were constructed by Lord and Burnham Company, horticultural architects and builders of such magnificent glass structures as the conservatories at the New York Botanical Gardens.

The gardens of Miralta were an interesting mix of classical Italian and Victorian ideals. From the house, a path lined with high-pruned trees led to a stone-columned arbor which supported roses and framed a grass tennis court. On the hillside below the greenhouse a Roman-style swimming pool was built into the slope, ornamented with sculpture and a rose-covered pergola. Below the pool was a vegetable garden decoratively laid out in parterres. In various parts of the property, flowering annuals were bedded out in decorative patterns, reflecting a Victorian style and making use of materials from the greenhouse. Here and there on the grounds were vignettes with benches and garden ornaments and paths lined with evergreen trees.

Downhill from the main house, the Smiths remodeled Frank Froment's carriagehouse in the style of a villa. This served as housing for Smith's stablemen as well as the crew of his cruiser, *Privateer,* which was anchored in the cove below.

At various times Smith had at least two power yachts by that name, the largest of which was a steel-hulled boat, 176 feet long. It is likely that this cruiser was used for commuting into New York during the summers spent in Greenwich, since these were also active times for Smith's career. In the year Miralta was completed he was appointed New York City's Commissioner of Docks and Ferries, a position he held for five years. In this capacity he obtained government approval for longer piers on the New York waterfront, enabling the city to build additional dockage for berthing the larger ocean liners which Smith accurately prophesied would be vital to the port's continued success.

Smith continued to be active in business until he was in his seventies. In 1933 he was in poor health when he and his wife sailed for England aboard the *Majestic* for what was to be a rest cure. Two days out of New York the tycoon suffered a stroke, dying only hours after docking in his native England. He left an estate of over $4 million. Ownership of the Greenwich house passed to his wife and was held in the family until the death of the elder Smith daughter, Mrs. Kerner Easton, in 1956. Much of Miralta's land has been subtracted, and growth of the trees has reduced the scope of the views; but the house remains much as it did at the time of the Smiths' ownership.

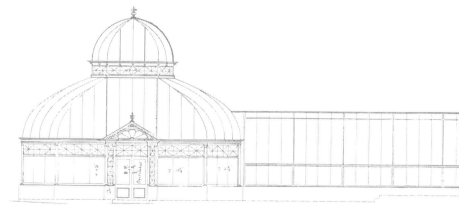

Milbank and The Towers

Milbank in the 1930s.

O N THE CORNER of Putnam and Milbank avenues stands an elaborate iron gate with massive pillars and archways, incongruously set into a low bluestone wall. Though it now encloses only a contemporary apartment building, it once marked the entrance to the largest estate in central Greenwich. This was Milbank, with land stretching from the Post Road to an inlet of the Sound, and from what is now Milbank Avenue to Indian Field Road, encompassing over three hundred acres.

The founder of the Milbank family in Greenwich, Jeremiah (1818-1884), began his business career as a wholesale grocer in New York in the late 1830s. A fortuitous meeting with Gail Borden in 1857 introduced him to the possibility of preserving milk by canning, and he financed the operation that was later to become the Borden Condensed Milk Company. Supplying this product to the Union Army during the Civil War brought instant wealth to both partners, and in 1863 Milbank further invested in the newly founded Chicago, Milwaukee and St. Paul Railroad. Soon his business life was so active that he turned the wholesale grocery business over to his son Joseph and devoted all his time to investment banking.

In the manner of other wealthy New Yorkers, Milbank decided to establish a suitable country house; that his wife, the former Elizabeth Lake (1827-1891), was from Greenwich surely influenced his choice of location. He purchased land opposite the Second Congregational Church, high above central Greenwich. It had been farmed until 1865 when New York politician William ("Boss") Tweed bought eighty acres from Philander Button, a principal of Greenwich Academy, to build Linwood, his summer home.

After Tweed's death in 1878, his widow sold the property to Jeremiah Milbank, who lived in it for a time, but the Republican was not interested in Tweed's house and had other plans for the site. He sold it to H. O. Havemeyer, who moved it several hundred feet to a lot on the Post Road. Local historian William Finch recalls that the Victorian house remained there (on property now owned by Temple Sholom) until it was razed in the 1930s. The only construction which survived from the Tweed era was part of the fine low bluestone wall which encircled the property, but even this wall would be interrupted by the grandiose gateway surmounted with the Milbank M, which Jeremiah Milbank had erected.

In the early 1880s Milbank engaged the fashionable New York architectural firm of Lamb and Rich to design his house. The partnership of Hugo Lamb and Charles Alonzo Rich later gained prominence for such projects as the Berkeley Preparatory School (now the Mechanics Institute) on West Forty-fourth Street in Manhattan. In the 1880s the two architects were becoming known mostly for their country house commissions, and Jeremiah Milbank need have looked no farther than Henry Mallory's house on Byram Shore for reference to their work.

Rich is generally credited with the Milbank design. It can never be known how much of such a house is architect's creation and how much is projection of a client's ego, but the result of the Milbank project was a suitable monument to the founder of a great American fortune. From the Putnam Avenue gate, visitors traveled a road shaded by elms and evergreens. At the end of the drive, in a broad clearing with manicured lawns, was the red-roofed mansion. Fortresslike, it stood near the brow of Putnam Hill overlooking woods and the Sound beyond. The heavily rusticated stone building was Romanesque-inspired with its suggestion of rounded towers. A broad roofed piazza swept across the front of the house and sheltered the main entrance.

From here one stepped into a wainscoted reception hall of baronial proportions, with panels elaborately carved in Renaissance motifs. Directly ahead was a handsome oak stairway leading to the second floor. A generous fireplace was decorated with Della Robbia-

The facade after the removal of the porch roof.

The garage, built in 1907 to replace the outdated stables.

Spence Cottage, built circa 1865 on land which became part of the Milbank estate.

style cherubs, carved in stone, who appeared to be warming their hands at the hearth.

The most ornate room was the parlor with its rounded bays. In this large salon—twenty-four by forty-four feet—walls lacquered deep red were hung with tapestries, and the exotic ceiling was coffered in bamboo. Across the hall the library appropriately featured built-in bookshelves and has been described as having been "quietly finished" in comparison with the more elaborate rooms. The lavish use of paneling in the hall extended into the dining room, where walls and ceilings were covered with carved mahogany.

The sense of being in a historic building, which visitors must have felt, belied the true character of the house, a comfortable and surprisingly modern dwelling for the 1880s. Many of the finest conveniences which money and engineering could provide were present: central heating, a laundry room in the basement, and an Otis elevator which ran from basement to attic.

The private second floor housed six large bedrooms and a family sitting room. The five bathrooms would have been comfortable in any era, with their silver-plated fixtures and walls adorned with six-inch, hand-painted tiles imported from China. On the third floor were a ballroom, a billiard room, and a playroom along with smaller family bedrooms and servants' rooms.

While the later garage/chauffeur's quarters echoed the architecture of the main house, other outbuildings scattered throughout the property were designed in a more pastoral fashion. Dairyman's cottage, carpenter's shop, and superintendent's house were all white-frame cottages built in the carpenter Gothic style with mansard roofs and "gingerbread" trim.

Although Jeremiah Milbank died before his house was completed, his descendants would use it until the 1950s. His wife saw the estate completed as planned, and as a memorial to her husband she donated the clock for the steeple of the Congregational Church directly opposite the entrance to Milbank.

From Jeremiah's wife the house and land passed to their son, Joseph (1848-1914), who deeded the holding to his sister, Elizabeth, in 1897 when he built his own summer estate in East Port Chester. Born in 1850, Elizabeth Milbank was the wife of Colonel A. A. Anderson, a noted portraitist whose studio was in New York. She was known as a generous woman whose beneficiaries included Barnard College and who founded, with her brother, the Milbank Memorial Fund devoted to charity. Elizabeth Anderson is remembered locally for many philanthropies. She donated the library to Greenwich and funded the town's first incinerator. Milbank was often the scene of gala charitable benefits, but given that she was a staunch temperance supporter, it is certain that no liquor was served at these affairs.

Over time Elizabeth Anderson acquired additional property until the parcel totaled 350 acres. (This, combined with other real estate she owned, made her the largest landholder in the Town of Greenwich by 1900.) She continued developing house and grounds in the manner her father had imagined. Under the direction of Thomas Pytell, the estate gardener for over thirty years, the grounds were planted with numerous specimen shrubs and shade trees — many of them rare and brought from distant places. In 1903 the town's first tree-spraying machine to control pests was developed at Milbank to protect the valuable plantings. Some of the statuary decorating the gardens were remainders of Tweed's ownership. Local legend has it that these pieces — like the building material for the estate wall — were intended for New York City parks but conveniently found their way to Greenwich as free adornment for Boss Tweed's property. A tennis court was added as well as a small playhouse complete with kitchenette and lavatory. A large greenhouse supplied off-season vegetables together with green plants for indoors. The lower part of the property was farmland including fields, stables, and poultry buildings requiring at least twenty farm workers.

The easternmost portion, along Indian Field Road, was left in its rustic state, with rocky forest and streams. The only dwelling in this area was a gatehouse known as the lodge. Located in the southeastern corner of the property where the woods opened into orchard and meadows, it was reminiscent of an English shepherd's cottage with a roof of thatch. This Adirondack-like portion of the property was the first to be subtracted from the holding. Elizabeth Anderson deeded the wild 273 acres to her cousin Albert Milbank in 1920, who in turn sold them to a developer, Arthur H. Waterman of Brooklyn and Rye. Now known as Milbrook, this was one of the country's first planned real estate subdivisions — a self-contained neighborhood with private club and golf course, designed to preserve much of the bosky setting. Only in the spelling of the subdivision's name, a play on the Milbank name, is any memory preserved of the family who once owned it.

The Andersons' daughter Eleanor was married briefly to John Stewart Tanner and later to Frederick B. Campbell. She became a physician and maintained a great interest in the field of public health. From her first marriage she had one daughter, Elizabeth. After the divorce this child was adopted by her grandmother as Elizabeth Milbank Anderson II. She spent much of her childhood at Milbank and attended Greenwich schools in the early grades before continuing her education in New York. It was she who inherited her grandmother's estate and as a young woman came back to Milbank in summers with her husband, H. Adams Ashforth, and children. Though Elizabeth Anderson Ashforth died very young in 1930, her husband and family continued to use the house, eventually making it their year-round residence.

Her son, Henry A. Ashforth, Jr., recalls it as a wonderful house in which to grow up, with views to the Sound from the upper windows and a spacious playroom for cold and rainy days. The gardens and farm provided plenty of entertainment for the children, and the remaining woods below the cliff still gave the house site a feeling of nearby wilderness.

But in 1940 the acreage was further reduced when the Town of Greenwich condemned sixteen acres of farmland to build the much-needed Julian Curtiss School. Even without the farm at least a dozen men were needed to maintain the grounds, and during the war years this kind of staffing was all but impossible. By the 1950s problems that afflicted many other large property owners — the lack of household staff, and the expense of heating such a cavernous space — were felt at Milbank, too. Weary of the burden, H. Adams Ashforth decided to sell, but on the contemporary real estate market the fine old house was a white elephant, more valuable for its property than as a residence. The house and land were purchased by developers, Chutick and Sudakoff of Forest Hills, New York, who would build apartments on the site.

Much of the sculpture and the furnishings were sold at auction. Bathroom fixtures and imported tiles, Renaissance-style paneling and mantels — appointments which Jeremiah Milbank had chosen for their look of permanence — were sold from the house before it was finally pulled down.

Little physical evidence of the estate remains to tell about it. The lodge is now a residence close on Indian Field Road, its thatched roof replaced by terracotta. The brick gardener's cottage has been incorporated into the Putnam Hill development, and nearby is the statue of Bacchus which once graced Milbank's lawn. Some evidence of the 1920s landscaping may be found in the towering trees — beech, elm, and sycamore — that have survived here and there in the real estate developments. And Jeremiah Milbank's grandiose gate still stands on the avenue, oblivious to the passage of time.

The main house of The Towers.

While Elizabeth Milbank Anderson maintained an estate on Putnam Avenue, her brother Joseph Milbank (1848-1914) was building a very different sort of estate on Byram Shore.

At the end of the nineteenth century the waterfront community now called Byram Shore was an isolated rural area then known as East Port Chester. Most of the land there had belonged to the Mead family for many generations, but as manufacturing developed along the Byram River and the little towns of Port Chester and East Port Chester grew, a few people recognized that this could one day become desirable real estate.

One of these individuals was William Tingue, owner of the Hawthorne Woolen Mills on the Byram River in Glenville. Among his real estate investments was a thirty-five acre tract along the water. This parcel would eventually be the waterside acreage of three of the most prominent estates of the Byram "gold coast": Marston, Milbank, and Hirschhorn. The development of Byram Shore as a summer watering place for wealthy and prominent New Yorkers proved to be beneficial to the town of Port Chester. Although the estate owners were only part-time residents, they developed a strong sense of community and contributed backing for such civic projects as the founding of United Hospital in Port Chester.

But this was many years in the future in 1886 when Tingue sold eleven of his acres to Matilda Starbuck. If she built a house on the land, no record of it remains, and in 1898 the tract was purchased by Joseph Milbank. Three years later, construction was begun on his summer home.

For design work he called upon the architectural

The main entrance gate.

The gate cottage.

firm of Howard and Cauldwell. John Galen Howard had apprenticed for the architectural firms of Henry Hobson Richardson and McKim, Mead, and White. He eventually moved to California where he became director of the School of Architecture at the University of California. While still in New York, Howard was associated for a time with Samuel Milbank Cauldwell, a Princeton graduate and cousin of Joseph Milbank. The two had been practicing together for only a few years when Milbank engaged them, but they had already enjoyed acclaim for their designs for the Hotel Renaissance and the Hotel Essex in New York, as well as for several distinguished residences.

This summer estate they planned for Joseph Milbank was known as The Towers. It was an enclave of house and dependencies unified by a theme of neo-Renaissance architecture. The common element was

provided by broad-eaved terra-cotta roofs which first greeted the visitor at the entrance gate and reappeared in various sizes and shapes on all of the estate's buildings. The structures were arranged on a twelve-acre site, giving the effect of a self-contained village nestled around the most important element, the grand manor house.

This imposing structure commanded the landscape from its waterfront site, and its bright red-tiled roof was visible at great distance across the Sound. It was a stucco-on-frame residence, its walls punctuated by windows with classical pediments.

The house's dominant feature was a four-and-a-half-story tower wing. At ground-floor level a porte-cochere extended over the driveway sheltering the main entrance. Three floors above was a balustraded loggia offering spectacular views in every direction. This porch was crowned with an exaggerated version of the peaked red roof and broad eaves.

The main floor held a large living room, a dining room, a card room, and a paneled library, as well as a pantry and a kitchen. On the second and third floors were nine bedrooms, each with bathroom, and the servants' wing held an additional eight maids' bedrooms. Presumably, while the Milbanks were living at The Towers, the latter bedrooms were always in use since a household staff of eight or nine were required to maintain the residence.

The house was planned to benefit from its waterside location. Besides the tower loggia there were three wide verandas (two of them screened) for warm weather sitting, and many of the rooms on the water side of the house had generous windows so that one could enjoy the view of gardens with the Sound beyond. On the south side of the house an old-fashioned formal garden, always planted in colors of blue and white, bloomed each summer below a large open porch. Just beyond was a traditional rose garden.

Outdoor amusements were easily found for the family and their guests. There was lawn bowling on a green near the beach, and the estate had a tennis court until 1962 when it was replaced with a swimming pool. A squash court was housed in its own building.

The gatehouse, a stucco dwelling, contains many design elements of the main house—hipped dormer, second-floor porch, stuccoed chimney—and has its own two-story version of the grand tower. The carriagehouse, containing stalls and tack room and, later, the garage, also carried the distinctive roofline. Even the tiny guest house interpreted the design theme on a small scale. This cottage, tucked away on the edge of the property, housed visitors in the summer and was used by the Milbank family on occasional winter weekends at the shore.

The only unrelated structure was the large glass-and-steel greenhouse whose art nouveau design was more sympathetic with the building's function. Here seedlings were started for the many gardens at The Towers, including vegetable gardens which covered an entire acre, and cutting gardens which provided flowers for the house.

Though architecturally interesting, The Towers is best remembered locally as home to several generations of the prominent Milbank family. The builder of the shore estate, Joseph Milbank, had worked closely with his father, the first Jeremiah Milbank, in grocery, railroad, and banking businesses. With his sister, Elizabeth Anderson of Milbank, he founded the Milbank Memorial Fund in memory of their parents.

After the death of Joseph Milbank in 1914, the Byram Shore estate passed to his son, Jeremiah (1887-1972). It was during Jeremiah Milbank's ownership of the estate that he had the yacht *Jem* constructed. This was a fast 75-foot vessel powered with two Rolls Royce engines which he used to travel between the summer house and New York. Named with Jeremiah Milbank's initials, it was a familiar sight anchored in the protected waters between Shell Island and The Towers' private beach. A larger yacht, *Saunterer*, was a cruiser used for family pleasure trips.

Just as the family estate passed from father to son, so did the tradition of philanthropy. Jeremiah Milbank founded and supported the Institute for the Crippled and Disabled, the first rehabilitation center in the United States and, with his brother Dunlevy (1878-1959), he was keenly interested in funding medical research. Like his father and grandfather before him, he was a staunch and active member of the Republican party, and his friend, President Herbert Hoover, was a frequent guest at the shore estate as well as on the Milbank yacht.

The death of Jeremiah Milbank in 1972 was also the end of The Towers as a family seat where generations of Milbanks had gathered on vacations and holidays and which, in recent years, had been a year-round residence. Of the three neighboring estate houses built on William Tingue's thirty-five acre parcel, The Towers had stood the longest, outlasting both the Marston and Hirschhorn residences. The era of enormous houses with loyal staffs was over, and the estate became another victim of the changing times.

The great house was torn down, and other homes were built on the site. Some of the dependencies survive as residences, and here and there between the trees one still has glimpses of the distinctive red roofs that signified The Towers.

"Jem," built in 1930.

II

THE MID-COUNTRY ESTATES

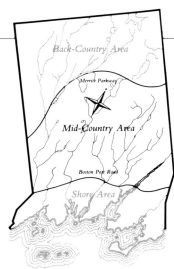

Rambleside

Rambleside, 1986. William Hubbell photo.

Principal Owner: Zalmon G. Simmons
Original Architect and Construction Date: Unknown
Architect for Renovations (1920s): Unknown

THE GREENWICH ESTATE created by Zalmon Gilbert Simmons (1871-1934) and his wife, Frances (1882-1964), included not only his magnificent English country manor house with its immediate landscaping but also five acres of iris gardens containing sixty thousand irises collected from all over the world. Woodlands, fields, and an eight-acre spring-fed lake made this property one of the most desirable in the area, and the Simmonses lived there year-round, seldom traveling far from it.

Zalmon Simmons became president of the foundering Simmons Company in Kenosha, Wisconsin, upon the death of his father in 1910. In that position he proceeded to revolutionize the "nighttime furniture" of the nation, and his company became one of the largest manufacturers of beds, springs, and mattresses in the United States. He bought North Carolina textile mills to improve the quality of his mattress ticking and added to his holdings companies already making fine furniture. An extremely creative man with a dynamic personality, he expanded his business from its regional status and moved into Canadian, English, and French markets.

When Simmons moved the executive offices of his firm from Kenosha to New York City in 1923, he began to buy land in the midsection of Greenwich. Alice C. Schwab sold him most of his acreage in March of that year, but he continued to add to it until late in 1929. After giving building sites to his sons Zalmon, Jr., and Grant, he still owned over one hundred acres.

The Schwab property originally had on it a shingle-style farmhouse which Simmons kept as the nucleus of his new house. He enclosed it with white-painted brick and added to it extensively. The resulting mansion, with its varicolored slate roof and seamed granite trim, is a stunningly beautiful home. Great attention was paid to architectural details, and the finest building materials were used, though neither the architect's name nor the builder's is known. Finally, to complete the interior of the house Frances Simmons engaged the talented Elsie de Wolfe, the interior decorator who revolutionized twentieth-century design in Europe and America and who also happened to be a personal friend of hers.

The original entrance to the property was on Clapboard Ridge Road at an old tumbledown red wooden gate which had been a landmark for years, particularly for fox hunters who often gathered there on their horses before the hunt began. When Simmons put his cinder road through, he had the old gate removed, but upon hearing that the hunters missed their landmark, he built stone walls at the entrance and put an iron archway overhead with a sign reading "The Red Gate." His road, called Woods Drive, led through beautiful forests, wound around the lake, and looped to the northeast before coming back down to his house and to those belonging to his sons.

The front door of Rambleside opens to a grand entrance hall which exhibits a classic de Wolfe touch: an inlaid copper and black marble floor. A family member who visited often remembers being encouraged in his younger days to "walk on the black squares." This beautifully paneled hall opens to the left into a study called the wood room. Paneled with pine brought from an old house in Bloomsbury, England, it has an unusual fireplace with accents of antique wood and silver inlay; and the Simmonses had its walls hung with extraordinary pictures, all of snowstorms. To the right, through a spacious white-paneled stair hall and music room, is the library, a handsome room finished in walnut. The floor is teak; the fireplace is black marble; and the recessed bookcases are punctuated by full-length engaged Corinthian columns. Oversized bay windows provide a panorama of lawns and gardens to the north, west, and south.

From the main hall one also enters both the drawing room and the dining room. The walls of the latter were covered with antique Chinese wallpaper.

The entrance hall, circa 1925.

The dining room featured hand-painted Chinese wallpaper, an Elsie de Wolfe trademark.

The clock tower gate.

A breakfast porch there, enclosed with glass windows, overlooks the rear terraces. Tall oriental folding screens were part of de Wolfe's decoration for both the dining room and the entrance hall, and bifold leaded-glass doors with glassed mirrored panels opened between the two rooms. Floors vary from the antique parquet of the drawing room to the Italian terra-cotta tile in the flower-arranging room. Dramatically placed mirrors added to the atmosphere of the downstairs, and a collection of paintings ranging from works by Sir Joshua Reynolds to those of Georgia O'Keefe reflected the owners' taste in art. Because of the east-west orientation of the house on a horizontal line, most rooms are suffused with brilliant sunlight, and the sense of openness is emphasized by the many arched French doors which lead directly to the broad rear terrace.

When the Simmonses lived at Rambleside, the service quarters on the ground floor consisted of a butler's pantry, a kitchen, a kitchen pantry, an icebox room, a laundry, a maids' sitting and dining room, a lavatory, and a servants' porch. Extensive family, guest, and staff accommodations were located on the second floor. The master suite included a sitting room with fireplace; two separate dressing rooms with baths; and a large, heated, glass-enclosed sleeping porch. Two other suites with bedrooms, parlors, baths, and one with a porch were available for guests. On this floor were also six maids' rooms, two baths, a lavatory, two large linen closets, and a serving room.

The third floor has two master bedrooms and baths, a billiard room, a children's playroom, two attics, and a built-in cedar closet. The cellar contains an unusual stone vault for wine and two built-in wine closets in addition to the usual furnace room, preserve closet, and other storage space.

A guesthouse, which could be used independently as a self-contained unit, is attached to the main house by a curved, covered arcade. It has a living room with a manteled fireplace, a dining room, a full kitchen, two bedrooms, a bath, and its own private courtyard as well as an attached three-car garage. In the farm group of outbuildings across the driveway from the main house were two 2-family cottages for the butler, the chauffeur, the chief greenhouse man, and the superintendent; two greenhouses; a six-car garage with apartment upstairs; and a small stable for four horses. Among the animals kept there over the years were two ponies, Tiddlywinks and Jingle Bells. They pulled the grandchildren in a pony cart and were hitched to a Russian sleigh in winter when there was snow. Behind the guesthouse was an aviary filled with exotic birds. A duck house at the lake provided shelter and a feeding place for hundreds of ducks, favorites of Frances Simmons.

The landscaping and the many gardens on the estate provided a spectacular setting for the Simmonses' mansion. Since Zalmon Simmons was not willing to wait for trees to grow on the barren land around his newly built house, he spent thousands of dollars trucking in fully grown elm trees and replanting them. Some of them were as large as two feet in diameter and so heavy to transport that Simmons had to have all the bridges en route checked to make sure they were strong enough to hold the load. Some residents still remember the accomplishment with amazement and comment on the beauty of the trees which flourished on the lawns until they succumbed to Dutch elm disease some years later.

Isabella Pendleton, a member of the American Society of Landscape Architects, designed the many gardens on the property. Boxwood bordered formal gardens near the house, and there was a large walled rose garden. A wisteria-covered pergola of stone-and-beam construction led to a garden named the Adam and Eve Garden for the statues there. Cut stone stairways separated the many terraces; stone walls and sculpted hedgework divided lawns and gardens into areas pleasing to the eye. Small patios and a mosaic-tiled fish pond were also part of the scene. Frances Simmons was extremely interested in flowers, and it was her passion for gardens that led to the magnificent collection, the so-called River of Iris. The hundreds of species, including water iris, were marked with metal tags, and visitors came from all over the world to see them. They were interspaced with walks and other plantings, laid out in an amphitheaterlike area of land with two artificial lakes. The superintendent was also head of the botanical department at Columbia University, and before the Great Depression eighty-three gardeners were said to have worked regularly on the property as day workers. Near the greenhouses there were also a vegetable garden, grape arbors, and a small orchard of apple and pear trees. Pear Lane, near the farm buildings, was named for the fruit trees which grew there.

Beyond the gardens, broad sweeping lawns surround the house. The expansive rear flagstone terrace provides large sitting areas accessible from many of the main rooms, and two grassy terraces sweep down to a 150-foot reflecting pool with a fountain in its center. Lawns continue behind it, ending at a forest of towering evergreens in the distance.

Zalmon Simmons loved his business and applied vision, creativity, and a great deal of time to it. He increased the Simmons Company's sales eightfold to $40 million, and pursuing his interests in finance and the stock market, he further increased his fortune. A successful businessman, he was also a good athlete, having gained local fame as a baseball player at St. John's School in Manlius, New York. In later years his hobby was yachting.

Frances Simmons, who had very definite ideas about how things should be done, presided over the estate in matriarchal fashion. Since the Simmonses' two sons lived in enormous houses on either side of Rambleside, children and grandchildren were nearby. Christmas was always an extravaganza with all the family at the big house for a huge Christmas dinner at midday. In the afternoon marionette shows and similar entertainment were provided for the children, who were fed again afterward and sent to bed. The adults then, as a family tradition, sat down to a formal dinner which lasted past midnight so that Zalmon's birthday could be ushered in on December 26. The Simmonses' social life included a great deal of entertaining, sometimes at musicales featuring chamber groups. They were regular members of the Round Hill Community Church and donated the organ that is now there. As could be expected, given her love of flowers, Frances Simmons was an active member of the Greenwich Garden Club.

Zalmon Simmons died in 1934, and the estate was gradually broken up. The main house was sold in 1938, although Frances Simmons continued to live in Greenwich until she died in her nineties. In 1951 the family gave seventy acres between Clapboard Ridge Road and Lake Avenue to the Greenwich Boys Club. The land has been used to provide the club's members, at that time numbering 1,300, with accessible camping grounds, a chance to enjoy the oudoors, to study woodcraft, and to fish, swim, and canoe. The mansion is left today on less than ten acres.

The Castle

The famed swimming pool of The Castle. Gil Amiaga photo.

Principal Owner: James C. Green
Architect: James C. Green
Construction Date: 1903-1906

HEN CATHERINE DENEUVE and Jack Lemmon danced in the empty swimming pool of a local castle, they were merely the last in a line of actors who have played their parts in an extraordinary real-life setting near the heart of Greenwich. Their film, *The April Fools,* was one of many shot at this site — among them the silent film classics *The Perils of Pauline, When Knighthood Was in Flower,* and *Cinderella* — but the history of the estate dates back to the beginning of this century.

James C. Green (1877-1927), a prominent architect and artist originally from Missouri, bought a little over three acres in 1903 from the Edgewood Park Land Company. On this relatively small piece of property rose his dream and creation — a reproduction in every detail of a fifteenth-century castle-fortress, a massive structure of Connecticut stone and brick, Italian Renaissance in style. He had studied at the Ecole des Beaux-Arts in Paris and spent considerable time sketching châteaus and cathedrals in Europe. He designed many large office buildings in New York, Chicago, and San Francisco and two other castles in Greenwich. He did not complete his own castle as it stands now, but he provided for future expansion in his original plans, so that the resulting building is a monument to his skill and imagination. Its gabled roofs, towers, parapets, spacious halls, galleries, intimate Gothic rooms, and labyrinths of stairways make it one of the most picturesque and remarkable of the largest homes in Greenwich. The most impressive feature missing at present is the building's tallest tower, which was hit by lightning twice and was never replaced. The moat with drawbridge, the gardens, swimming pools, waterfalls, and statuary complemented, in its heyday, the astonishing edifice. From the heights of its towers the view to Long Island Sound in the distance is spectacular, and in the immediate foreground are the varying angles and pitches of chimneys and roofs, the hues of their tiles ranging from orange and soft red to bluish green.

In 1916 its second owner, Henry L. Brittain (1874-1959), bought The Castle. A self-made man, he became one of the industrial leaders of what by 1925 was known as the New South. He owned shipbuilding corporations in Mobile and Tampa, drydock companies in Savannah and Jacksonville; he participated in the syndicate which in 1939 put together a $13 million deal to buy twenty-two steamships and freighters of the Luckenbach Line in New York. He formed an explosives company in New York and headed a real estate development company in Florida. His obituary in the *New York Times* noted one of his first accomplishments which happened to take place at a refreshment concession he had at the 1898 World's Fair in St. Louis. It was reported that he obtained some small, sweet pancakes from an Armenian's neighboring stand, inverted them over scoops of ice cream, then sold them to some girls standing nearby, and thus created the first ice-cream cone.

Brittain and his wife, Gertrude, lived with their two small children at Castle Breatann, as it was called by the *Greenwich Press* in 1923. They filled it with innumerable treasures — rare furniture of the fourteenth, fifteenth, and sixteenth centuries; priceless tapestries and statues; magnificent rugs; valuable paintings; and other pieces of art. The numerous rooms, the majority of which were Spanish Gothic in style, were unusually imaginatively furnished.

One of them was the altar room, which was on the ground floor and served as the entrance to the central part of The Castle. To reach it one had to pass under an arch connecting the two main wings of the building and then walk through the Spanish courtyard. In this altar room a baptismal fountain and many statues of saints added to its cathedral-like atmosphere. Passing on to the meditation room and from there to the reception hall furnished with fifteenth-century wooden figures of St. Peter and St. Mary, a twelfth-

The Castle with tower intact, circa 1917.

The great hall or music room during the Mitchells' ownership.

The crenellated towers from the rear courtyard.
Gil Amiaga photo.

century Spanish primitive of Christ, and many pieces of antique Spanish furniture, one ascended the spiral stairway of stone to the main floor.

On this level the Dante room had walls of white paneled stone, a low ceiling, and small windows. The furniture was of the fifteenth century, procured from Umbria, Tuscany, and Venice, with the exception of one beautifully carved Spanish rosewood bed with twisted posters. At its foot was a marriage coffer six hundred years old. Included in the furnishings were a thirteenth-century tryptich (a small altar closed after use) and early Spanish paintings of St. Anthony and St. Francis.

From the Dante room an old Ecuadorian Spanish room provided passage to the Venetian chamber occupied by Gertrude Brittain. An antique Venetian bed with a green silk coverlet bore the coat of arms of the Orleans family and other gay decorations. Abreast of the bed was a raised alcove-chapel for her private use. A Venetian bureau was richly painted with scenes of the Adoration of the Magi.

The living room with its warm chestnut paneling and beehive plaster ceiling was furnished with antique Florentine and Tuscan furniture, and a magnificent Kirmanshah rug covered its polished oak floors. Yellow damask draperies framed the leaded windows inset with small diamond-shaped pieces of stained glass. Candle supports were of Spanish gilt. A rare Grecian marble bust of the fourth century B.C. from the Stanford White collection stood over the fireplace.

Originally the house numbered about fourteen rooms, including the living room, the dining room, the kitchen, a butler's pantry, bedrooms, and servants' rooms. Under the ownership of the Brittains and, after 1927, of John T. H. Mitchell (1875-1930) and his wife, Anna, the size of the mansion doubled. Arcaded porches on various levels were enclosed and in some cases enlarged, and many rooms were added.

Today there are seven bedroom suites in the main house. When they are added to other rooms there and to the four in the cottage (formerly the chauffeur's, now a guesthouse), the total is forty. There are fifteen fireplaces and nine chimneys. Including necessary additions by the present owners, there are now fourteen bathrooms. Some eighteen different levels from one room to another have been counted.

One of the most important additions was the great hall, or music room. It is an enormous, stately room with twenty-foot ceilings, Tennessee marble floors, and plaster walls painted white and grooved to look like stone. Tall vaulted windows reaching from floor to ceiling allow light to stream in from two sides and provide a beautiful view of trees and gardens outside. A tremendous fireplace dominates one end of the room. Its opening, large enough to walk into, is surmounted by an old and magnificent stone carving featuring two major panels of what appear to be biblical scenes. Two gigantic baroque columns flank it. Opposite the fireplace a marble staircase leads up to the minstrel gallery with its spiral banisters painted gold. Certainly when the Mitchells owned the house, and perhaps even before, an organ occupied the space below the gallery. The great hall was the scene of musical soirees and grand entertaining by the Mitchells. Their daughter Ann made her debut at a large ball there. Probably reflecting the interests of Anna Mitchell, who was a pianist and composer known as Hart Mitchell, a small stone teahouse elsewhere on the grounds was fitted out with a sound box especially constructed to reproduce the music of the organ in the great hall.

A most unusual change in a small part of the castle took place when the artists Leon Carroll and Jacques Darcy were given carte blanche to modernize a long narrow room called the sunroom. They designed a lighting system which illuminated a mirror-based fountain made of ground-glass planes and produced shimmering blue-and-white phosphorescent effects suggesting will-o'-the-wisps or moonlight on polar glaciers. Equally unusual was their treatment of a bas-relief, *The Sun Worshippers*, carved in plaster and set in one wall. Nearby, a niche enshrined a statue by Alexander Archipenko, the figure standing in solitary beauty, lit from below by a concealed brilliant green light. Stark Art Deco furniture, a floor tiled in simple geometric patterns, and a blue-and-white glass soda fountain completed this incredible scene.

Outside this room is a swimming pool which was formerly a sunken rose garden. A double row of white columns, square on the outside and round on the inside, line one side of the pool. Backed by a row of tall cedar trees, the columns at one time supported a grape arbor, and the Brittains placed marble statues of ancient emperors and kings here and there. A cabana with half columns and classical figures in relief occupies the other side of the pool. Garlands and cherubs decorate similar columns on the outside of the castle itself, and Della Robbia-like insets add color to its stone walls. The Mitchells put sand at the far end of the pool

The pool gate flanked by caryatids. Gil Amiaga photo.

for their daughter to play in. At that time water was piped from the swimming pool to a reflecting pool down the hill on the other side of the driveway. From there it splashed in the form of a waterfall into another large, shallow pool below and was then recirculated to the swimming pool.

In 1930 Mitchell, who at the time was president of the advertising agency Lennen and Mitchell, Inc., in New York City, died suddenly of a heart attack at the age of fifty-five. His wife and daughter continued to use The Castle for years. The *Greenwich Time* reported in 1957 that "They have other houses both in Europe and in Florida—all in the Italian style which marks their Greenwich residence—where the large scale entertaining has continued unabated." They traveled frequently to the Riviera and to Palm Beach, taking world cruises in between, often staying in Greenwich only a few months of the year. Consequently, many of the rooms were more or less permanently swathed in dustcovers. In her last years Mrs. Mitchell lived in Palm Beach or alone in the Greenwich mansion except for one Japanese servant and a dog. Her daughter sold the house in 1972 to its present owners, who have repaired, restored, and carefully refurnished it to approach its former splendor.

Magnificent tapestries installed by the Croft family are the focal point of Grahampton's dining room. Gil Amiaga photo.

Principal Owner: Henry W. Croft
Architect: Johnson and Abbott
Construction Date: 1917

HENRY WILLIAM CROFT (1865-1947) had no particular ties to Greenwich when he decided to build a home here. Born in Allegheny City, Pennsylvania, he went to local public schools and then took a commercial course at Iron City College in Pittsburgh. One of nine children whose father died at a young age, he worked first as a bookkeeper when he was sixteen, then was employed by the firebrick company which became the Harbison-Walker Refractories Company of Pittsburgh after several mergers. Under his skillful management the enterprise developed rapidly, for not only was he knowledgeable concerning the details of the brick-manufacturing business but he was also an expert in finance and administration. He remained actively associated with that firm from 1887 until 1938, when he retired as chairman of the board. Thus, he was an extremely wealthy and successful man when he began to think about where he would like to retire. His wife urged a location some distance from the business in which he had worked so hard. One of his daughters recently related that "they chose Greenwich out of the blue."

In late 1915 the *Greenwich News and Graphic* reported that "One of the largest real estate deals ever made in Greenwich has just been completed and so quietly was it done that very few people are yet aware of its magnitude. A block of land, embracing nearly three hundred acres, valued at from one to two thousand dollars an acre, comprises the sale." By February 1916 Henry Croft had obtained the deeds of five farms in the Clapboard Ridge section of town, originally known as Clapboard Tree Ridge. They had belonged for some time to the families of George M. Mead, Henry De Kraft, Hannah E. Peck, Elbert M. Reynolds, and Julia A. Reynolds. On the north the resulting estate was bounded by Clapboard Ridge Road, on the south by Parsonage Road, on the west by Lake Avenue and Parsonage Road, and on the east by Northbrook Farm.

The land was for the most part rolling, picturesque country, much of it cleared farmland, some of it in orchards or forests. The fact that the Merritt Parkway did not later cross Greenwich right through this area, where it logically should have, is due to the efforts of the Crofts and other landowners who were able to block the plan.

The press had been reporting fears that the high prices of building materials would have a depressing effect on construction, but by mid-1916 a reporter for the *Greenwich News and Graphic* wrote that "apparently the tidal wave of prosperity that has swept across the country took everything with it, even any scruples that prospective builders may have had regarding the additional expenditures required because of the advanced cost of labor and material." Henry Croft was no exception as he planned his substantial mansion. Finished in 1917, it was built of brick with a slate-and-tile roof; it had eight bedrooms, eleven fireplaces, and six chimneys. The architectural firm Johnson and Abbott of Pittsburgh designed the house; William H. Nye of New York was the contractor, and John Greenleaf was the landscape architect.

The main block of the house has a broad chimney at either end and dormer windows in the second story. The front door opens into a wide entrance hall with a staircase both to the right and to the left leading upstairs. Directly ahead, through four large arches, is a spacious room which the Crofts called the living hall. A marble floor designed in squares covers the entire area, and on it they arranged an oriental rug at the entrance and large square and oval rugs of a solid color in the living hall. Steps lead down to that room, which they furnished with groups of plush velvet sofas, armchairs, and a piano. Handsome fireplaces are the focal points at both ends of the hall.

Other important rooms in the sections of the house flanking the main block are the dining and the living rooms, both quite grand. The striking feature of the dining room is the beautiful tapestries which the

The approach to Grahampton.

Crofts found in England, brought back, and had framed with additional woodwork on the walls. An extremely wide fireplace is centered in one wall, and huge logs to supply it were stacked nearby. They were brought up from the cellar through a trapdoor which the ever practical Henry Croft had designed for the front hall. The dining room is large enough easily to accommodate a breakfast table by the bay window. Here the family sat when they were not using the formal dining table. The living room is magnificent with its oak paneling and intricately detailed plaster ceiling molded in bold relief. The Crofts furnished their house with English antiques and many paintings. One of their daughters remembers it as an extremely livable and comfortable home, dearly loved by her parents.

Henry Croft's office, a rather dark, half-paneled room, in his day furnished with leather furniture and an enormous moose head on one wall, is at the left end of the house. He devised a machine there, which amplified music so that it could be heard throughout the house, long before modern stereophonic equipment was available. A door from the office leads directly out to one of the magnificent gardens.

Augusta Graham Croft (1870-1949), for whom the estate was named, was, in her daughter's words, a great gardener. She worked closely with John Greenleaf, with a British superintendent from Blenheim Palace for a while, and with the local gardeners she employed to create the spectacular gardens of Grahampton. She studied catalogues, brought plants back from England, grew her own seedlings, and when she felt the first garden was insufficient for her flowers, she planned and planted a second. A stone, slate-roofed summerhouse, complete with wrought-iron seats and railings, graced one of them. From it could be viewed fountains; pools; boxwood-lined paths; and lovely beds of flowers — delphiniums of different shades, canterbury bells, foxgloves, irises, the scene ending with steps leading up to the pedestal where a graceful nude Diana restrained her leaping dog. Flowers surrounded a square lily pool. Everywhere the beautifully tended walks, shrubs, flowers, and stonework transformed the pastures, orchards, and marshy ground originally surrounding the house. The Crofts also planted elm trees, some of which survived the blight. Unfortunately, most of the boxwood were killed during one particularly hard winter.

The esplanade at the rear of the house.

The living hall as furnished by the Crofts.

The Crofts spent much of their time at the south side of the house, described by one family member as the living side. The terrace was there with its tubs of hydrangeas, the screened porch to keep the mosquitoes away, and the sweeping views to the Sound; in fact, the family could watch the Fourth of July fireworks in Rye.

The land in that direction embraced the fields and orchards of the old farms. A stable and a garage were built on the property. Cows and chickens were kept for a while. The twin daughters enjoyed riding horseback, and local fox hunters often galloped through their property, riding almost up to the edges of the gardens. Golf was Henry Croft's favorite sport; he pursued it at a number of clubs in various parts of the country and used his own lawn as a driving range.

The Crofts wintered in Pittsburgh and summered in Greenwich for years, but they chose to spend the last years of their lives on their beautiful Connecticut estate. They had come a long way from the small Pennsylvania towns where they were born. Harry Croft, as he was called, died at Grahampton at the age of eighty-one. His wife died two years later while in Pittsburgh visiting two of her daughters. Most of the land has since been sold, but the names of such roads as Beechcroft, Pinecroft, and Meadowcroft are reminders of the family's ownership. The acreage with the house today has been reduced from almost 278 to not quite 5, the property of the original estate having been subdivided into residential lots.

The view toward the Sound.

Fountain, sundial, and Diana.

Northway

Rigidly sculptured trees frame the approach to Northway.

Principal Owner: Laura Robinson
Architects: J.E.R. Carpenter; Walter D. Blair
Construction Date: 1910-1913

*T*WO MILES out of town on what the late architect Alan Burnham called "the Fifth Avenue of Greenwich," there is a startling sight. Here, possibly with a sense of déjà vu, one immediately recognizes the Petit Trianon from the gardens at Versailles. While such a phenomenon would not be surprising in New York City, it is certainly out of context in Greenwich, Connecticut. Northway, or The Petit Trianon Deux, as it is more commonly called, was the result of a whim. It was built between 1910 and 1913 by Laura Robinson (d. 1964), a lady in her middle thirties, born in Chicago, who was an heiress to both the Diamond Match and the Goodyear Tire fortunes. In June 1910 Laura, her mother, Eleanor, and her sister, Henrietta, bought a little over fourteen acres of land with the intention of building their own personal palace on it.

Why these ladies wanted a château is a mystery, but such an extravagance is perfectly possible with great wealth and is certainly the prerogative of any princess. In August 1910, after a falling out with her sister, Laura became sole owner of the land and sought permission of the French government to construct a copy of one of France's architectural treasures. Her request was granted, and Robinson hired the New York architects J. Edwin R. Carpenter and Walter D. Blair to adapt the design of her chosen château. Henrietta returned to Chicago and built her own mansion—without the blessing of the French. This unauthorized and unauthentic château is now the Chicago Medical Museum on Lake Shore Drive.

To understand the Robinson estate, one must first understand the time and the architecture of France during the reign of Louis XV. Architecture was a principal distraction of French monarchs in the seventeenth and eighteenth centuries, and the prestigious post of Le Premier Architecte du Roi was a coveted title. When Jacques-Ange Gabriel achieved this distinction in 1734, the royal purse was in severe straits and vast new architectural works were out of the question. The royal interests were therefore directed toward remodeling existing structures or creating additions to them or to their grounds. One such revision was the design for the Gallery of Ulysses at Fontainbleau which Gabriel undertook for Louis XV. His major effort, however, was the Place da la Concorde in Paris, and it is here that his ability to manipulate tremendous areas of open space with a minimum of building mass is best articulated. Gabriel made clever use of the proportional relationships between surrounding structures, that is, the Tuileries, while maintaining subtle control over the entryways into the square.

The Petit Trianon, Gabriel's second most famous work, was conceived as a small, independent pavilion in the garden of a larger château. Louis XV intended it as a gift for Madame de Pompadour, but she died before its completion in 1769, and the exquisite little palace became identified with others, most notably Marie Antoinette. This building marks the break with the rococo tradition, for Gabriel's design is characterized by simplicity and severity of line, by the stress given to the cubic mass of the structure, and by the classical beauty of the whole with its harmonious relationship to its site. The château is totally integrated from any viewpoint—each of the four facades restates and echoes the other by a delicate adjustment of proportions and fine variations of detail. For the main entrance, Gabriel used a frontispiece of pilasters after the Corinthian order over a rusticated basement. The rear facade has full columns in the same style, while half columns decorate the sides. The horizontal line of the cornice is uninterrupted; there are neither statues in wall niches nor garlands above the windows. In the Petit Trianon, Gabriel translated English Palladianism into French elegance with a noble simplicity. The pure white limestone walls of this château reflect the air of perfection that is characteristic of Gabriel's classic vocabulary.

The simple elegance of Northway's facade.

It took three years and $1 million to complete the Greenwich version of the Petit Trianon. Both Carpenter and Blair had studied at the Ecole des Beaux-Arts in Paris and were well qualified for the challenge. They created a near-perfect copy of their model, making certain modifications to retain the perfection of proportion dictated by the smaller acreage. The design is scaled down from twenty-six rooms to thirteen, and Robinson had two lower wings added, one on each side. The outer walls are brick, covered with plaster or stucco, but they are white. And the reflecting pool with its fountain is located in front of the divided staircase to the entrance. While Robinson's pool is rectangular, the original is circular and sits at the head of the long lawn, flanked by the drive on either side. The trees at Versailles that edge the drive are shaped with an upward scoop; those along the approach in Greenwich are clipped into strict rectangles. It was necessary for Robinson's gardeners to climb sixty-foot ladders to prune these trees, creating what Laura Robinson called her *bosquet*.

The interior design of Northway remains faithful to Gabriel's work. One enters between two small salons into the spacious front hall where a pipe organ once played beneath the graceful staircase that sweeps away at the right. The staircase at Versailles, of which this is a replica, shows the gentle modification of the rococo used throughout the château and is considered the loveliest of the Louis XVI period. Delicate paneling continues the Louix XVI style in every room. On the left of the hall is the living room with a gallery or loggia. On the right is the handsome dining room and the most famous of Laura Robinson's few deviations from the French master; in one of the murals adorning the dining room walls, the likeness of Marie Antoinette was replaced with that of Miss Robinson.

For fifty years this magnificent residence was the scene of glittering entertainments and delightful musicales. The furnishings were exquisite eighteenth century, either authentic pieces or excellent reproductions. Every detail was reproduced from the original, including the doorknobs. The floors were parquet on the first floor and hardwood above, all covered with the finest of carpets. There were seven bedrooms and seven baths. The three chimneys served eight fireplaces. A garage and stables with five servants' rooms were built in 1913, as was a potting shed and the greenhouse, the latter with three bedrooms and a bath. The formal gardens were famous, a tribute to both the eye of the owner and the skill of her many gardeners.

Laura Robinson married William A. Evans in 1915, two years after the completion of her château. Evans was the scion of an old South Carolina family, a graduate of Hobart College, and a prominent New York lawyer. Incredibly, his mother's name was Marie Antoinette. Laura and her husband had one child, William Alexander, Jr., who was killed in an automobile accident in 1939 shortly before his twenty-fourth birthday. Evans died two months later, but his widow lived until 1964. Laura Robinson Evans willed half of Northway to Christ Church in Greenwich and the other half to the Greenwich Hospital. These institutions in turn sold the estate to two New York City antique dealers, whose sole interest in Northway was the furnishings. They were apparently unaware that Parke-Bernet had a contract for these treasures; nearly $100,000 was realized from their sale at auction in 1966. The château was sold again in 1967, empty of antiques but as solid in structure as when it was built. Today the Petit Trianon Deux remains a stunning monument to a woman whose dream it was and who brought a bit of eighteenth-century France to Greenwich.

SOUTH ELEVATION

Percy Rockefeller's 64-room mansion, Owenoke Farm, completed in 1912.

The William G. Rockefeller Estate
Principal Owner: William G. Rockefeller
Architect (before 1889): Unknown
Architect for Renovations: (1905): William G. Rockefeller

Owenoke Farm
Principal Owner: Percy Rockefeller
Architect: Hiss and Weeks
Construction Date: 1907-1908

EW PEOPLE are aware that the Rockefeller family with its "residential park" influenced the orderly development of the central part of Greenwich more than any other landowner. The existence of the two Rockefeller mansions is now a mostly forgotten part of the town's history, but the concerned and wise subdivision of the brothers' vast holdings has proved a priceless legacy for the Greenwich they loved. One must begin with the holdings of William (1841-1922), brother of John D. Rockefeller. He began to accumulate land in the 1870s, buying six acres here, thirty there, as much as two hundred elsewhere, from such early residents as John Denton, Eli Perry, and John Sniffen. One of the best known of his purchases was the thirty-seven-acre farm of the lifelong recluse David Husted for $25,000. Husted, descended from Angell Husted, one of the original patentees of the town in 1665, had lived alone there all his life in a building which included a cowshed in the basement, carriage and living rooms above, and a hayloft on top. On October 14, 1903, the *New York Times*, in reporting the sale, stated that Husted's "farm is so rocky that it was said one could jump from one stone to another all over it without touching ground." William's son, Percy, later built his mansion on this land, on the east side of Lake Avenue, north of North Maple Avenue.

William Rockefeller made another important purchase in 1899 — on the west side of Lake Avenue — a little over forty acres from Theodosius Secor, brother-in-law of Joseph Husted. Rockefeller's primary Greenwich residence, until he built a mansion on his Tarrytown holdings at about that time, had been his home called One Elm on what is now Milbank Avenue. Secor's house later became the home of his son William Goodsell Rockefeller.

In 1880 the same Joseph Husted had sold William Rockefeller almost forty-three acres for $15,000, this being the land which became the famous Deer Park. By the time William moved to Tarrytown, having sold One Elm, he had accumulated over four hundred acres in central Greenwich. His two sons, William G. and Percy, continued to buy acreage to add to their father's holdings; and much of his land was transferred to them — most notably the sites of their houses and also Deer Park, which, however, they owned jointly.

William Goodsell Rockefeller (1870-1922) was the older of the two brothers. After his graduation from Yale, he went to work in his father's office. His father was a principal founder of the Standard Oil organization, but although William G. was for a time treasurer of the New York Standard Oil Company, his interests led toward copper rather than oil. His marriage to Elsie Stillman (1872-1935) in 1895 was one of the notable social events of the year. James Stillman, her father, for many years president of National City Bank and largely responsible for its development, was one of the most powerful figures of his generation in American finance. Consequently, her wedding was of more than just social interest. The couple lived at first in the Madison Avenue house given to them by her family, and they went to Greenwich only in the summertime. However, in the spring of 1905 the *New York Times* reported that "William G. Rockefeller is spending $40,000 on work on his father's former residence [the Lake Avenue farmhouse] near his Deer Park.... He is his own architect in the present case and almost daily visits the place to give instruction to the 100 men employed there by the day." He had the old farmhouse cut in two, half of it moved, and another house of three stories with a cupola on top built in the center to join the parts. It was a white frame house, with a tin roof and shutters at the windows.

When the improvements were done, Elsie and William G. moved out to Lake Avenue year-round, and it was in this comfortable, rather than elegant, house that their five children grew up. The house was, in general, roomy and homey, with wallpapered plaster walls and comfortable furniture, not antiques but of

This view of the William G. Rockefellers' Lake Avenue farmhouse before renovations suggests the simplicity of both home and grounds.

good quality. On the ground floor were the living room, a billiard room, Mrs. Rockefeller's office, a dining room, a children's dining room, a library, a nursery room for the children to play in, a pantry, an enormous storeroom for food and supplies, a kitchen, a scullery room behind the kitchen, and other miscellaneous closets and small rooms. Family bedrooms and bathrooms, guestrooms, and some servants' rooms as well were on the second floor.

The third contained the housekeeper's and children's nurse's rooms; other servants' rooms; and two large bedrooms with a connecting bath for their sons, Sterling and Stillman. There was also the huge water tank that served the whole house. The elevator ran from the basement to the cupola. Trunks and closets on this top story were a source of unending fascination for the children, who also liked to climb out of the windows and run around on the roof, though doing so was against the rules. Stillman remembers that his brother, Godfrey, a radio buff, kept his equipment in one of the cupola rooms and, on that fateful night in 1912, picked up distress signals from the *Titanic*. He remembers, too, sighting Halley's Comet from that vantage point.

The outbuildings were extensive, in order to provide the family of seven with the way of life to which they were accustomed. The laundry was housed in a building separate from the main house. The stable was three stories after having been remodeled when the work was done on the house. Two families of servants lived there, and at one time one of them included ten children. The iron stalls and hardwood floors gave way in 1906 to changes allowing the space to be used for automobiles of various designs. Nearby were a big shed for tools and numerous cold frames. In addition

to the outdoor tennis court, Elsie Rockefeller had an indoor court built in 1930. Still standing, it is a one-story building made of steel and stucco, complete with dressing rooms, showers, lockers, a kitchenette and lounge, as well as the court itself.

The site of the main house provided a spectacular view; it was high enough so that one could see Long Island Sound. Lawns and informal plantings surrounded the building, except for the west side where there were large vegetable and flower gardens. Porches on both the north and the south sides of the house were open and often used. The driveway led in from Lake Avenue to a porte-cochere under which carriages and, later, cars could drive, keeping their passengers dry in inclement weather. "The place has all the appearance of an extremely well-managed and prosperous farm," stated the *Greenwich Graphic*. "These characteristics together with the fact that it is beautifully situated, commanding a superb view to the north and south, render it one of the most attractive situations in Greenwich." It went on to say that the Rockefeller places "are not only beautiful in themselves but make all neighboring land more desirable and valuable." The land directly surrounding the house amounted to about 132 acres when its owner died.

William G. Rockefeller, a man who did not like newspaper publicity and who claimed to be "just a plain, ordinary American citizen," according to the *Greenwich Graphic*, caught a cold while watching the Yale-Harvard football game in the fall of 1922 and died of pneumonia shortly thereafter. By that time he had resigned his position at Standard Oil Company and had withdrawn from many of his business connections. He had gained for himself, however, the reputation of being a hard worker and of attending thoroughly

Summer view of the farmhouse.

Elsie Stillman Rockefeller serves one up on the outdoor court.

and conscientiously to whatever duties he undertook. The *New York Times* reported at the time of his death that he was six feet tall, portly, with sloping shoulders, and that he wore, "or did until recently, a small dark beard" and that "he used to affect strikingly tall collars with big wings." His wife was not with him when he died, as she had gone to Europe to care for Godfrey, ill with typhoid fever in Belgium.

Elsie Rockefeller continued to live at the Lake Avenue house where she died at the age of sixty-three. She had shown particular interest in the Greenwich Shelter, and she actively supported not only this home for small babies but also the Greenwich Day Nursery, established to care for children of working mothers. She contributed money to both and gave them the use of two buildings on Arch Street. Widely admired, she was described by a family friend as a woman with "a lot of style and a lot of humor."

Percy Rockefeller (1878-1934), eight years younger than his brother, William G., also graduated from Yale and then went to work for his father. He became a leading industrialist, at one time serving as a director of fifty-one corporations, many of them outside the areas of his father's direct interest. In 1923 he was one of the five men in this country whose lives were insured for $3 million or more. However, he too disliked publicity. The *New York Times* wrote that, as an individual, he "remained in the background. He was little known as a personality except to a small circle of intimates, but his boldness and sagacity as a financier were felt definitely in the financial district." He married Isabel Stillman (1876-1935), Elsie's sister, in 1901, and like his brother's wedding, his was an event of great social importance and public interest.

Percy and Isabel decided to make Greenwich their place of primary residence and proceeded to plan a great house to be built practically on the site of old David Husted's hovel. The *Greenwich Graphic* predicted that "it will take a year to complete the building and surrounds, as it will be of more than usual pretensions." Indeed it was. The New York architects Hiss and Weeks designed the house, and H. W. Dededrick of Elizabeth, New Jersey, one of the most famous builders in the United States, directed the work. It was begun in the fall of 1907 and, when completed the following year, it was billed "Our Stateliest Mansion" by the *Greenwich News*. It was 212 feet in breadth, 68 feet in depth, and had altogether 64 rooms. Since Percy wanted absolute safety from fire, the construction was unusual, with not a piece of wood in the outside double walls. Each of the two walls was built of hollow terracotta blocks, with four inches of airspace between them. This confined airspace was intended to make the house cooler in summer, warmer in winter, and drier year-round than any ordinary construction. The fireproof walls were covered on the outside with stucco, and the roof consisted of red tile. The completed mansion cost $500,000 and was called Owenoke Farm after the Cos Cob Indian chief of that name.

The main portion of the building was four stories high and had wings on either side of two stories. There was a large portico in front with pillars of white freestone, this entrance opening into a library. To the right of the library were the dining room, the breakfast room, the kitchen and related areas; to the left were the sitting room, the flower room, and Rockefeller's private office.

Elsie Stillman Rockefeller ready for the hunt.

The log cabin in Deer Park.

A partial description of one of these rooms will give some idea of the grandeur of the house. The library was some sixty feet long and about half as wide, finished in dark, weathered oak with bookshelves of the same material built into the walls. The ceilings were paneled and hand-decorated. At either end were huge fireplaces with exquisitely carved Cannes marble mantelpieces. Most of the other rooms were finished in cherry wood enameled in white. There were other fireplaces of French and Italian marble and some unusually intricate oak carving. Floors were of fine hardwood.

Since cost was no problem, the butler's pantry and kitchens contained the most modern culinary equipment, including one white metal sink which alone reportedly incurred a bill of $700. All the rooms on the second and third floors were elegantly furnished and adequately provided with fourteen bathrooms and innumerable closets. Rockefeller's bathroom was some twenty feet square, with a shower of marble and glass. Even the dozen-odd rooms in the servants' quarters were excellently appointed.

In the basement were the furnace rooms, the great laundries and washrooms for the family, a servants' washroom, a huge ironing room, and a drying room to be used when weather did not permit clothes to dry outside. Three tremendous boilers with mammoth fireboxes generated the vapor which heated the house—a new system that did not require pressure. There was adequate space for carriages, besides room to store coal. Three elevators served the house: an electric one for passengers, a hand hoist for freight, and a third for use as a dumbwaiter.

A thirty-by-sixty-foot veranda on the eastern end of the building was open to breezes and afforded a magnificent view of the Sound. From this site it was possible to see the surrounding country for miles, yet it was easily accessible from Greenwich.

One of the many social events which took place at the estate was the reception following the wedding of one of the Rockefellers' four daughters, Isabel, to Frank Lincoln in the fall of 1925. Over 4,500 invitations were issued, and newspapers reported that thousands were present. After the ceremony at Christ Church, guests were received at Owenoke Farm in the library, which had been decorated with Easter lilies. Fragrant lilies of the valley were placed in the dining room, where fifty-four people were seated for dinner. Buffet refreshments were served on the south veranda, made festive for the reception with orange trees, while the east porch was transformed into a dancing pavilion with blooming vines as the decorative feature. John D. Rockefeller drove over from Pocantico Hills for the occasion.

Seruccio Vitale landscaped Owenoke Farm's grounds, his plans providing for spectacular plantings and gardens. Carefully selected shrubs and trees were tended by the many gardeners who weeded, trimmed, and transplanted. Horses wearing leather shoes drew the mowers which kept the lawns cut to perfection. An enclosed one-acre vegetable garden supplied the family with vegetables. In 1911 Rockefeller, in a burst of enthusiasm to learn about unfamiliar trees, hired a forest engineer to set out thirty-nine species of evergreens and hardwoods so that he could observe their characteristics and growth.

The unique part of their father's land known as Deer Park, eventually owned jointly by William G. and Percy Rockefeller, deserves description of its own. A writer for the *Greenwich Graphic* wrote, "what nature has not done, money has secured. Beautiful drives wind in and out among the groves of trees, and artificial lakes upon which swans and ducks sail gracefully along, have been made here and there about the park. Brooks wind picturesquely under overhanging rocks in which shining trout swim peacefully, with no fear of the angler's fly. Tame deer run to visitors and eat from their hands, and silken-haired Angora goats eat from the fertile pastures. The western log hut, made from logs cut in Michigan expressly for the purpose, is a cool and comfortable retreat."

The half-mile racetrack used for years for both racing and gymkhanas was situated in Deer Park. William Rockefeller and his two sons as well were excellent horsemen, and riding had become an important part of their lives. William G. had famous kennels of beagles and foxhounds in the park. The dogs he bred won many ribbons, but he closed the kennels in 1910, giving the animals to the kennel master, because their barking near his home got on his nerves. Deer Park also had large stables for the workhorses used on both estates. Cows and pigs were kept there too; the superintendent and his family lived in the park; and a carpenter's shop and enormous hay barn were used jointly by the brothers. The high wooden fence surrounding the park to keep the deer from escaping was a landmark in Greenwich for years.

The strikingly beautiful stone walls on the Rockefeller properties are another familiar feature to residents of Greenwich. By 1899 about eight miles of walls marked roadside boundaries and divided fields. Most of the roadside walls were double, the field walls single in width. Greenwich workers employed during the spring and summer collected the many stones from the fields and to make their work easier, used a huge, ingenious machine described by the *Greenwich Graphic* as "gallows-like." They were so skillful at fitting the pieces of rock together without the use of mortar that today many of these walls remain in excellent condition.

The *New York Times* declared in 1908 that William G. and Percy Rockefeller were preparing to buy up land in Greenwich "which in area and value will perhaps outrival the vast estates of John D. Rockefeller at Tarrytown, New York. It is reported that they intend to open a residential park with their own residences as a centre." Their ideas came to fruition in the years that followed, but not exactly as they had planned. After Elsie died in 1935, thirteen years after William's death, her house was torn down, as it proved difficult to sell. Percy died in 1934, and Isabel died eleven months later. Since the market for such vast homes was limited, Owenoke Farm was demolished three years later. Pneumatic hammers, steam shovels, and dynamite were used. Parke-Bernet Galleries auctioned off oriental rugs; early Flemish and French tapestries; French salon suites; Renaissance carved walnut furniture; and Chinese porcelains, silver, crystal, and paintings.

The development of a "residential park" has, though without its two grand houses, proceeded over the years. Small estates and other parcels of land were sold with restrictions set and building plans approved by the Rockefeller family. This farsighted policy was instituted before the town adopted such restrictions of its own. Thus, the sale of lots and the construction of substantial homes has taken place in an orderly manner on an enormous amount of prime property in central Greenwich. The business acumen, financial resources, and foresight of William Rockefeller and his two sons, combined with their love of Greenwich, have left a legacy to the town which its residents continue to enjoy today.

Beausite

The rear facade and rose garden of Beausite. Gil Amiaga photo.

Principal Owner: George E. Learnard
Architect: Unknown
Construction Date: 1919-1920

LTHOUGH THEY WERE destined to enjoy it for only twelve years, George Edward Learnard and his tall, impressive wife, the former Elinor Nye of New York, created in Greenwich a beautiful English-inspired estate on the land which they purchased in 1919 and 1920. He was a dynamic, self-made man, born in 1874 in Boston and educated in public schools. He became an engineer and finally president of International Combustion Engineering Corporation of New York City. Also associated with businesses involving pulverized fuel, grates, water tube boilers, and coal oil extraction, he traveled often in Europe as well as the United States. Although he was reported to have used all his fortune and his wife's jewelry to save his company, unfortunately it did not survive the 1929 stock market crash. In 1931 he was forced to sell his Greenwich property and rent a home on North Street where he and his wife are said to have lived, childless, until he died.

In the more prosperous period of their lives, however, the Learnards bought land in Greenwich amounting to over 150 acres. There they built the country home they called Beausite and used it summers and weekends. The property had belonged to the Mead family, some of it to Edgar Mead, the rest to A. Newton and S. Christy Mead. A large part of it, known locally as the old Russell place, had been a farm used primarily for growing wheat and had an apple orchard, a grape arbor, and a root cellar. The original farmhouse and a smaller house both burned. The stone base of the former was used as the foundation for Beausite; that of the latter, for the gardener's cottage. The beautiful stone manor house built by the Learnards in 1919 still stands on a slight knoll overlooking rolling meadows which were formerly pasture, gardens, and orchards. It was originally approached by a long gravel drive marked by stone columns supporting wrought-iron gates. Stone walls flanked the drive on both sides. To the southeast of the main house, in the lee of a hill,

the farm buildings were clustered: two barns, a silo, a seven-car garage with staff quarters above, and two tenant houses. These outbuildings, constructed of stone and shingle, blended easily into the landscape. The tenant house known as the bungalow, which predates the Learnards' ownership, is the only one truly visible from the main house. Its heavy log construction lends a rustic quality to the view from the hill above.

Grand in concept if not large in square footage, Beausite is a two-story Tudor house with a balanced four-gabled facade which provides a harmonious blend of scale and design. The formal facade is composed of natural fieldstone; stucco and half-timbering accent the second-floor gables. The roof is variegated slate, and the windows are made of leaded glass set in limestone mullions.

The main stone-gabled entrance of the house faces north. The visitor enters the front door from the circle at the end of the driveway, passing through a small foyer into the entry hall from which the other public rooms of the house open. It is almost austere in its simplicity, but for the richness of the smoothly cut travertine stairs and supporting wall. Although the other walls are plaster, exacting workmanship has made the transition from stone to plaster nearly impossible to detect and leaves the impression of a travertine room. Light flows softly down from a second-story window and highlights the simple vaults and subtle textural changes of stone and sand plaster, creating an ethereal effect. Wrought-iron and wood stair railings, lightly decorated with grape leaf motifs, relieve the almost monastic simplicity of the room.

To the immediate right of the stair hall is a small library paneled after the French rococo style. Floor-to-ceiling bookcases, the fireplace, oak parquet floors, and honey-colored paneling make this little room one of the most intimate on the first floor. Its style contrasts sharply with the Gothic style of the rest of the house.

91

The living room as furnished by the Learnards.

The reflecting pool, later filled in, circa 1935.

*The main stairwell
made of travertine.*

Beausite's living room reflects the superb craftsmanship to be found throughout the house. It is a large, double-height space which runs along the south side of the house overlooking the formal garden and meadows. As in many Tudor-style homes of this era, the glory of the room is its paneling. Dark-stained oak, carved in linen folds and exquisite medallions, covers two-thirds of the walls' height. Between sections of paneling the carving also features stylized figures on bases and under canopies, reminiscent of Gothic church portals. The panels contain motifs of busts, twining vines, fanciful fish, and urns similar to those found in ancient Rome. A large brick-lined fireplace is set in the north wall. Much of the paneling in the house, and the fireplaces as well, are thought to have been purchased by the Learnards in Europe and installed by European craftsmen.

The living room is lit primarily by a large, full-height window looking out to the rose garden. In the upper halves of its five vertical parts are handsomely painted modern glass panels made for the house. They depict events in the history of the United States, including Pilgrim scenes, Washington at Valley Forge, General Putnam's ride, and a tribute to World War I veterans. Other windows overlooking the south lawn are inset with stained-glass panels of various styles and different ages, the provenance of which is unknown. Also in this room is one of the more endearing sculptures to be found at Beausite—a smiling peasant carrying two faggots of firewood. The figure is more roughly carved than the paneling figures and is obviously from a different source, and he livens up the formality of the room as a smile brightens a face.

The dining room is also richly paneled. The wood extends all the way from the random-width, pegged oak floor to a plaster ceiling, which is boldly traced with ribs and pendants evocative of English High Gothic style. An antique carved and painted limestone fireplace is set in the paneling, and many of the original colors are still visible on its decorative figures.

West of the library lies a large, sunny sitting room, used by the Learnards as a game room. Above linen-fold oak wainscoting, large plaster panels with floral reliefs adorn its walls, and the ceiling is set with dropped, square oak beams beautifully carved with fruit and flower patterns. Doors set in carved stone jambs and inset with leaded glass have linen-fold carving to match the wainscoting and are decorated with large L-shaped hinges, themselves painted with designs in muted colors. The simple richness of this one-and-a-half-story room is enlivened with magnificent eight-panel leaded-glass windows overlooking three sides of the property. Set in them are large stained-glass medallions which depict the twelve signs of the zodiac. On the north windows two additional medallions feature French caravels of the late sixteenth century. The Learnards also installed in this room two stained-glass panels from Sulgrave Manor, the ancestral home of George Washington, in England. Both panels have since been removed for safekeeping. A large, simply carved limestone fireplace decorated with heraldic reliefs faces the length of this unusual room.

All of the ten bedrooms are on the second floor. The largest, part of the master suite, is in the original section of the house. A sitting room and a bath adjoin this bedroom, complete with its own fireplace and a balcony overlooking the living room. There are six additional bedrooms with five more full baths, most of them added later, as were the servants' rooms on that floor.

One of the loveliest parts of the grounds outside the house is the walled garden, which can be seen from both the sitting and the living rooms. It is protected on its north side by a tall stone wall; to the south the wall is low and affords a view across the meadow to the bungalow. The garden area is long and rectangular, terraced near the house in flagstone. A low stone perimeter in the center marks the boundaries of what was formerly a blue-tiled reflecting pool, which had a fountain in its center. Today it is a rose garden. Marking the openings in the garden wall are pairs of tall, slim, stone columns, each pair topped with matching sculptures such as eagles, griffins, and lions. Beyond the former pool, steps lead to a second level, also adorned with sculpture-topped columns. A small gazebo marks the far corner of the lower level. The two levels must have at one time provided a deep vista to the west.

The Learnards made their estate into a self-sufficient gentleman's farm. They hired an Englishman, Claude Peake, to bring his prize Guernsey cows and work for them. Peake and other hired help, many of them Polish or Russian immigrants, rotated crops of corn, wheat, and hay; raised vegetables and chickens; and built the dairy herd up to forty cattle. In fact, George Learnard's hobby became raising purebred cattle, although his enthusiasm may have been dimmed by an incident of erroneously administered inocula-

The farm buildings of Beausite.

tions which killed his best bull and a number of cows.

When the Learnards' efforts to stave off bankruptcy failed in 1931, William and Mary Dewart bought the house with over eighty acres of the property and renamed it Wilmary Manor. William Dewart (1875-1944) was, as George Learnard had been, a self-made man. He began his business career while still in his teens by founding a button factory. Hard work over many years earned him the presidency of all the Munsey corporations including, eventually, the *New York Sun*. A very successful man financially, he too had a residence in New York and summered in Greenwich. The Dewarts added the servants' quarters and additional bedrooms to the main house, as well as a garage which had a terrazzo floor and blue-tiled walls to make it more appealing. Their house, as described by the Greenwich *Daily News-Graphic*, was "a notable combination of architectural beauty and domestic comfort." They filled it with fine English and French furniture, oriental rugs, tapestries, magnificent sterling, china, and crystal, beautiful objects of art, and a library of books, some of them rare.

The Dewarts did extensive landscaping, especially tree planting and stonework, and sold most of the cows, though they kept many chickens. The frogs in the reflecting pool made so much noise that William Dewart could not sleep, so he had it filled in and planted a rose garden. He closed off Dewart Road with large boulders, changed the stone entrance, and began to sell parcels of land.

Some fifty years later, only a little more than nine acres remain with the house, but it is fully intact and continues to reflect the original architectural intent. The outbuildings are still there and cared for; the remains of the orchards are visible, and many of the stone walls stand today.

Three Oaks

The forecourt and main entrance of Three Oaks. All Three Oaks photos by Gil Amiaga.

Principal Owner: Robert P. Noble
Architect: Phelps Barnum
Construction Date: Circa 1930

I N 1923 the Lifesaver mint candy business was sold by a Cleveland manufacturer for $2,900. Although few people understood why the brothers wanted to venture into candymaking with this purchase, Robert P. and Edward J. Noble, originally from Gouverneur, New York, formed the Mint Products Company, Inc. With working capital of $900 they got production of candy under way in a one-room Manhattan loft where six girls were employed. Problems with cardboard packing that stuck to the candy almost swamped the little business, but Edward devised a new, easy way to open a foil wrapper, and those difficulties were solved. Robert was the engineering expert, with experience at Westinghouse; Edward brought advertising expertise to the enterprise and was convinced that he could sell his product successfully. Fourteen-carat gold Lifesavers planted for a while in many of the packages led to enormous increases in sales, and the little rolls of sugar mints with the hole in the middle grew in popularity until the Noble brothers, because of their well-managed company, became multimillionaires.

In 1920 Robert Peckham Noble (1881-1973), the older of the two by a year, came to Greenwich, where he lived to be ninety-two. Aside from his distinguished business career, he was extremely influential in a wide range of community activities including the Greenwich Hospital, the Greenwich Boys Club, the Greenwich Chamber of Commerce, Greenwich Academy, the Putnam Trust Company, and the Round Hill Club. At Indian Harbor Yacht Club he was commodore and an ardent sailor. When this "quiet giant of the community" died in 1973, in *The Nutmegger* it was said of him that "Few succeeded so well in so many aspects of living."

Noble lived in the Belle Haven section of Greenwich for a number of years before he bought a lot of almost twenty-six acres in mid-country Greenwich and made plans to build a house there. In 1934 he added another parcel of land, slightly over seventeen acres, to his first purchase. The location was far enough north to seem in those days a great distance from the center of town. The land had, in fact, been a farm and had therefore been cleared for crops. Since there were few trees of any size on the property, the place was named for the three magnificent oaks growing at the building site. Now, however, the broad lawns in front are scattered with large handsome trees, and an apple orchard planted by the Nobles flourishes.

The original farmhouse was torn down. To take its place the architect Phelps Barnum was engaged to design the beautiful Georgian home which still stands today. It is built of rusticated brick and has a slate roof. Most of the windows have green shutters and are six over six, eight over eight, or in the instance of the large one over the main entrance, ten over ten. Some have brick, some limestone sills. On the second floor of the service wing there are unusual dormers faced with slate. The main block of the house, slightly recessed, is balanced by two sections containing on the one side the dining room, on the other side the living room, both of which have magnificent views of the back lawns from the rear of the building.

The house is known especially for its living room, called the Adam room because of its elegant style associated with the two Adam brothers, architects in late-eighteenth-century England. The woodwork in this room, brought over from Hamm Court, Upton-on-the-Severn, England, is rich in details characteristic of its period. The beautifully carved doorframe matches the window frames. The carved mantel is decorated with classical garlands over the marble surround, which is veined in delicate shades of pink and beige. Above the wainscoting and the chair rail the plaster walls are crowned with an ornamental cornice applied as a ceiling molding. The carved shutters inside the windows are also typical and fold back into the window casements when not in use. This sophisticated room is extraordinary for the restrained

The beautifully carved Adam doorframe from the main hallway.

The Adam mantel in the dining room.

yet intricate beauty of its details.

Mrs. Noble, the former Meta Buehrer, worked with the Chicago architectural advisor Watson and Bowler to find the old paneling for the house. She engaged Nancy McClellan of New York City to help her with interior decoration such as wallpaper and fabrics; the fine antique furniture she collected complemented the exquisite taste of the architectural details. Other interesting and lovely touches enliven different parts of the house. Cabinets with inset butterfly shelves above and paneled doors below are built into the green-paneled walls of the dining room. The family displayed a fine selection of Crown Derby china there as well as early silver pieces. The dining table was a Sheraton divided table. The paneled library has a fireplace with a broken pediment instead of a mantel and originally contained trophies from Noble's sailing days. Bookshelves are recessed in niches, and the end of the room is slightly bowed, giving it a very warm feeling. The floors are teak. Phelps Barnum designed the paneling here; however, his blueprints indicate that seventy-seven and a half feet of antique woodwork were used throughout the house.

Beautifully carved French paneling was imported for the large downstairs powder room. The door there, when closed, becomes invisible as part of the wall.

The charming little butler's pantry has a series of tiles running along the wall—hand-painted scenes of monks at work: picking apples and grapes, drawing water, and hoeing. The large kitchen still has the original flowered tiles in part of its floor. In the front hall a church-sized organ, something Noble had always wanted, is built into the house. Made by the Skinner Organ Company of Boston, its huge wooden pipes are hidden behind a wall. The Nobles' daughter took organ lessons from the organist of Christ Church; Noble could not play very well but had rolls for it that made it work like a player piano.

A low stone wall fronts the property. Only a short distance from it a low brick wall defines the forecourt in front of the house. Before reaching this entrance the drive forks to the left, sloping down and away from the main house to a brick building of surprising charm. In earlier days this was the stable, with its slate roof, brass-topped cupola, a weather vane, and stone-walled courtyard—a little gem of a structure now converted to a private home. Past the stable is a house which includes the original gardener's cottage,

Detail of the mantel.

A brick wall encloses the forecourt with formal planting beyond.

a greenhouse, and a garage. Now too a residence, its fieldstone exterior resembles an ivy-covered English cottage.

Meta Noble was deeply interested in the grounds around her house. Her great pride was a lovely walled garden in the English style designed by Marian Coffin. It was surrounded by brick walls of varying height. Originally the beds were all square, lined with boxwood hedges, and there was a little fountain at the garden entrance, enlivened at one time by two bronze ducks designed by the sculptor Wheeler Williams. Flowers included delphiniums, irises, poppies, phlox, balloon flowers, salvia, digitalis, nemesia, heliotrope, and clematis. Tulips were to be followed by bellflowers, which gave way to snapdragons. Perennials bloomed in borders, and the center beds contained the glorious rose garden.

The landscaping in general was quite formal, very English. There used to be a boxwood garden in the back of the house, perennial gardens, and a sunken garden. Lawns slope down the hill from the terrace behind the house; the surrounding areas were planted in spruce, boxwood, azalea, and other shrubs with stone walks leading through them. Still there and growing is a long row of espaliered apple trees. Behind

them, near the gardener's house, were extensive vegetable gardens.

Unlike many of the other Greenwich estates, there were no farm animals, only the horses which the family used for riding. The Nobles were part of a group of enthusiastic fox hunters in town, and Teddy Wahl, the well-known horseman who ran Round Hill Stables, remarked of Mrs. Noble, "she was a sharp little fox hunter and hunted well. Little bit of a thing. I used to have to have the reins made specially small for her because her hands were so small."

Three Oaks remained intact for almost fifty years. Two years after Noble's death, however, the property was broken up, and his house now stands on a little more than eight acres of its former total of forty-three.

Lochwold

Architect's renderings of front and rear elevations of Lochwold.

Principal Owner: Edward J. Noble
Architect: Lewis Colt Albro
Construction Date: 1923-1924

DWARD JOHN NOBLE (1882-1958) with his older brother Robert bought a tiny, failing candy company and built it into the multi-million dollar Lifesavers business. His business career, however, was not limited to candy. Besides acting as chairman of the Lifesavers firm, which merged eventually with Beech Nut Packing Company, in 1941 he purchased the Blue Network, which he renamed the American Broadcasting Company. He served as its first chairman, then as director, and in 1953 he was responsible for the greatest radio/television transaction ever negotiated: the merger of his ABC network with United Paramount, Inc. During President Roosevelt's administration, he also became chairman of the new Civil Aeronautics Authority from 1938 to 1939 and Undersecretary of Commerce from 1939 to 1940. An extraordinary capacity for hard work made him one of America's outstanding businessmen and philanthropists. His native northern New York was always closest to his heart, and he established three hospitals in that rural area. His concern for people found expression through acts of philanthropy of a particularly constructive kind, especially in the fields of health and education.

Edward Noble bought most of the land for his building site in 1923, and he eventually ended up with approximately one hundred acres in mid-country Greenwich. A large and spectacular part of his property was the Lake Avenue tract owned by Ernest Thompson Seton after he sold Wyndygoul and before he left Greenwich for New Mexico. Architect Lewis Colt Albro designed an English style country house for the Nobles. It was completed in 1924, though not without difficulties, for Albro died before it was finished. The Nobles aptly named their estate Lochwold, loosely translated "lake, hills, rocks."

The curving driveway leads in from the main road past tall old rhododendron bushes, yews, and large evergreens, swinging by the former garage which is now remodeled as a home. Made of stone and brick with a slate roof, it was the only outbuilding on the place. At the circle in front of the house, the main impression is a residence not of great size, but of great charm. It is built of dressed fieldstone and has a slate roof. The main chimney has a two-thirds brick capping, and bricks have also been used as window frames and arches. First-floor windows are primarily in-wall, with leaded-pane casements, grouped in twos, threes, and fours; second-story windows, except in the main gable, are dormers. To the left of the three-story gable, which contains the entry hall, the living room, and the sunroom on the ground floor, is the main section of the house, with a dining room and a study. Again to the left, but slightly set back, is the kitchen and the service wing. This left wing with its saltbox roof forms an L with the rest of the building, following the line of the driveway.

The interior of the house is meticulously finished and gracious in feeling. The rooms downstairs are large but not cold, and there is plenty of light. Throughout, both structural and decorative details bring great pleasure to the eye. In the entry hall, the oak staircase to the second floor has a graceful, carved pheasant as a newel post. The lower half of the wall is paneled in oak; the upper half is plaster with intricate moldings. The French doors leading to an outside terrace have unusual grillework including a peacock in the center. Noble's wife, the former Ethel Louise Tinkham, collected antique English furniture with which she furnished the house, and she became an authority on early oak pieces.

The living room is warm with handsome, oak-paneled walls. The plaster ceiling is decorated with floral borders and plants and animals in relief—oak leaves, a pig, a griffin, and a peacock among them. In the fireplace are its original very tall brass andirons incorporating in the metalwork figures of people surmounted by crowns. The floor is random-width pegged oak, raised in one corner of the room to define

The rear facade from the pond.

The loggia off the living room during the Nobles' ownership.

that space as a library area for reading. The dining room, striking because of its large central rosette in the plaster ceiling, has teak floors.

Beyond the living room is perhaps the most unusual room of all, the loggia. With its four sets of French doors, the impression is of glass and light all around. The fireplace is extraordinary: tall, gracefully shaped, and made of limestone with a crested escutcheon above flanked classical figures in plaster. It also has a pair of large andirons unique to the house. The original wrought-iron-and-gilt lighting fixture hangs from the high-beamed ceiling. The multi-colored slate floor adds subtle tones to the room with its soft green, red, and gray squares.

Features of particular interest upstairs include a bedroom with barrel-vaulted ceiling and unusual moldings and a long hallway, its walls covered with murals of delicately painted pastoral scenes, ending in an arch. A third-floor playroom has cartoon figures of the "Alice in Wonderland" story decorating the walls.

The grounds around the house are spectacular. The land is studded with huge rock outcroppings and planted with rhododendron, laurel, azaleas, yews, and andromeda. Ethel Noble was a knowledgeable horticulturist and took great interest in different varieties of plantings. There are little paths everywhere which she called meditation walks, lined with labeled rare trees and shrubs and often leading to sitting areas. The spacious lawn slopes downhill from the terrace at the back of the house to a pond and forest beyond. The site is quiet, private, and quite lovely.

Noble died at his home in 1958 after a long illness. His wife continued to live there, and after her death in 1975 it was sold. Only about three acres of the estate's total are still with the residence today. However, the rest of the original property remains, separately owned, completely intact, currently classified as forest land.

Murals line the walls of the upstairs hall. Gil Amiaga photo.

The murals of the third floor playroom. Gil Amiaga photo.

The pheasant newel post of the main staircase. Gil Amiaga photo.

A gentle grassy slope and informal plantings frame the rear facade of Chelmsford.

Principal Owner: Elon Huntington Hooker
Original Architect: Unknown
Architect for Renovations (1908-1911): McKim, Mead, and White

T IS SINGULARLY pleasing to recognize that a particular house reflects its owners' personalities, tastes, and way of life. Such an estate is Chelmsford, owned by Mr. and Mrs. Elon Huntington Hooker, together from 1906 to 1938, and, after his death, by her until 1956. It is a lovely and livable home, billed as one of the showplaces of Greenwich in the 1930s, but never pretentious or overbearing. The living space and the ten bedrooms are gracious and roomy; and countless closets, shelves, and odd nooks provide storage and conveniences almost beyond belief, for Mrs. Hooker ran an efficient household in a careful and meticulous manner. The grounds, with her beloved gardens and his tennis court, as well as one of the earliest and largest swimming pools in town, enabled them to enjoy their leisure in what was then the country. Finally, such an estate provided an ideal way of life for their four daughters, with whom they spent a great deal of time.

Elon Hooker (1869-1938) was born in Rochester, New York, a descendant in direct line from the Reverend Thomas Hooker, who was instrumental in the founding of the state of Connecticut as one of the thirteen original colonies. Elon Hooker earned degrees from the University of Rochester and Cornell University, where he won highest honors and was awarded a fellowship which took him to Europe. Armed with a letter of introduction while in Rome, he was able to meet Blanche Ferry of Detroit, daughter of Dexter M. Ferry, banker and owner of large flower and seed properties. One of the Hooker children relates that they fell in love in twenty-four hours but that he postponed marriage until he had finished his education and could support a wife. Though the object of many suitors' attention, she waited for him, and they were married in 1901.

The eventual result of his aptitude for engineering and science was the Hooker Electrochemical Company, founded in the early 1900s. From property best described as a shanty in a dead pear orchard, he developed what became the largest enterprise of its kind in the world, an immense plant covering thirty-two acres located at Niagara Falls, New York. He loved his work and was an engineer at heart; however, he also taught Baptist Sunday school; and he was a Greek scholar and a very good, very competitive athlete—a champion college tennis player and an avid fisherman.

Blanche Ferry Hooker was a bright, capable woman who with her sister was one of the first girls from Detroit to go east to college. She excelled at Vassar, was president of her class, and was involved all her life in many cultural and social activities. At the time of her death she was also known as a leading horticulturist. In addition, she possessed a financial turn of mind and ran Chelmsford in a very businesslike way.

After living for some time on North Street in Greenwich, the Hookers decided to move in with their good friends Mr. and Mrs. Charles Lanier, who in 1898 had bought land close to town from Alexander and Cynthia Mead. The Hookers bought from them their house and a little over fifteen acres in 1906, adding almost four more acres in 1912. They engaged the outstanding architectural firm of McKim, Mead, and White to design additions to the rather small house they had purchased. Accordingly, a wing containing the spacious drawing room and the master bedroom suite was built in 1908, and by 1911 the service wing and more bedrooms had been added. During the course of the latter construction the Hookers took their four little girls to Europe to avoid the confusion of the work in progress, and when they returned the addition was finished.

The resulting house is a long, rambling structure built of stone and clapboard with a ludovici tile roof, in what might be called Dutch Colonial style. All the rooms, with the exception of the library and a small room upstairs, have either an eastern or a

Chelmsford's informal setting is apparent in this aerial photo.

The swimming pool shown at the upper left in the photo above.

southern exposure, so that the sun fills room after room during the course of the day. The atmosphere, even in the third-floor servants' rooms, is therefore light and airy, and as the site is high, almost any window allows a view through the woods punctuated with rocky crags, down the steep hill to Horseneck Brook, or over lawns and gardens.

The living and dining rooms, both part of the original house, differ in style from the additions made by McKim, Mead, and White. The very large entrance hall, serving as a living room, is a replica of a Tudor room with a beamed ceiling and an ornately carved Norman-style fireplace which has a stone surround.

It contained the dark English furniture appropriate to the period. The paneled dining room walls were always painted white. When the Hookers moved the fireplace from one side of the room to the other, a large window overlooking the property's extensive back lawns was put in its place. The wall around the new fireplace was then covered with tiles depicting biblical, mythical, and Dutch scenes, done in mauve, rather than the usual blue tones. The effect is striking.

The drawing room, on the other hand, is Neoclassical in design. It is a large and elegant room with a marble fireplace and decorations including dentil molding, egg-and-dart detail, and Ionic columns. The Hookers furnished it with Chippendale furniture. Long draperies hung from brass rods and were changed summer and winter according to the careful schedules made out by Blanche Hooker for the running of the household. When not in use they were kept upstairs in unusually long drawers designed especially for their storage.

Bedrooms on the second floor — for parents, the four daughters, governess, and guests — are all connected, one to the next, through bathrooms and alcoves with extra sinks and mirrors for greater convenience. All the bedrooms except two have fireplaces; figures of animals adorn the tiled fireplace surround in one child's bedroom. The differing heights of sinks and mirrors, tailored to the tall Elon Hooker and his petite wife, are typical of the special touches that are noticeable.

Showers are marble; stained-glass insets illustrating La Fontaine's *Fables* adorn a child's bathroom. Bookcases extend down the long hall, and there are innumerable closets: tiled closets for cleaning supplies; a carpenter's closet with drawers of built-in, labeled boxes, and shadow pictures of tools painted on the wall (according to a daughter, if a tool wasn't put back in the right place, you were in trouble); a closet for wrapping packages, complete with iron holders for rolls of paper and drawers for string and other necessities. An enormous fuse box identifies the sewing machine light and the elevator light, among countless others.

The service wing was a world of its own, complete with the servants' dining room including paneled cupboards and shelves; the laundry room with cement floor and big machines that washed and ironed; a two-room, tiled servants' bathroom with not only the usual facilities but also a large slop sink for waste water; the storage room where huge iceboxes held the blocks brought in through an opening; and the dumb-waiter as massive as an elevator and with doors on two sides. Finally, the spacious kitchen and butler's pantry were fitted out with all the necessities: huge stoves (first coal, later gas), sinks, a large central preparation table, and always storage and more storage—cabinets, substantial wooden drawers with brass pulls, endless shelves. In addition, there were marvelous conveniences, such as an enormous plate warmer with a marble top; cutting boards that pulled out when needed, then disappeared; a large inset slab of marble mounted with a strong light overhead for making bread; porcelain doorknobs and white tiles everywhere, some decorated with blue designs. Rows of bells for summoning servants were arranged on a big wall panel.

The original landscaping of the grounds was done by Charles Gillette of Richmond, Virginia, but Elon Hooker was responsible for designing the curving driveway which wound around the stately trees, leaving them intact. After the initial planning, Bryant Fleming made further changes including the unusual long grassy steps he designed in back, resulting in a more gradual slope down the hill, because he felt it gave the house more composure. The gardens were not arranged in a stiffly formal manner but overflowed with flowers. They were tended by fifteen to twenty gardeners, mostly Italian, who walked an hour and a half to work through back fields every day from the Port Chester area. The two-acre vegetable garden supplied more than enough for the Hookers, and all extra produce, flowers, and milk were regularly given away to those employed on the estate or, often, to Greenwich Hospital.

The Hookers enjoyed an active social life and over the years invited many guests. To accommodate visitors the picturesque Rose Cottage was built. A cozy, warm house made of stone, it had four or five bedrooms, a dining room, a small living room, and its own kitchen and maid's room. It is occupied as a separate home today.

There were other outbuildings. The garage, also of stone construction, contained a tiled area large enough for several big cars, space to wash them, the chauffeur's apartment and the Hooker girls' art studio above, and a gasoline pump outside. The superintendent, John Rutherford, who had married the girls' Scottish nurse, had a cottage for his family. The chicken coop housed as many as two hundred chickens. There was a barn for cows and horses. The daughters were accomplished riders—one of their favorite horses was named Beacon Light—and before automobiles were widely used, a team of aging horses bought from the Greenwich Fire Department used to take Elon Hooker down the hill to the railroad station at a full gallop.

During their first decade in the house, the Hookers stayed in Greenwich year-round. However, Elon Hooker became weary of his daily commute to New York. Consequently, he and his family adopted a routine involving four moves a year, enabling them to spend winters in their Fifth Avenue apartment; May, June, September, and October at Chelmsford; and the hottest months, July and August, at either Southampton or East Hampton. Blanche Hooker, an incredibly well organized person, managed the logistics efficiently, making sure that the cook, the butler, the governess, and the children, to say nothing of clothes and such essentials as silver, arrived safely at each destination. Every third summer they took the girls to their grandparents' six-hundred-acre farm in Unadilla, New York.

Thus, Chelmsford became a place to be enjoyed during the most pleasant months of the year when much of the family activity was outdoors. The girls became excellent tennis players, horsewomen, and swimmers. The brook was stocked with fish, and Elon Hooker was fond of walking down the so-called fisherman's trail to fish there at six o'clock on Sunday mornings. Among others who were invited to enjoy the pool and the gardens were all the New York employees of the chemical company. Every summer they were graciously entertained by the entire Hooker family.

Residents of Greenwich may also remember Elon Hooker for his efforts in helping found the Field Club. He was interested in having a club where entire families could enjoy competitive sports together. Old-timers recall the early days when mothers and nannies sat under the famous apple trees, knitting, while their offspring and husbands played tennis.

Today the main house and almost nine and a half acres continue to be beautifully maintained by the present owners.

Northbrook Farm

Artist's rendering of Northbrook Farm, after an early postcard photograph.

Principal Owner: John H. Flagler
Original Architect and Construction Date: Unknown
Architect for Addition: Frank Ashburton Moore

OHN HALDANE FLAGLER (1838-1922), described by a local newspaper at the time of his death as a "noted captain of finance," and a year earlier by the *New York Times* as a "multimillionaire steel and iron man," was born in Cold Spring, New York. He refused, after earlier education, to go to college and instead went to work for his uncles, who were iron dealers in New York. Showing marked executive and organizational ability, he was made manager of the Boston branch of their business. Soon afterward, however, he started his own firm of John H. Flagler and Company to manufacture iron and steel. His operation gradually became noted for its production of tubing, and to further the development of this specialty Flagler also founded the National Tube Works in East Boston. This plant was soon the principal American manufacturer of tube products, its business growing as the oil fields of Pennsylvania were opened and a demand was created for large quantities of tubing. When this vast concern was later merged with the U.S. Steel Corporation, there were 4,500 men on its payroll.

Flagler was not only a successful executive, he was also known for the invention of certain scientific processes of great value to the iron-and-steel industry. He introduced to iron manufacturing the use of a gas furnace which until then had been known only abroad and which had been restricted there to the manufacture of glass. He also improved the use of uniform heat in the treatment of iron and steel until he had evolved a process which by the early 1920s was almost universally used.

Not willing to limit himself to his iron, steel, and tubing interests, for many years he was president of the Hegeman Company, which operated a large number of wholesale and retail drugstores and chemical houses. In 1911 by a series of mergers he created a company which controlled perhaps the most extensive line of drugstores in the world. This firm later became associated with the Liggett interests and merged with them.

John Flagler's first marriage of more than thirty years to Anna H. Converse of Boston ended at her death. They had only one daughter, Anna, who in 1889 married a Baron Harden-Hickey and by 1907 had become an invalid, hospitalized in Stamford, Connecticut.

In 1897, at age fifty-nine, Flagler fell in love with Alice Mandelick (1879-1918), a young contralto of twenty-three, after hearing her sing at a concert. A year later he married her, but for some reason the marriage was not announced to the public for another twelve months.

John and Alice Flagler expanded their already busy social life when they acquired about forty acres of choice land in northern Greenwich and proceeded to build an enormous mansion there. The property had been owned by Jared Reynolds and was later run for some years as a dairy farm by Mrs. Grace Camman and a Miss Willard. Flagler actually bought it in 1905 from S. Stanwood Menken.

The house was made of stucco in the Spanish Mission style with a red-tile, hipped roof. Arcaded porches, wings of varying levels, roofed chimneys resembling small bell towers, curvilinear and decorated parapets, long stretches of stone balustrades, and arched portals all contributed to the rather exotic flavor of the building. In the heat of the summer, awnings shaded the windows, many of which opened outward from the bottom.

The greatest expanse of manicured lawns was divided into four geometric shapes by walkways. The grass was surrounded by balustrades and punctuated by formally clipped ornamental shrubbery and large plants in urns. A fountain splashed into a circular pool in the center. The estate also contained huge glassed conservatories and greenhouses, chickenhouses and other farm buildings, a tennis court, a guest cottage, the superintendent's house, and garages.

John Flagler and friend.

Northbrook Farm's entrance was unpretentious.

Alice Flagler continued to pursue her musical interests during her married life. She performed regularly as contralto soloist at the Church of the Ascension in New York City and gave many concerts and recitals at her Greenwich home, some for the benefit of organizations such as the Greenwich Equal Franchise League. On one notable occasion in 1916 she was hostess at Northbrook Farm to eight hundred socially prominent people of Greenwich and New York for the benefit of Sing Sing inmates. A dramatic play was performed by ex-convicts on a raised platform at the far end of the spacious veranda, which was enclosed in glass for the event. According to the *New York Times*, it was the first time a performance of this kind had ever been given by ex-convicts for the benefit of those still inside prison walls. It raised $1,200 to be used for educational work at the prison. In connection with this affair, Mrs. Flagler gave a luncheon for fifty-eight ex-convicts and their wives in a garage on the estate.

John Flagler was an enthusiastic yachtsman and a member of both the New York and the Larchmont yacht clubs. He owned several large steam yachts during the early 1900s, among them the 63-foot *Dorothy*, the 124-foot *Allita*, and the 106-foot *Esolanie*; and

Its greenhouses were more impressive.

when time permitted, he enjoyed cruising on these comfortable yachts. In 1913 the delay of *Esolanie*'s departure on a November trip proved newsworthy, for when the time came for the well-provisioned vessel to sail, the chef was found to be in jail as a result of some drunken and unruly behavior the night before. Interestingly enough, members of the crew contributed the $100 bond so that he could be released.

Alice Flagler died in 1918 at the Flaglers' Park Avenue residence in New York. In January 1920 it was announced that Flagler had agreed to sell his Greenwich property for between $300,000 and $400,000 to Walter C. Teagle, president of Standard Oil of New Jersey, who reportedly wanted to give the estate to his wife for Christmas. However, before the title changed hands the mansion caught fire and, together with its beautiful furnishings, tapestries, and pictures, burned to the ground.

Among the items in the house not included in the sale was a pipe organ. Organ experts had arrived from New York to prepare it for shipment, and in order to have the house warm and comfortable, the caretaker started a fire in the furnace. It was believed that a defective flue was responsible for the blaze that resulted. Firemen were delayed because of roads blocked with snow, and frozen pipes further hindered their efforts when they arrived. Consequently, except for the organ cabinet, a large grand piano, some books, and a few pieces of furniture, everything was lost.

Undaunted, John Flagler not only began to build a new mansion, to be of Italian Renaissance design, but in the spring of 1921, at the age of eighty-three, married for a third time. The bride was a painter who specialized in watercolors, thirty-three-year-old Beatrice Wenneker of Brooklyn; the ceremony took place in a small town at the edge of the Berkshire Hills. Although an effort was made to keep the marriage a secret, the news was out within a week and attracted much attention.

Seventeen months later Flagler was dead of pneumonia. He and his new wife had been staying at the guest cottage on the Greenwich property before moving to their New York residence for the winter. His new house was never finished as he had planned. He left an estate unofficially estimated at $2 million. His will disclosed that after providing generously for his widow, family, servants, and some of his friends, he had left $1 million to be divided equally among New York, Columbia-Presbyterian, and St. Luke's hospitals in memory of his second wife, Alice Flagler.

Khakum Wood

High-Low House from the Pleasaunce.

Principal Owner: I. N. Phelps Stokes
Architect: I. N. Phelps Stokes
Construction Date: 1908-1910

HIGH-LOW HOUSE, the oldest occupied house in the United States in 1912, was to be found in Greenwich on the estate of Mr. and Mrs. Isaac Newton Phelps Stokes. Phelps Stokes (1867-1944), as he was familiarly called, was a noted architect, designer of Woodbridge Hall at Yale University, St. Paul's Chapel at Columbia University, the Music School at Harvard; housing expert, appointed by President Theodore Roosevelt to the State Tenement House Commission; and historian, author of the six-volume *Iconography of Manhattan Island*. In 1900 he bought almost 177 acres of land, which had been the W. A. Husted farm, from William Smith, and from that date unfolded a most interesting story.

Phelps Stokes and his wife selected the highest part of their property for a building site and decided on the placement of the house they would build. The more important rooms would face a little west of south, so as to get the full benefit of the prevailing summer breeze. The dining room would be situated to make it possible, during the greater part of the year, to enjoy the setting sun through the high windows of the great hall at dinnertime.

Phelps Stokes completed the general plan of the house and its surroundings in 1905, and work was immediately begun on the north wing, including the service quarters and the pleasaunce (literally, a "pleasure ground"), a level sunken area of closely clipped turf which met the low-walled gardens adjoining the house. His intention was to complete the development in three parts, over a period of perhaps ten years, and to occupy the house as soon as the first section was finished. Meanwhile, when they were in Greenwich, Mr. and Mrs. Stokes and their baby daughter, Helen, lived in a building already on the property which they called the Old House.

The first section of the gray stone, Tudor-style house was finished in 1908, built by only a few carefully picked workmen; the second section, including the octagonal tower, in 1910. This tower had a stone post in its center supporting a circular stairway made with triangular pieces of stone cut to form the steps. Neatly fitting together like pieces of a pie, they spiraled upward to a room at the top which had a magnificent view over lawns, gardens, and the surrounding countryside.

The family had just settled comfortably into their enlarged quarters with the full expectation of waiting another five years before beginning work on the last section when, in the summer of 1910, an advertisement in *English Country Life* magazine caught Phelps Stokes's eye. All the materials of a little half-timbered Tudor manor house, called High-Low House and built in 1597, were offered for sale. Standing near Ipswich in Suffolk, England, the house had been condemned so that some municipal improvements could be carried out. In Stokes's own words, "I was struck at once with the charm of the old woodwork and with the possibility of using this material in the completion of my own house." Subsequently he arranged with an English firm to take the house down, put everything in proper repair, pack, ship, and re-erect the house in Greenwich, in accordance with his own working drawings. Some 688 cases and bundles arrived at a pier in New York and were then transshipped to a Greenwich wharf engaged for the unloading. They were hauled to Round Hill Road and piled on the Stokeses' lawn.

The English foreman who had demolished the house found in the New York vicinity half-a-dozen masons and carpenters, also English, who were experienced in work of such unusual character. A total working force which varied between twelve and eighteen men began reconstruction of the old house in the spring and finished before cold weather set in. They followed the age-old, painstaking building methods of sixteenth-century England wherever practicable; and where additional materials were required

I. N. Phelps Stokes and his daughter Helen.

The breakfast room of High-Low House.

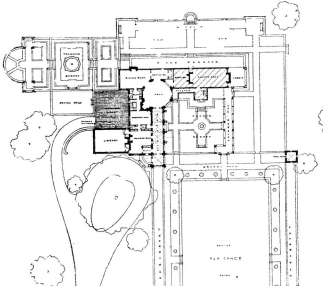

they were found in other old houses in the neighborhood of Ipswich or, in the case of some flooring and timbers, in the wreck of an old English ship on the New Jersey coast. The only new materials used were mortar, terra-cotta furrings on the outer walls replacing the original oak lath, tiles under the flooring, and window frames and glass. While the old frames were in good condition, they would not have withstood the horizontal rain and sleet of Connecticut winters, so they were discarded.

The resulting building, finished in 1912, was a beautiful and harmonious union of its two parts. The old manor house stood as it had in England, each timber, tile, and chimney brick in its original place, preserving all the mellowness and irregularities that come only with age. The weathered red-tiled roof and the soft tones of the aged wood and brickwork contrasted, yet blended, with the gray stone of the main body of the house to which it had been skillfully connected as a wing. The house, when completed, included a drawing room, a dining room, a reception room, a library, a billiard room, a writing room, a loggia, a kitchen and other service quarters, nine master bedrooms, seven servants' rooms, and eight bathrooms and lavatories. The Stokeses liked to spend time searching for antiques, and to furnish the house they bought fine old furniture, English for the most part. One exception, in the dining room, was the long antique walnut refectory table which was Spanish in origin.

Outside the house the exceptional gardens and plantings were laid out by Frederick Law Olmsted, Jr., well-known landscape architect, city planner, and son of the designer of New York City's Central Park. He trained with his father and maintained with his stepbrother their father's firm after the senior Olmsted's death. The land immediately surrounding the house was developed into a landscape as typically English as was the residence. Low-walled gardens clustered about the old wing, and the pleasaunce, quite unusual in the United States, was, as proposed by Stokes, "so closely related to the house as to form almost an outdoor part of it." This finely clipped carpet, stretching toward a screen of trees to the north, was surrounded by a high stone wall, for the greater part screened by masses of foliage and flowering shrubs, and bordered by clipped yew and boxwood. Across its far end was a pleached alley of clipped English linden, under the edge of which

The Great Estates / 112

was a rectangular swimming pool with broad steps descending into it, and beyond the pool was the tennis lawn.

The Stokeses named their estate Khakum Wood after a spring on the property used by the Indians, and they called the house itself the High-Low House, since it was the original name of the old wing. They arrived from their New York residence each summer and stayed for the season but used the house only on weekends in the spring and fall, closing off the old wing when cool weather made the coziness of the stone portion of the house desirable.

Mrs. Stokes, the former Edith Minturn, was responsible for the running of the estate. Her husband was busy with his architectural firm and his writing, so it was she who directed the staff and made sure that daily life ran smoothly. Her daughter states that it was also really she who loved the animals, the gardens, and the country life. To help inside, she had a cook and two maids, all Irish, and outside, a man who served as chauffeur, a gardener for the vegetables, a dairyman, and a general handyman. A Japanese gardener cared for the flower gardens. Day workers were also employed when needed, for the estate produced great quantities of vegetables, milk, poultry, and eggs. Edith Stokes usually drove her husband to the railroad station in a carriage pulled by their mare, Mabel. It took only twelve minutes to get there but forty minutes to return home, as the horse then had to be walked to cool down. The Stokeses, as did other commuters, used a paddock near the station where they let their horses stay until they became accustomed to the noise of the trains. Even so, pandemonium often broke loose as horses reared and tried to run away with their carriages when the 5:49 steamed in from New York.

In 1925 Phelps Stokes began to sell plots of his land according to a plan he had developed with Olmsted for a highly restricted residential estate. By 1937, when Edith Stokes died, thirty had been sold, with twelve remaining. They were from two to seven acres in size and had town water as well as underground electric and telephone service. A little over twenty acres were kept with High-Low House. Phelps Stokes died in 1944 at the age of seventy-seven. His estate was bought purely for the property and the view; the house, half of which was three and a half centuries old, was thereupon torn down to make way for a modern structure.

The English wing under construction.

The completed English wing.

The compatible join of the old and the new.

Fort Hills Farm

The imposing Tudor facade of Fort Hills Farm. Gil Amiaga photo.

Principal Owner: Reinhard Siedenburg
Architect: William F. Dominick
Construction Date: 1917-1920

N 1927 THE HOUSE belonging to Reinhard Siedenburg (1876-1927) was described in his obituary in the *New York Times* as "a show place in the Round Hill section" of Greenwich. A member of the cotton brokerage firm of Reinhard Siedenburg and Company of New York, he had just died "following a stroke of apoplexy," at the relatively early age of fifty-one. For a number of summers he and his wife, Paula, had rented in Greenwich and in 1914 decided to purchase Harriet Willson's more than eighty-two acres of land consisting mainly of apple orchards. They then proceeded to plan for their own summer home there, the one later mentioned at his death.

Siedenburg chose as his architect William F. Dominick, well known in his day for designing many private residences, and other types of buildings as well, among them Riverside School and Christ Church in Greenwich and St. James Episcopal Church in New York City. Hvolbeck Construction Company of Greenwich was the builder. The result is a grand manor house, Tudor in style, of stone and half-timber construction. The Siedenburgs named their property Fort Hills Farm because his parents lived in a section of Staten Island known as Fort Hills.

Construction began on the outbuildings first in 1917, but as it was thought to be unpatriotic to use large numbers of men and the necessary material to complete work during World War I, the main house was not finished until 1920. In the meantime, the Siedenburgs and their four children lived in the superintendent's quarters, while the servants used the garage.

The manor house remains today an imposing, extremely well planned and constructed building, approached by a roadway bordered by tall evergreens and huge rhododendrons. As seen from the front or north side, the first story is built of granite, all of which came from a quarry on the property that is now completely grown over. Italian stonemasons were hired to do the work. The half-timbered frame construction of the second story overhangs the first, and it not only gives a picturesque effect but also increases the floor space for the bedrooms there. The long lines of the roof, which is made of variegated rough slate, are broken by the gables and the five strong brick chimneys. The single chimney of the living room, with its stone-stepped offsets, seems to anchor the house firmly at that end, balancing the low roof of the service wing at the other. In the angle formed by that wing, the stonework of the first story has been continued up to form the stair tower, and there is an interesting distribution of casement windows at various levels. The rooflines have been softened from their severe straightness by subtly giving them the effect of the sagging that age produces; and both the irregular design of the timber beams and the rough texture of the stucco between them add to that effect.

The south side of the house overlooks beautiful gardens and landscaping. Two levels of terraces were originally banked with honeysuckle and rambling roses, and there was a perennial garden backed by shrubbery, as well as large areas of lawn. Steps at both ends connected the top with the bottom level. Doors on this side of the house open onto a terrace of tile and flagstone that extends the length of the building and is covered at one end by a wing which thus forms a part of the porch.

Inside, one of the most interesting features of the house is the handsome oak paneling throughout much of the first floor. The main entrance opens into a large hall with its own fireplace; a wide carved staircase leading upstairs; and various closets and other wall compartments hidden behind the wood facade. A carved oak panel with an open arch in the center and doors on either side divides the entrance hall from the living room but serves in effect to draw the visitor from one large space to the other. This partition was

Rear facade and upper terrace wall. Gil Amiaga photo.

Main staircase and front entrance hall. Gil Amiaga photo.

The living room from the entrance hall. Gil Amiaga photo.

on occasion removed to accommodate large gatherings. In the living room there is also a fireplace approached by a step and flanked by wooden seats, once covered with cushions. The ceiling is beamed. Bookcases along one wall were built to conceal an organ, but it was never purchased.

A small, intimate study contains a mantel carved with the initials of Mr. and Mrs. Siedenburg; the Siedenburg coat of arms crowns the library fireplace. In the latter room there are four particularly interesting wood carvings along the cornice of the walls—a musician playing a lute, a writer, an artist painting with palette and brush, and a man reading a book. The dining room, originally painted a soft green, opens onto a bright sun porch of wood, plaster and stone, with a tile floor. Throughout the first floor there are impressive examples of stained-glass and leaded windows, many inset with colorful medallions depicting animals, objects, or people.

The service wing contains a spacious kitchen, its walls lined with varnished cabinets; the servants' dining room; a large pantry with bins big enough for a barrel of flour, sugar, or the like; a dumbwaiter; a luggage elevator; and a safe for silver, as big as a closet.

In the basement there is a sizable playroom, or billiard room, with a fireplace. This room was enjoyed by Siedenburg as well as by the children, who sometimes performed plays on a stage at one end of the room. On that level there was another room which the children thought to be "secret" because they were never permitted to go into it. It was storage space for the gas kept on hand in case the electricity failed. The fixtures for gas lighting were recessed in little cabinets in the walls upstairs. The rest of the basement is a labyrinth of rooms—a laundry (the huge original gas dryer is still there), a wine cellar, coal storage rooms (enough coal was brought in during one week each summer to last the whole winter), a wood storage room, a furnace room, a mudroom, a preserves closet, and other miscellaneous storage rooms. A central vacuum cleaner served the entire house.

Most of the bedrooms are on the second floor. They include the master suite with its two bathrooms; four full-sized bedrooms for the children; two guestrooms, one called the green room and one the chapel room because of its angled ceiling; and the sleeping porches where the windows could be opened by pushing the sashes up into the attic walls. The fresh air of the porches was thought to be very healthy, especially for growing children. Each bedroom door

Mrs. H. Danforth Starr, the former Kathryn Siedenburg, and her daughter Eleanor with pony Prudence, in the early 1930s.

has a different knocker depicting a character or a scene from a book. Five servants' bedrooms are also on this floor, each with its own washbasin. They are connected by stairs with the kitchen and other parts of the service wing downstairs.

On the third floor an enormous room with a fireplace was considered by the children to be a wonderful place to play, as in it were kept, among other things, costumes and trunks. There were two bathrooms and three bedrooms besides, including the view room, so named because of the distance one could see from its windows. The governess slept in one of these bedrooms.

Fort Hills Farm was never a year-round residence for the Siedenburg family. Their New York City apartment was their permanent home, and they came out to Greenwich to live from May until November. During the period when school was in session the children accompanied their father to New York on the train in the morning and returned each afternoon. During the rest of the year the family came only for weekends and holidays, while several servants stayed to watch over the house during the week. When everyone was in residence, however, a number of servants were on hand to take care of the family's requirements. There was a butler, a cook, a kitchen maid, a parlor maid, the ladies' maid who spent much of her time ironing in the second-floor sewing room, a laundress, a chambermaid, a houseman, a chauffeur, and a man who lived in the coop and took care of the pigeons.

The outbuildings were substantial, especially the one which included the superintendent's quarters on its left side, a barn for horses and cows in the center, and on the right the chauffeur's quarters above and the garage below. In the garage there were areas for carriages and also for the summer and winter automobile bodies. This building is now a private residence, as is another sizable barn. In addition, there were two pumphouses, a coop, and a pigsty. The trees, flowers, and grounds were well cared for; there was a tennis court down from the second level behind the house and bridle paths through the woods.

The life-style made possible by such a house with its grounds and staff was an enviable one indeed. According to the *Greenwich News and Graphic*, "The first brilliant society wedding of the early fall season" in 1926 was Paula Siedenburg's, one of the two daughters, and "a large reception followed the ceremony." This event took place in the gardens. Her sister Kitty's coming-out party was also held at Fort Hills Farm, and on this occasion the hall panels were removed for dancing. When she was married, the gardens were again the site for the reception.

As was true of many of the Greenwich estates, the Siedenburgs' home was not merely a showplace; it was also a working farm. There were fruit orchards of quince, crab apples, peaches, and apples, and a vegetable garden which produced everything the family needed. Cows supplied milk, and there were usually a carriage horse, a workhorse, three or four cows, a pig, chickens, ducks, and pigeons in residence.

As is also true of so many of these estates, although the houses have survived largely intact, the same is not true of the land. In 1922 thirty-three of the original Siedenburg acres went to the newly formed Round Hill Club. In 1933 Mrs. Siedenburg divided approximately thirty-four acres among her two daughters and a surviving son. When she sold the house itself in 1937, the sale included almost fifteen acres. Today this imposing manor house is left with just under three.

The Johnston Estate

The approach to the Albert Wheeler Johnston estate. Gil Amiaga photo.

Principal Owner: Albert W. Johnston
Architect: Carrère and Hastings
Construction Date: Circa 1916

LBERT WHEELER JOHNSTON (1871-1952) was born in Brooklyn, New York. A man of tremendous energy and with a brilliant mind, he was exacting, complex, and an exceptional organizer. Johnston made a fortune as a mining engineer and served for many years as president and chairman of the board of the Canadian company Teck-Hughes Gold Mines Ltd. His study of metallurgy took him over much of the world and into areas where he could pursue his passion for fishing and hunting. While he enjoyed the solitude of a quiet lake, he also gave a great deal of time to civic and cultural affairs, serving as a trustee on the boards of both the Greenwich Hospital and his alma mater, Wesleyan University. In his retirement years Johnston turned to publishing and in 1936 at the age of sixty-five he bought the *Daily News-Graphic* and changed the name to *Greenwich Time*. Four years later he became its publisher and, in 1943, bought the competing weekly paper, the *Greenwich Press*, and eliminated it. His ties with the mining world remained strong, however, and in 1948 Johnston established the Munitalp Foundation for scientific research.

Albert Johnston began buying land in mid-country Greenwich in 1909 and had accumulated a total of fifty-four acres by 1916, when he retained Theodore E. Blake as architect for the sprawling English manor house he envisioned. At that time Blake was associated with the New York firm of Carrère and Hastings; he was well known for his part in designing the New York Public Library and the United States Senate and House of Representatives office buildings. While in independent practice during the last twenty years of his career, he designed the Rosemary Hall School in Greenwich. He knew the area well, for his family had lived in Greenwich for more than two hundred years. He also knew Albert Johnston, as both were members of the Field Club. The rambling cut-stone mansion he created for Johnston reflected both Johnston's and Blake's insistence on perfection of detail within an uncluttered space.

Seen from the fieldstone wall that bounds the property, the house appears deceptively simple; it resembles an overgrown cottage. The grand dimensions of Blake's design become apparent as one approaches the house down the curving graveled drive past the stone pergola covered with grapevines. Since Blake's work included the landscaping as well as the designs for the main dwelling and outbuildings, the result is a harmonious blend of texture and line. The great stone walls of the house rise comfortably from a base of rock and evergreens above the gentle terracing, which contains rhododendrons and pachysandra at the foot of towering oak trees. Free-form lawns flow off toward the deep woods, which in 1916 were truly wild and the denning place of many foxes.

The three-story house is slate-roofed and is faced with random-coursed ashlar, a hewn-stone finish made popular by the nineteenth-century American architect Henry Hobson Richardson. It shows a masterful handling of heavily textured masonry. Typical of this "Richardsonian-Romanesque" style are the small-paned windows, double panels of eight hung in horizontal bands. Johnston had special bronze fittings made for all the windows and doors to ensure that his mansion would be well locked, a caprice considered odd in those days when security was not a problem. Richardson's influence is also discernible in both the casual wanderings of the arched verandas and the impulsive placement of the balconies. The curiously irregular siting of the four tall chimneys reinforces the impression of understatement; it is an excellent example of the Edwardian period, with its emphasis on assured informality both indoors and outdoors.

The great entrance hall, with its generous fireplace and grand staircase, was a requisite of the English country house of the time. The floor plan is Queen Anne, open and informal despite the opulent size of the rooms. There are fourteen fireplaces in the house,

The facade as originally designed before the addition of balconies.

Arched entrance to the back gardens.

many of magnificently carved stone or marble. A stained-glass window on the landing of the sweeping stairs repeats the delicate leaf pattern in the wrought-iron railing. The library, the drawing room, and the banquet-sized dining room contain exquisite pegged or parquet floors, wood paneling, lofty ceilings, and plaster fireplace friezes. Under the stairs is a flower room where Mrs. Johnston arranged the flowers each day, freshly cut from the gardens or the greenhouse. The gardens themselves were modeled on those of Leningrad's Winter Palace and are set off by spectacular borders of azaleas.

Upstairs are six family bedrooms and four servants' rooms. The master suite covers an entire wing and includes two bedrooms; a dressing room; a tiled sunroom; and an imaginatively paneled library, reputed to have once been part of the quarters of a ship's captain. A shooting gallery with a fireplace is in the basement.

The four-car garage/stable surrounded a stone courtyard and included three standing stalls, a box stall, a carriage room, a machine shop, and quarters for "the man," a chauffeur or other employee. It also contained a billiard room—but without fireplace for reasons of

The garage and stables after remodeling as a residence. The original plan is shown below.

safety. The architecture of this building is similar to that of the main house, and the landscaping was equally well thought-out, with pyracantha gracefully espaliered upon the stone walls.

Little is known about the personal lives of the Johnston family. Mrs. Johnston (1874-1954) was born Constantine Julier in Cleveland, Ohio. She was known to be a reserved, extremely proper woman, who entertained in her home at small dinners and teas. But the *Greenwich News and Graphic* notes that on Saturday, January 7, 1922, Mrs. A. W. Johnston gave an informal dance for "about one hundred of her intimate friends" at the Field Club. The Johnstons also gave one, if not two, wedding receptions at their estate for their only child, Constantine Eugenie, who was married twice. Her first husband, John K. O'Meara, was killed in 1941 at the age of thirty-two while testing a sail plane for an aircraft company in California. In July 1944, Constantine married John A. Beach in a quiet ceremony at Christ Church. A photograph in the March 3, 1952, issue of the *Greenwich Time* shows a smiling Mr. and Mrs. Beach aboard their forty-foot ketch, *Fessona*, at the Nassau Yacht Club. The Bahamas were a favorite retreat for the Johnston family; Mrs. Johnston died there in January 1954.

Albert Johnston died in August 1952 at the age of eighty-one. Of his many achievements, his enchanting mansion remains much as it was in 1916, although it is now situated on only three acres. The stable building is no longer part of the property, but a pool and a pool house have been added. The azaleas, rhododendrons, peonies, and roses have grown lovelier with time, and the estate continues to demonstrate the imagination and charm of a gentler age.

121 / *The Johnston Estate*

Greyledge

Greyledge in the winter of 1920.

Principal Owners: Colonel Raynal C. and Anna P. Bolling
Architect: Carrère and Hastings
Construction Date: 1912-1915

HEN THIS WAR is over, I am going to take any balance of years belonging to me in complete enjoyment of all the little things of life...and keep my heart mellow with the love of my wife and children and the joys of my own home." So wrote Colonel Raynal Cawthorne Bolling (1877-1918) in 1918, according to Henry Pearson's *A Business Man in Uniform*. However, he had little time left, for during the spring offensive of the Germans in France, he was the first American officer of high rank to die on the field of battle.

The home to which he longed to return was a large stone mansion located in what was then the back country of Greenwich, set on land that he and his wife, the former Anna Phillips (1880-1961), began to buy in 1909. The first parcels, purchased in January of that year, were two pieces of farmland of about thirty acres each, one from Rebecca and J. T. Lyon and one from Thomas N. Cooke and Guy D. Mead. Additional parcels, acquired in 1911-13, brought the total to almost a hundred acres.

The Bollings engaged the architect Theodore E. Blake, a Greenwich resident and a member of the New York firm of Carrère and Hastings, to design their house, which is set far off the road at the end of a long driveway. Excavation began in 1912, and the family moved in during 1915. The building has three stories and is faced with the native stone excavated from the cellar. It was originally roofed with wooden shingles, which were replaced in the 1970s with slate. The bulk of the house is softened by the angles at which the wings are attached and by the extensive gable in front, the three smaller ones in back, and the dormer windows on all sides. Large arched openings to the porches with half-timbering at either end keep the main body of the house from looking too massive. Five stone chimneys are needed for the thirteen fireplaces. Local men did the work, and during the construction they staged a strike which was successful in raising their wages from $1.00 to $1.25 a day.

Inside, the house was finished in a simple manner with natural chestnut wood used for all the doors, moldings, and bookcases. The library, which was used by the Bollings as their living room, had floor-to-ceiling bookcases. The warmth of the wood made it a most inviting and comfortable room. The paneling of the music and dining rooms gives them a more formal feeling, though none of the fireplaces or moldings is ornate. All the rooms face south toward lawns bordered by large trees and open onto long halls that run the length of the house in the front. Off the living room is a light-filled porch, or loggia, with windows, glass doors on three sides, and a big stone fireplace on the fourth. A wide terrace outside connects this large porch to the smaller one at the other end of the house, which was used as a breakfast room. This room can be entered from the pantry or from the main dining room. The service wing constitutes the rest of the first floor and included a pantry, an ample kitchen, a laundry, a dining room, and a back hall with a freight elevator running from the basement to the third floor. There was also a back porch and a large area, enclosed by a stone wall, used for drying clothes.

The second floor contains the master bedroom suite with its large dressing room opening onto a porch. Encircling the suite is a back hall where there are many closets and a secret stairway to the children's playroom on the third floor. When the trap door was shut and covered with a rug, this entrance could not be seen. There were four guest rooms and baths. The one nearest the master dressing room ("the bachelor's guest room") has doors opening onto the master bedroom porch; and its bathroom still has the original white tiles, pull-chain toilet, bathtub, basin, and little fireplace. There were four maids' rooms with a bath in the second-floor service wing.

Mrs. Raynal Bolling and Greyledge, 1920.

The facade during that same winter.

A softer view of Greyledge the same year.

The third floor consisted of four bedrooms and three bathrooms for the children, a sleeping porch, a playroom, a linen room, and a substantial attic at each end of the house.

The basement ran the whole length of the house and included a furnace room, a coal room, a laundry, a wine cellar, storage rooms, Colonel Bolling's thirty-yard pistol range, his large sporting den with a fireplace and a bath, and two servants' rooms with a bath.

When the original barn was destroyed by fire in 1926, a new barn was designed by the Jamesway Farm Supply Co. The latest type at the time, it had a distinctive roofline and a unique ventilating system. The upper floor contained two large hay lofts with a wide ramp, between which the horse-drawn wagons could pull up a load. The fork lift, pulled on a track from the ceiling, could swing the hay into either side. Below there were twelve stanchions with troughs, outfitted for milking cows. Surplus milk was sold to the Round Hill Dairy.

Five horse stalls and a tack room in the barn were the center of activity for the family, as all but one of the Bollings were riders. Nearby was a schooling ring with about twelve show fences used for practice. The last fence, if one wanted to jump it, led out of the ring onto the road; then it was away and gone over hill and dale and fences, up into the back country for fifteen miles or more.

The Bolling children, three girls and a boy, learned to ride on their ponies, one of which they coaxed into the house and up to the second floor once when their mother was away. Getting the pony down was quite a problem. As they grew older they rode the team horses around the farm and sometimes hid behind trees to watch the fox hunters go by. The day was special when they could ride the horses downtown to be shod at the blacksmith's shop. As the two youngest daughters became experienced riders, they owned thoroughbreds and, in the words of a neighbor, were "absolutely stunning on horses." They competed in many horse shows and hunter trials and whipped-in for the Fairfield and Westchester Hounds as well.

There were four chicken houses on the farm, the largest two stories high and almost two hundred feet long. Raynal Bolling, Jr., started a commercial poultry farm on the property, first selling eggs to the mothers of Brunswick School students and later delivering by van all around town. With twelve thousand chickens, it became a $100,000-a-year enterprise known as Bolling Farm.

Other outbuildings included a root cellar, an incinerator, a work shop, a pump house with a 15,000-gallon water tower (which still stands), a windmill 80 feet high with a 14-foot wheel, one closed shed, three open sheds, and an ice house next to a swimming pool enclosed on three sides with natural rock. The children had two playhouses, one of a type called a Hodgson House, sold in pieces to be assembled.

In 1929 a three-acre pond was dredged at the upper end of a brook on the property. Not too far away was a fairly large house with a barn and a shed. The house was usually lived in by one of the help. The six-car garage, with an engine pit and a 500-gallon underground gas tank near the main entrance, contained two apartments for the farmers. This and the superintendent's house off the main driveway were finished in the same manner as the main house, with the stone taken from the excavation sites.

The property embraced a beautiful piece of the countryside composed of pastures bounded by stone walls, extensive apple orchards, and many evergreen and hardwood trees. Lilacs, laurels, rhododendrons, and evergreen shrubs grew around the house. Many of the elms have since been killed by Dutch elm disease. There were times during ice storms when fires were built around those trees close to the house in order to melt the ice. Extensive lawns surrounded the house and stretched down either side of the driveway to the entrance. To keep the grass from being damaged when mowed, the lightest team horse was fitted with special leather boots when pulling the large mower and its rider.

Near the main house to the left of the driveway were planted hundreds of daffodils, which bloomed in the spring. Further down near the entrance the large flower garden, lined on two sides with white pines, was designed and planted by Adah E. Barton, the children's constant companion and guide over the years. She divided the large flower beds with a strip of lawn ten to twelve feet wide, leading to the naturally shaped pool. On the hillside where the pump house and the water tower stood she planted a rock garden extending the entire length of the ledge. Across the driveway from the flower garden was a large vegetable garden with a trellis for grape vines down its center.

Raynal Bolling, descended from an English family that settled in Virginia in 1660, was born in Arkansas in 1877. He himself said that because he had been frail as a boy and of an apprehensive nature, he began in his early teens to try to do all the things he was afraid

A portion of the living room.

The garage and servants quarters, 1915.

The "Jamesway" barn in later years.

Edward C. Potter's memorial statue of Colonel Bolling.

of doing. As time went on, this attitude came to be a rule in his life to the extent that the presence of any challenge became an invitation to meet it. He planned a different adventure every summer. He and his sister once rode horseback the six hundred miles from Charleston, West Virginia, to New York City in twenty-eight days. He finished Harvard College in three years and then went on to Harvard Law School. He began his professional career in the office of Guthrie, Cravath, and Henderson in New York at the age of twenty-five but had an opportunity to work for U.S. Steel Corporation, and by 1913 had become general solicitor there.

Bolling was a pioneer in military preparedness, and after war broke out in 1914, he organized a machine gun unit which he took to the first Plattsburg camp. That summer he learned to fly, at his own expense, and later organized a flying squadron for the New York National Guard. He flew many times from Mineola across Long Island Sound and often landed at Conyers Manor, owned by E. C. Converse, not far from his home. Colonel Bolling's activities in the preparation of the air service campaign and his knowledge of aeronautics were soon recognized by the government in Washington. In 1917 he was appointed head of the Aeronautical Mission which was sent to Europe to select the type of aeronautical engines to be manufactured in this country. He went to England, France, and Italy. Later he was given the rank of colonel and placed in charge of all air service activities for the Allies in what was then called the Zone of the Interior, A.E.F. He was killed when he was sent to the front to study actual combat conditions.

Colonel Bolling also made significant contributions to the Town of Greenwich. As chairman of its Board of Health, he pushed for a pure milk supply, mosquito protection, and better order in local administration. He was also interested in better roads, harbor improvements, and training Boy Scouts. He was a governor of the Field Club (which he and his wife helped to found), and of Manursing Island Club in Rye, New York. They loved to play tennis and often met for a game before going home to dinner. He was elected the first master for the Fairfield and Westchester Hounds when it was organized as a hunt in 1913.

In 1922 a bronze statue of Colonel Bolling was erected on the grounds of what was then the Havemeyer School in Greenwich. The sculptor was Edward C. Potter, whose best known works include the lions in front of both the New York Public Library

Family portrait in 1915, just after completion of Greyledge.

and the Pierpont Morgan Library, and equestrian statues of Grant in Philadelphia, Washington in Paris, and Hooker in Boston. The unveiling of the statue in Greenwich took place at a large ceremony with a parade led by the architect, Colonel Aldridge Twachman. After World War I Bolling Field in Washington was named in Colonel Bolling's honor.

In 1907 Raynal Bolling married Anna Tucker Phillips of Boston, the sister of his classmate, William Phillips. Left after his early death to raise four children alone, she too established herself as an important contributor to the life of Greenwich. As described by her close friend, the Rev. Dr. Daniel Bliss of the Second Congregational Church, "she felt an obligation to nurture in the community where she lived those values of learning and of culture that she and her family had by birth and training made a part of themselves." To this end she was instrumental in creating the Greenwich Choral Society and served as its president for twenty-six years. The motto she coined for the society was "To encourage the art of singing and the love of hearing great music." Her open houses at Greyledge after concerts were fabulous not only for their display

of food and refreshments, but also for her warm friendliness, her effervescent sense of humor, and her indomitable spirit. In addition to numerous other worthy causes, she served as chairman of the Greenwich Academy Board for thirty-seven years. Under her leadership there both Century Hall and later the present school on North Maple Avenue were built.

Anna Bolling continued to live at Greyledge for many years, but a year before her death in 1961 the house was sold, and it remains today quite unchanged, with just under six acres. All the outbuildings are gone except the garage and the superintendent's house, which are separately owned residences.

Wyndygoul

The gates of Wyndygoul. C. Christopher Semmes photo.

Principal Owner: Ernest Thompson Seton
Architect: Unknown
Construction Date: Circa 1909

N 1912 a transaction billed by the *Greenwich Graphic* as "The largest single sale of real estate ever made in Greenwich" took place. The property which changed hands remains today one of the most important pieces of land, over one hundred acres in the middle of Cos Cob, to survive in unspoiled condition, largely undivided except within one family. The man who created the estate, Ernest Thompson Seton (1860-1946), did so for reasons which were part of his unusual and colorful character. The man who bought it from him, Maurice Wertheim (1886-1950), was also a complicated and unusually interesting personality, though of quite a different cut. A deep love for this land still lasts among members of his family.

Seton emigrated with his parents and nine brothers from England to western Canada when he was six years old. He developed a fascination for the wild outdoors, which was reinforced by his solitary trips through the Canadian wilderness during his youth. Although his later schooling took him to the finest academies of Canada, the United States, Britain, and France, he abandoned the more formal artistic career on which he had embarked as a young man. Instead, he decided to learn independently the language and the methods of nineteenth-century biologists and naturalists, resolving to use his ability as an artist to support him in this endeavor. In the long run he succeeded in both fields. At the peak of his career he was considered to be one of the best all-around animal and bird artists in America; by the early 1900s he had received almost every honor that could be bestowed upon a naturalist. Along the way he hit upon the knack of telling a story that appealed not only to children but also to people of all ages who love the outdoors and wild creatures, and most people remember him now for such entertaining books as *Wild Animals I Have Known*.

Seton was a spellbinder, a man of grandiose dreams who liked the company of illustrious people.

He was also of a very independent mind. Not once did he hold a full-time job, and during his life he passed through alternating periods of poverty and prosperity. Characteristically, in an attempt to associate himself with a Scottish ancestor holding a claim to nobility, though unproven, he changed his given middle name, Evan, to Thompson in 1901.

Ernest Thompson Seton, as he was thereafter known, wanted most of all to live on a homestead in the wilds of Manitoba. When this plan proved to be economically unfeasible, since he felt he needed to be near New York City, he began to search for land close to what he called America's great ganglionic center. He rejected Staten Island because of the ferries, New Jersey for its mosquitoes, and Long Island and Westchester County because of the prohibitive cost of real estate. He found what he required in Connecticut—a hundred acres of splendid forest, a sparkling brook (Strickland's) running down a rocky valley, marshes, gorges, meadows, and abundant wildlife. He was able to buy seven different parcels of land in Cos Cob, mostly from local farmers, between 1900 and 1907, and then he at last owned the place he considered his wild kingdom. In the magazine *Country Life in America* he later wrote, "I felt like Moses on Mount Pisgah looking over the Promised Land."

In 1896 Seton married Grace Gallatin, an independent young Californian whom he had met in Paris. She was a personality in her own right: an active feminist, writer, book designer, inveterate world traveler, explorer, big-game hunter, interviewer, war worker, and campaigner for the Republicans in 1928 and 1944. She was also interested in psychic research, in numerology, and in alchemistic experiments; and she believed in reincarnation. The *Greenwich News and Graphic* proclaimed admiringly in 1931: "From Jolo to Mindanao—By Elephant and Cattle Boat—From Vice Regal Palaces to Fever Ridden Jungles—This Amazing Woman Traverses the Globe to Find Material for Her Stories—And to Collect Bats." This unusual cou-

Sketch of the original house after a postcard photo dated 1909.

The main entrance as it looks today. C. Christopher Semmes photo.

ple had one daughter, Ann, called Anya by her parents, who preferred that she use an American Indian name. As Anya Seton she became the author of such fine novels as *The Turquoise, Green Darkness,* and *The Winthrop Woman.*

Having bought their property, which they called Wyndygoul (after an erstwhile "Seton" estate in Scotland and meaning "Windy Gulch"), the Setons turned their attention to building a house on it. They engaged an architect whose identity is unknown, accepted his plans on the strength of a watercolor sketch, and left on an extended trip. When they returned, they were extremely upset with the work to date, and Seton took over. The resulting house, described as Tudor-Indian by Anya, was three stories high and had a red-tiled roof. The basement and the first floor were constructed of fieldstone as smoothly laid and plastered as possible. Seton, with his artistic bent, put a little paris green and yellow ocher into the cement so that a faint olive green tone prevailed.

The second story was of stucco on iron lath, and here again Seton directed the mixing of the cement. To each of three bins he added either red ocher, yellow ocher, or lampblack and left a fourth bin uncolored. A mixture of these provided a faint rose terra-cotta color in general, and he was very pleased with the beautiful play of what he considered soft and agreeable tints.

The house as Seton conceived it reflected his fascination with Indians and with nature. His Painted Sun Gallery was a long room blazing with light and color and decorated with Indian frescoes. A frieze of horses ran around the house and under the third-floor windows, drawn in the stucco like Indian picture writing. His study was high on the third floor where he could observe the birds. The room contained a natural history library of three thousand volumes and some three thousand skins of mammals and birds, some of the latter contributed in the early 1880s by Theodore Roosevelt. The large porch on the ground floor was constructed of massive oak and chestnut timber hand-hewn on the place and was furnished as a hunting lodge. With heat available from its stone fireplace Seton claimed to have used it as his headquarters eight months of the year.

Seton's hardest-won triumph at Wyndygoul was the successful completion of a dam which created a tranquil lake a third of a mile long and twenty feet deep. To find a proper foundation it was necessary to keep a steam pump going night and day for six weeks in order to dig through eighteen feet of gravel to a clay substratum. Seton felt that his creation was worth the bill of five times the original estimate. The winding channels, the islands, the reflections in the water of his magnificent forest—all were the answer to his dream. He stocked the lake with brook trout, black bass, and twenty-three species of ducks and geese.

To his grounds he introduced imported rabbits, pheasants, guinea hens, and peacocks. Anya grew up with skunks, properly deodorized, and usually had one in her bed instead of a kitten. He planted birch and pine seedlings in old pastures in an effort to include

Ernest Thompson Seton holding forth in characteristic style.

Wyndygoul road and bridge. C. Christopher Semmes photo.

as wide a variety of nature as possible within the boundaries of his land, which were marked with a ten-foot pig-, rat-, and poacher-proof wire fence.

Seton built on the estate an Indian village including tepees similar to those of the Sioux, Blackfoot, and Cheyenne Indians. He interested local boys in his knowledge of Indian lore, partly to keep them out of trouble, partly as an extension of his own enthusiasm. Known as Woodcraft Indians, or Seton's Indians, they met regularly, held ceremonies at the large council ring surrounded by Seton's mammoth rock paintings, wore Indian costumes, paddled birchbark canoes, and learned important lessons about how to survive in the woods. Around the campfires they listened spellbound to this tall man with his great shock of hair who wanted to be known at these occasions as Black Wolf. By 1903 there were over fifty such tribes of boys in the United States. Their organization was observed, revised, and later packaged by Robert S. S. Baden-Powell as the Boy Scout movement.

Despite the Setons' professed love for their property, they sold all of it in 1912. Some said that he consented to sell because he could spend so little time there, some that his wife preferred the more fashionable Lake Avenue address where they subsequently built a second home. In any case, they moved and later on were divorced (1935). Seton left Greenwich after buying a two-thousand-acre ranch in New Mexico and, at the age of seventy-four, married his longtime secretary, Julia Buttree, who at the time was dean of the College of Indian Wisdom in Santa Fe.

Maurice Wertheim, who purchased the estate from Seton, was quite a different sort of person from the "eccentric lord of Wyndygoul," as Seton was once

described. He was an investment banker who had begun his business career with the United Cigar Manufacturers Company, a philanthropist, the publisher of the liberal weekly the *Nation*, and director of a number of industrial firms. He preferred, however, to be known as a sportsman. He was a trustee of the American Wildlife Foundation, a noted fisherman, and a tournament chess player. In addition, he was a founder and director of the New York Theater Guild, a patron of exhibitions sponsored by the Sculpture Guild, and on the advisory committee of the New York University Institute of Fine Arts.

Just before his fiftieth birthday in 1936, Wertheim began collecting French impressionist and postimpressionist paintings on a highly selective basis. During the next fourteen years he succeeded in assembling one of the most remarkable and focused collections of late-nineteenth and early-twentieth-century European art in America. A member of the Harvard class of 1906, he bequeathed "the Collection," as he always referred to it, to Harvard for the use and benefit of the Fogg Art Museum.

One of the unusual outbuildings. C. Christopher Semmes photo.

The stream leading from the lake created by Seton.
C. Christopher Semmes photo.

In contrast to Seton's fascination with wild animal and native Indian life which led him to reenact tribal dances at Wyndygoul in full costume, Wertheim, who wore a fresh carnation from his own greenhouse in his lapel every day, was immersed in the worlds of business and art. He enjoyed his beautiful estate tremendously but in his own way. It augmented his status and expanded the life he and his family could lead, and it became more than just a summer place for them. For years it was an integral part of their life. He too stocked the lake with fish but enjoyed it as a sportsman rather than as an observing naturalist. Furthermore, though he left the bulk of the property in its wild state, he was always interested in improving things and, as in so many areas of his life, was very energetic at it. He concentrated on the broad, level valley floor below the rocky crags on which the main house was set. There he had Edward Palmer build stables which included stalls for horses and quarters for the groom. He built a cow barn and a pony barn and not far from the stables a large greenhouse with a potting shed, a gardener's house, and a chicken coop where pheasants were also kept. A sizable vegetable garden was maintained and a very old orchard of fruit trees as well. A riding ring completed this well-tended part of the property. The Wertheims also added a small house to the right of their front gates for their chauffeur. To the left their superintendent lived in an eighteenth-century Mead homestead which Seton had moved and rebuilt for use as a gate lodge.

At some point after he acquired Wyndygoul, Wertheim engaged the British architect Henry E. Woodsend to make changes there. Woodsend was recognized for his designs of many large country houses and for his interest in harmonizing them with their natural surroundings. It is known that he designed the pumphouse and stone bridge on the place; but as no records can be found, and since a huge fire destroyed a wing and the whole third floor of the main house in 1931, it is impossible to tell what changes he might have made to it. It is likely that the big porch was removed, and certainly the most extreme aspects of the original rustic atmosphere were not the Wertheims' style. The basically simple, unsophisticated rendering of most of the downstairs rooms with their adobelike details was, however, retained. Rough stucco walls, inset wooden bookcases bounded by rounded corners of plaster, simple fireplaces (one with no mantel), random-width pegged floors, deeply paneled wooden doors, hand-hewn baseboards, leaded casement windows — all these details contribute to the personality of the house. Most of the rooms are small and intimate. The exception is the living room, which Mrs. Wertheim used as her music room. Large and full of light, it has a huge fireplace with a stone mantel of unusual design and big windows overlooking the sweep of the lawn and enormous oak trees.

The flower gardens were Mrs. Wertheim's domain, in particular the Italian garden, which had been the only bit of formality on the estate under Seton's ownership. Its beautiful flowers, trellises, and statuary, all overlooking the expanse of the lake, were her special pride. Alma Morgenthau before her marriage, she was an artistically talented woman, energetic in her own way, who had her own strong interests. She had wished fervently to be a singer, but her family did not think this ambition was suitable for a well-bred young lady. She did study music, however, and performed in recitals. For her the most important room at Wyndygoul was the music room, where she kept her piano. Besides managing two households, one in Connecticut and the other in New York City, and supervising the lives of her three daughters, she was actively interested in the development of American music. The *New York Times* quoted her as saying that "composers need their own people to believe in them, to stand by through the long, slow grind, to take a chance, to encourage and to perceive." She did not believe that the public really wanted to hear "only foreign composers and foreign music, sprung from Continental life, morals, and manners" (also quoted in the *Times*). Consequently, she lent her support to many young composers and musicians, among them Aaron Copland, and founded the Cos Cob Press to print music manuscripts that might not otherwise have been published.

For almost twenty years the Wertheims came out to Wyndygoul from their New York residence for four months in the summer and every weekend for the rest of the year. Their middle daughter is the author and historian Barbara Tuchman, who received the Pulitzer Prize not only for *The Guns of August* but also for *Stilwell and the American Experience in China*, and who has written most recently *A Distant Mirror* and *The March of Folly*. She has strong memories of her life

there — of summer mornings when she and her sisters were small, spent riding ponies followed by a groom on foot up Cat Rock and Cognewaugh when those roads were dirt. When they were older, they spent hours with their horses on the trails in the woods and training in the paddock for horse shows. They swam and canoed in the lake. She remembers her mother gardening, her father rushing out the door with a plate of scrambled eggs and a cup of coffee to catch the train. She recalls pumping the player piano up in the third-floor playroom and sitting in the library window overlooking the lake when lightning struck a nearby tree with a terrifying jolt. The familiar pattern of time spent in Cos Cob was a schedule that remained ingrained even after she had her own family. The ancient rocks, the forests, the running brooks, the flowers and fields, the beauty and the quiet have continued for many years to be one of the most important factors in her life.

The main house still stands on its magnificent site, but after the fire one of its wings and the third story were never rebuilt, so that its appearance is greatly altered. Miraculously, to someone coming upon it for the first time, this property in the heart of Cos Cob still resembles the wilds of the Adirondacks or Canada.

Wildwood Farm

The approach to Wildwood Farm.

Principal Owner: Alexander L. Dommerich
Architect: Unknown
Construction Date: 1916

N A BITTERLY COLD January night in 1967, firemen were called to the fifty-room mansion bought four years before by the Roman Catholic Diocese of Bridgeport from the estate of Clara S. Dommerich (1882-1962). When they arrived, flames were roaring through the inside of the house, and there was little hope of saving it. Before the fire could be brought under control some twelve hours later, the interior collapsed, and all the upper floors fell into the basement. Before that night the vibrant life of one of the great estates of Greenwich had, in fact, already ended with the deaths of Alexander L. Dommerich (b. 1881) and his wife in 1961, and 1962, respectively. Now the house itself, empty except for some building materials stored there, was destroyed.

Alexander and Clara Dommerich had come to Greenwich in 1909, shortly after they were married, living first on Milbank Avenue and then on Benedict Place. By the end of December 1914, they had bought from Raymond B. Thompson, Kate G. Hyatt, and Anna P. Bolling most of the nearly forty-four acres which were to be the site of the home they planned to build. They engaged the Charles T. Wills Company to be their builder. Charles S. Wills, who, like Alexander Dommerich, was a graduate of Lawrenceville School and also lived in Greenwich, was president of the firm his father had founded. It was one of the leading construction companies of New York, having among its accomplishments the New York Stock Exchange, the Pierpont Morgan Library, the Standard Oil Building, and the Gorham Building, all in New York City, and the chapel at West Point.

In 1917 the Dommerichs moved into their new home, which was, according to the *Greenwich Time*, a mansion "built in the grand style of the era." As a partner of L. F. Dommerich and Company of New York, a prosperous factoring concern, it was fitting that he and his wife live in such a residence and see

their children grow up there.

A hardworking man, he commuted to New York every day on the Club Car of the railroad. So determined was he to get to the office one stormy day that he had a horse and sleigh hitched up to take him to the Cos Cob railroad station, but to no avail. The snow came to the horse's belly, and the sleigh kept sinking.

For Clara Dommerich, called Claire, the focus of life was bringing up her four children, two girls and two boys. She managed her large household of servants, often visited her father and mother, who lived in a little house nearby on Stanwich Road, and spent much of her free time reading and doing needlepoint. She was noted for her work transcribing reading materials, ranging from actuarial tables to books of the Bible, into Braille for the blind.

The Dommerichs' grand house was of stucco and half-timber construction with a green-tiled roof. A long driveway, shaded by many large trees, curved up a hill from Stanwich Road to approach it. Tall rhododendrons grew at the entrance, and low ivy-covered walls made of vertically set stones bordered the roadway on the steep hillside. The front of the house faced a forest of small trees, the spaces between them grassy and well kept, while the back, actually the more important side, looked out over a gracious expanse of sweeping lawns with Long Island Sound in the distance beyond.

The boulders in the foundation walls were gathered from the property, and many were chosen for size one by one by the Dommerichs so that there would be no chisel marks on them. The result was an imposing and substantial base for the house that rose above it. One entered the first floor through a large front door, its glass window hung with tatting. Inside was a vestibule with a tiled floor, which in turn opened into a large paneled front hall stretching both to the right and to the left, its fireplace made of stones, again from the property. A paneled staircase with a

Aerial view toward the rear elevation.

Alexander L. Dommerich, Jr. in 1935 with his first car, a 1920 Model T Ford. With him are assistant driver Valentine Bolmer at the wheel and chauffeur James Lonergan.

landing led upstairs. Also on the first floor were a billiard room, a den, a "ladies' coat closet" or powder room, another long closet for coats, a "telephone room," the dining room, the conservatory, a pantry, a kitchen, a laundry, and a servants' dining room. The furnishings were beautiful. There were hardwood floors with many oriental rugs, and the details were lovely; the blue-and-gold silk moire wallpaper in the living room and the marble fireplaces both there and in the dining room are notable examples. A family member has described the atmosphere of the house as "informal formality."

On the second floor were the seven main bedrooms, the bathrooms, Claire Dommerich's sitting room, and the sleeping porches, one double for the parents, one for their two daughters, and one for their two sons. There was also a wing of servants' rooms. In the third-floor attic were stored such things as winter curtains. The children loved to play there, riding bicycles they brought up in the dumbwaiter and romping through this great room in the top of the house. Additional servants' rooms were on this level too.

The basement contained storage rooms, a playroom, two furnaces, and enormous bins for tons of coal. Logs and kindling were brought regularly from the woodshed back in the woods and stored there for use in the various fireplaces of the house.

A porch to the right of the front door extended around the end of the building and across the back of the house. In order to take full advantage of the magnificent view toward the Sound, the terrace there was raised level with the first floor as the land sloped downward. The terrace walls were of the natural stone, covered with ivy; its floor was made of tiles. Imported from England, the first shipment of tiles sank on the way across the ocean, and another order had to be sent. Outside the dining room, also in the back, was an area the family called the breakfast porch.

The grounds in back of the house were primarily lawns, kept absolutely manicured. Gardeners cut the grass two days a week in summertime, rain or shine, driving a large mower, pulled by Dudley or Alex, horses humorously named for the Dommerich boys. There were groups of shrubs on the lawns and scattered lovely trees; in the spring hundreds of daffodils bloomed. There was, as well, an area devoted to more formal gardens where both daughters were married—a magnificent setting of great natural beauty.

South of the road to the main house, but also on

The view to the south from the main house.

Stanwich Road, was the driveway leading to most of the outbuildings. White board fences surrounded pastures where cattle grazed. There were fruit trees on the left, and a sizable vegetable garden and a cutting garden of flowers on the right. At the end of the driveway a large garage contained the chauffeur's quarters on one end, the superintendent's quarters on the other, with sufficient space between to hold six cars easily. Before the family had horses, the stable behind the barn had been a piggery with, among others, a pig named Longfellow in residence. After they bought horses, the Dommerichs did a great deal of riding, and all four children became accomplished equestrians. In this area of the property there were also cold frames, a chicken house, and a dairy.

Other buildings on the place included the dairyman's cottage, still standing on the corner of Stanwich and Cat Rock roads; pumphouses for the two wells; and a cabin built in the woods which had one ample room and a kitchen. Claire Dommerich often practiced on the piano which was there. When the Dommerichs bought the property, the North Cos Cob schoolhouse stood just north of the main driveway. Later when the town gave up one-room schoolhouses, the family bought it and tore it down, but they saved

the school bell and hung it under an awning in back of their own home to summon their children.

Although much of the property was wooded, it was nevertheless carefully tended. There were cinder roadways through the woods and many paths, one called the spring path because it was bordered by wildflowers. Children from many parts of town came up to play hockey when the pond was frozen. It was kept cleaned and a little house was provided so that the skaters could have hot soup there and store their skates. The tennis court was regularly used by family and friends.

Those days, however, did come to an end with the deaths of the owners of the estate; and after the main house burned, the Greenwich Catholic Elementary School was erected on the site. The large garage with chauffeur's and superintendent's quarters has been rebuilt; it is now St. Agnes Church and Rectory.

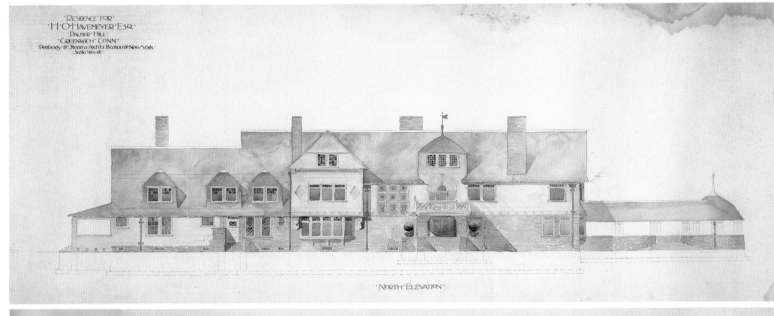

·NORTH·ELEVATION·

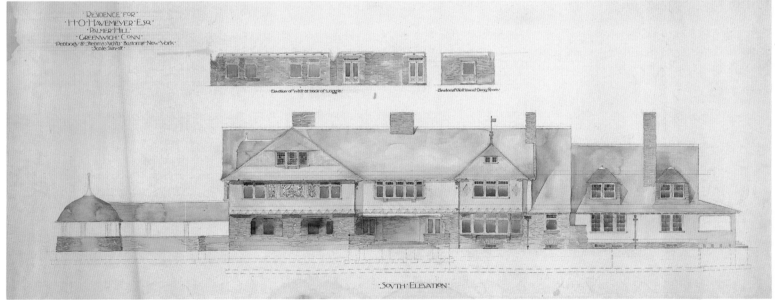

·SOUTH·ELEVATION·

Principal Owner: Henry O. Havemeyer
Architect: Peabody & Stearns
Construction Date: Circa 1889

ENRY OSBORN HAVEMEYER (1817-1907) is remembered today primarily for two reasons: first, for his career in the sugar business, for which he was called the Sugar King; and second, for his art collection, remarkable not only for its size and variety but also for the quality of the objects included in it. These two facets of the man deserve attention, especially during the last twenty-four years of his life. This period began with his marriage in 1883 to Louisine Waldron Elder (1855-1929), a most interesting woman.

Louisine's name was originally Louise, but as Henry Havemeyer had previously been married to her aunt, whose name was also Louise, she changed hers to Louisine in order to avoid confusion. Havemeyer adored his second wife; influenced greatly by her, especially where art was concerned, he provided her with virtually anything she wanted. At the time of their marriage, his father's sugar factory in Brooklyn (founded by his grandfather, a German immigrant) was prospering. He and his brother inherited it along with several million dollars in 1891, and Henry's shrewdly brilliant operation of the business produced additional fortunes in the years that followed. He had been the chief factor in the organization of the American Sugar Refining Company as a trust; and in his successful campaign against the Arbuckles, whom he defeated for the control of the sugar business, he displayed the energy and the resourcefulness that were considered to be typical of his career. His trust not only virtually monopolized the sugar industry in this country for many years, but was also at the forefront of most of the speculative movements in the New York stock market. For a time it was commonly said on Wall Street that the market brought to the sugar trust as much profit as did the sale of sugar.

Havemeyer combined his almost unlimited resources and aggressive nerve with his wife's lifelong love of art and her taste for objects not yet generally recognized as valuable or fashionable. The pair became a remarkable collecting team. The painter Mary Cassatt was an intimate friend of Louisine Havemeyer, and her perceptive advice added yet another invaluable ingredient to their activities. Neither of the Havemeyers bought without the other's approval, but Mr. Havemeyer often gave in to his wife's whims and enthusiasms. By 1889 they had begun to buy from the impressionists, many of them friends of Miss Cassatt. Their collecting passion spilled over into many other fields of art, as they bought Chinese porcelains and Persian lusterware; Venetian glass; Japanese tea jars; Ming bronzes; Renaissance and Oriental sculpture; rare manuscripts and prints, ancient and modern; and, starting about 1900, they began to find paintings of old masters. The resulting collection, which was left to the Metropolitan Museum of Art when Mrs. Havemeyer died, is one of the most magnificent donations ever made to a museum of art.

By 1889, with both their family and their fortune expanding, the Havemeyers engaged the architect Charles Haight to design a massive and daringly simple house at One East Sixty-sixth Street in New York. It was conspicuously unlike its fancier neighbors on the outside and, with the interiors done by the Tiffany Studios, bore no resemblance to others in fashion at the time. In short, the Havemeyers had the means, the courage, and the taste to be different. They enjoyed their original and extraordinary home in the city and the full social life they led there, but they were also fond of country life.

The year after they were married they decided to have a house in the country, specifically in Greenwich. Henry Havemeyer bought Boss Tweed's house from Jeremiah Milbank and had it moved from its original site to what is now Temple Sholom's property on Put's Hill. He had the nearby cemetery belonging to Christ Church moved so that he would not have graves in his backyard. However, in the spring of 1888 a large tract of land with a magnificent building site,

so high that one could see Long Island Sound, came to his attention through a real estate agent. By the end of May, Havemeyer had bought 85 acres from the Seth Quintard estate and by 1906 had acquired 118 more acres from seven other property owners. The land was in the Palmer Hill area, a short distance east of the Mianus River, mostly on the south side of Palmer Hill Road and primarily in Greenwich, though it did extend over the Stamford line.

Before any building could be done, the land had to be cleared. Sarah Morrow DeForest remembers that her father was hired as a gardener by Havemeyer before there was "even as much as a shingle to sleep under." According to her, the Peter Mitchell Company brought a crew of workmen who labored for months chopping trees with axes. They cleared the enormous areas which were to surround the house as lawns and built stone walls on some of the boundaries.

The house which the Havemeyers constructed was a large three-story country home, built in the shingle style popular in the last two decades of the nineteenth century and associated with the Boston architectural firm of Peabody and Stearns. It had stone foundations, shingled sides, a multigabled roof, and six large stone chimneys. The sash windows had wooden shutters which could be folded across the panes when necessary. To one side of the building was a long porch; at its end was a small conical-roofed conservatory with typical hip knob and finial. The porch, open at first, was later glassed in with windowpanes, and its stone walls became covered with ivy. The lines of the house were strong and simple, and the interior

was also kept free of the opulence which characterized the Havemeyers' New York City house. Their grandson recalls unimposing furnishings—some bedroom furniture done by Tiffany, but in a simple manner; rattan furniture and Chinese urns with ferns in them on the porch; some of the curtains and floors stenciled by his grandmother. He also remembers that the dining room was decorated in seventeenth-century Dutch style, Henry Havemeyer's favorite, with a tile floor and very dark paneling. It is clear that the house was completed by 1889, as there are existing records of all the sheets, blankets, and kitchen inventory done by Louisine Havemeyer in 1890.

The *Greenwich Graphic* reported in 1907 on "the large and valuable property on Palmer's Hill," saying that "the residence here is particularly fine, and the surroundings include all the elaborate features of a gentleman's extensive country estate." The gardener had three greenhouses at his disposal, one of which he called a grapery, where he grew white grapes, and figs in big pots. He had three men working for him and won prizes at flower shows for his entries—roses, gardenias, and orchids. The superintendent's cottage and stable were both substantial stone-and-shingle structures. A coachman, whose duties included driving Havemeyer to the Stamford railroad station every day, lived in quarters over the stable. A dairyman fed and milked the cows, and the supervisor's brother rode around throughout the summer with a horse and lawn mower cutting the grass. However, Louisine Havemeyer liked the simple country life for her husband, three children, and herself when they were at

Detail of what was probably the carriage house.

A typical outbuilding in shingle style.

Hilltop, and there were probably never more than three servants in the main house. She enjoyed doing her own cooking and especially liked to bake, preferring a change of pace from their more formal city life with its full social calendar.

Although when seeking a rest and a change the Havemeyers also spent time at their three-hundred-acre Long Island estate known as Merrivale—in fact, the family was there for Thanksgiving when Havemeyer died in 1907—they were warmly considered benefactors of the town of Greenwich. Henry Havemeyer paid $250,000 to build what was then known as the Greenwich School, now the Havemeyer Building housing the Greenwich Board of Education, and presented it to the district. He gave $5,000 of the cost of the Sound Beach School and made large contributions toward the lot, the organ, the manse, and the mortgage of the First Presbyterian Church. He improved the road described in an 1892 issue of the *Greenwich Graphic* as "the road over the hill and down toward Dumpling Pond, past Old Orchard Mill. One of the good things is a much needed drinking fountain by the roadside, part way down the Hill." This watering place for hot and thirsty horses remains today as part of the stone wall by the side of Palmer Hill Road.

In accordance with his wishes, Louisine Havemeyer and her children sold the three-cornered plot at Arch Street and Greenwich Avenue to the government for the site of the present post office, placed the purchase price in trust, and directed that the interest be used toward the upkeep of the school he

had built. At the time of his death, in 1907, the *Greenwich News* stated that "The sincerest grief was felt in Greenwich as in other places where he was known. Mr. Havemeyer had been generous in his attitude toward the town and shown an interest in the community beyond the giving of money. He had won a place in the hearts of Greenwichites which will not be readily taken by anyone else."

After her husband died, Louisine Havemeyer continued to spend time at Hilltop, her favorite of all their homes. She loved to work with flowers, was especially fond of her rose gardens, and kept bees. A woman of great liveliness, she was never still for long. She was a fervent suffragist, an outstanding fighter for women's equality with men. She became one of America's most effective speakers for this cause and in 1919 even went to jail in Washington, D.C., for setting fire to a portrait of President Woodrow Wilson during a demonstration.

The estate remained the property of her three children for almost twenty years after her death in 1929. But by the time 195 acres of the original property were bought by Gene Tunney and Arthur Starch, the buildings were falling into disrepair. The house was torn down, and the land was developed into an area of single-family dwellings which were sold for little more than cost to returning World War II veterans.

Henry O. Havemeyer.

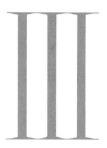

III

THE BACK-COUNTRY ESTATES

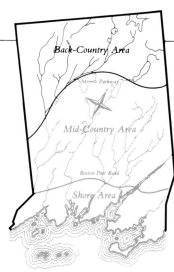

Dunnellen Hall

The rear facade of Dunnellen Hall.

Principal Owner: Rhea Reid Topping
Architect: William B. Tubby
Construction Date: 1916-1918

RISING TWO-AND-A-HALF magnificent stories on one of the highest hills in Fairfield County, the brick walls of the Topping mansion dominate the rolling countryside. Possibly the most famous and certainly the best-documented estate in Greenwich, this extraordinary creation was designed in 1916 by William B. Tubby for Daniel Grey Reid, financier and president of the American Tin Plate Company. Reid, known as the Tin Plate King, commissioned the work as a present for his only child, Rhea (1886-1947), who in 1910 had married Henry J. Topping, son of Reid's friend and associate, John A. Topping, president of Republic Steel. The mansion was completed in 1918 at a cost of $1 million.

William Tubby was well known in architectural circles. His designs, which ranged from American Colonial to classical, exhibited the eclecticism of the period and included substantial country estates, schools, hospitals, and the Greenwich Library. His outstanding work, however, remains the spectacular Jacobean manor in back-country Greenwich, a gift only a king could give.

Built originally on a mere forty acres, the twenty-eight-room mansion faces east, providing a panorama of Long Island Sound from both front and rear. The approach is a sweep of white gravel drive outlining an oval of green lawn which is centered by a reflecting pool and fountain. The heavily carved oak entrance door is topped by a great limestone pediment in the Roman style. The walls, laid in Flemish bond and eighteen inches thick, are decorated with gables and two-story bay windows and stand up past the eaves of the red-tiled roof to end in crenellations above both east and west facades. The steeply pitched roof is studded with eight towering double-stacked chimneys, each finished in a different design of molded terra-cotta. The effect is truly baronial.

The vestibule opens into an awesome forty-seven-foot hall whose travertine marble floors and limestone walls lead to a porch and the terrace beyond. An eighty-six-foot gallery crosses this hall at right angles, stretching from the kitchen wing on the south to the alcove at the north end where an Aeolian pipe organ once stood. The palatial dimensions are continued in the forty-five-foot living room whose teak floors are surrounded by walls covered with yellow silk brocade. A pair of French doors opens to a porch at the far end of this room, and in the center of the west wall there is an imposing fireplace with a ten-foot opening. The ornate mantel is supported on either side by a pair of Ionic columns topped by elaborate entablatures. The overmantel consists of double panels, each carved with an escutcheon. The oak-paneled library is entered from the living room as well as from the entrance hall and is also teak-floored. A fifteenth-century carved stone mantel highlights this room, and the great bay windows fill it with afternoon sun. A full-length portrait of the Toppings' first two sons, Henry, Jr., and Daniel, once hung above the mantel.

An archway of vaulted stone opens from the entrance hall into the dining room where the travertine marble floor once held an eighteen-foot table and a matching sideboard of equal length. Here a carved wooden mantel graces the eight-foot fireplace, and another set of bay windows sends light to reflect on the carved oak walls. A breakfast room, also marble-floored, opens from the dining room.

A twenty-two-foot-square smoking room with a fireplace and an adjoining service bar lies opposite the breakfast room. The bay windows in this room are identical in size to those in the library; small alcoves on either side of the windows hold statuary. This room and the breakfast room are the only rooms on the first floor without paneled walls or molded plaster ceilings.

A butler's pantry, complete with silver vault, leads from behind the breakfast room to the capacious kitchen where the walk-in "butcher's box" once stored full sides of beef. Beyond are the servants' dining room and the laundry.

147

Dunnellen Hall during the Washburn ownership in the 1950s.

The living room during the same period.

Aerial view in 1980. C. Christopher Semmes photo.

Two hundred feet of flagstone terrace border the west side of the mansion outside the living room, the library, and the dining and breakfast rooms. As one leans against the stone balustrade of this terrace, one looks across rolling fields and towering treetops to magnificent views of Long Island Sound.

The grand staircase, whose marble steps and ornamental wrought-iron railing sweep up from the center of the entrance hall, divides into a double landing on the wide corridor of the second floor. Here the entire north wing is given to the master suite, consisting of a spacious bedroom, a dressing room, and two baths. Both the master bedroom and the dressing room have fireplaces with carved marble mantels. The larger bath, which was once Mr. Topping's study, has been refinished by a later owner in shining pink onyx.

There are six family bedrooms—four with fireplaces—and six baths. The three bedrooms on the east side are connected by a small hall, making it possible to enter one from another without going into the center hall. On the other side, the two bedrooms south of the stairs may be turned into a suite by means of another small hallway. Beyond these rooms are a sewing room and the back stairway. The servants' quarters on the south wing complete the second floor and include seven bedrooms and two baths. There are two more bedrooms and a bath on the third floor as well as a cement-floored handball court.

Reid spared no cost on his daughter's mansion, and she lovingly named it Dunnellen Hall for her mother, Ella Dunn. Tubby fulfilled his assignment with the finest of materials incorporating perfection in every detail. Built of steel and reinforced concrete, the 23,000 square feet of living space are virtually fireproof.

Rhea Reid Topping added four parcels of land to the estate, and by 1927 it totaled 208 acres, 20 of which included a lake stocked with perch and black bass. There were a stable for riding and carriage horses, an eight-car garage, a swimming pool, a tennis court, a greenhouse, and a seventeenth-century marble pavilion imported from Italy in the formal gardens.

Like many of the country manors of the period, the Topping estate was also a working farm, providing most of the produce and dairy products required by the family and their retainers. There were a vegetable garden, potato and corn fields, two barns, and a silo. A herd of registered Guernsey cows gave milk and the cream from which butter was made. Chickens supplied eggs, and the pigs supplied meat. During the winters, when the Topping family moved into New York City, boxes full of their farm products would be put aboard the baggage car of the 8:15 train out of Greenwich, which was met by one of the family's chauffeurs at Grand Central Station.

Twenty-three servants lived in the main house, and seven families were housed on the estate. The two chauffeurs each had their own apartments at either end of the garage. The head gardener and the coachman lived above the stables. There were separate cottages for the farmer; the dairyman; and the engineer, who was responsible for the machinery that ran the ice plant and the pumps for the two wells. It was an enormous complex, nearly self-sufficient, and was impeccably maintained as a world of its own.

Rhea Reid was born July 8, 1886, in Richmond, Indiana, and moved to New York City with her father and his second wife in 1898. After their marriage, Rhea and Henry Topping lived in a large country home in Port Chester, New York, and in 1916 Daniel Reid deeded his handsome six-story residence on Fifth Avenue to his daughter—the same year that he engaged William Tubby to design Dunnellen Hall.

The Toppings had three sons: Daniel Reid was born in 1912; Henry J., Jr., in 1914; and John Reid in 1921. They lived quietly, with little involvement in community affairs. They belonged to the Round Hill Club, and Henry Topping, a dapper man and class of 1907 at Princeton University, was an avid golfer; in 1923 he won the Connecticut state championship. His one venture into the business world, a halfhearted promotion of golf clubs, ended in failure. Rhea Reid Topping, on the other hand, inherited her father's business acumen and spent much of her time in her New York City office overseeing the management of her vast wealth. In 1926 she took over the guardianship of her sons' trust funds which their grandfather Reid had set up in 1919. (Daniel Reid died on January 1, 1925.) In 1929, six months before the stock market crash, she sold the Fifth Avenue house at a substantial profit and bought an apartment in the city; the family lived in New York during most of World War II when rationing made it impossible to heat adequately the Greenwich estate. (The mansion and its outbuildings required 23,000 gallons of oil and two carloads of coal annually.)

Although Rhea and Henry Topping took little advantage of the entertainment possibilities of Dunnellen Hall, their sons did, and they gave it a reputation as the scene of lavish parties. The young Toppings also provided the press with extravagant copy through their numerous marriages. Dan, at one time co-owner of the New York Yankees, had five wives, the most famous of whom were actress Arlene Judge and Sonja Henie, the champion iceskater. Henry, Jr., who was called Bob, had four wives, one of whom was Lana Turner. He also married Arlene Judge, ten years after her wedding to his brother. Jack was the only son to remain with his first wife. His mother willed him all the silver, china, glass, and books from her estate and also gave him seventy-eight acres of her Greenwich land in July 1947, three months before her death.

Rhea Topping died of pneumonia on November 2, 1947, at Lenox Hill Hospital in New York City. She left $250,000 to each of her sons as well as equal shares of her residual estate, $35,000 to her husband, and bequests to each of her servants and secretaries. Henry Topping died in Clearwater, Florida, in 1951. Dunnellen Hall was sold for the first time in 1950 and for the ninth time in 1984. Through the years the ivy continued to creep up the walls while the acreage shrank from subdivision, bringing considerable income to local brokers. A five-thousand-bottle wine cellar was installed in the basement, and an Olympic-sized swimming pool was added below the terrace. An English-style pub adjoins the game room (smoking room), and air-conditioning and indirect lighting have updated the utilities. There are now more than one hundred wall outlets in the gallery alone to illuminate individual works of art. It has been suggested that the mansion be converted to a museum, which might be a viable alternative to the constant turnover of owners and the escalation of upkeep and taxes. Yet, despite the alterations made to the interior, Dunnellen Hall remains a stunning example of architecture in the grand manner and a reminder of the gracious living that flourished in the United States in the period between the two world wars.

Chieftans

The fox head knocker and boot scraper at the left are remainders of the Chieftans-Gimbel hunting legacy. Gil Amiaga photo.

Principal Owners: Alfred Whitney Church / Isaac Gimbel
Architect: Augustus D. Shepard, Jr.
Construction Date: 1911

AIL BORDEN was living in Connecticut at the time he invented the process to condense milk and subsequently founded the Borden Milk Company. He was the grandfather of Alfred Whitney Church (1878-1953), who was born in Elgin, Illinois, and became an heir to the Borden fortune. A 1901 graduate of Cornell University, Church married in December 1907. Four years later he purchased 250 acres of land in Greenwich and commissioned Augustus D. Shepard, Jr., of New York to build a complete estate.

The estate, constructed over a period of four years, was named Chieftans, the name it retains today. It consisted of a main house, garages, stables, barns, a dairy, a broodhouse, a laundry, a superintendent's house, and staff quarters. The resulting collection of varied outbuildings is stylistically similar to the main house in the use of fieldstones from the property, cedar shingles, and slate roofs.

The Churches' marriage ended in divorce in the early 1920s, and in 1925 the estate was sold to Isaac Gimbel (1857-1931), the co-owner of Gimbel Brothers department store in New York City. It is the Gimbel family that is most widely associated with Chieftans, as three generations lived there for over sixty years. The family liked the name Chieftans and kept it. Soon after buying Chieftans, in 1926 Rachel Gimbel hired the New York firm of Nicholas and Hughes to make some minor interior changes to the house. The firm was also responsible for the interior decoration of that period, and most of the furniture came from the Hearst collection. During the renovations, the second-floor bedrooms were rearranged to accommodate not only Isaac and Rachel Gimbel but also their son, Bernard; his wife, Alva; and their five children. The three generations lived together happily over the years. Bernard (1885-1966) and Alva Gimbel were given title to Chieftans as a twentieth wedding anniversary gift, on April 4, 1932. After the death of the senior Gimbels and that of Bernard Gimbel, Alva Gimbel continued to live at Chieftans until her death at the age of ninety in 1982.

One of the prime interests of the Gimbel family was horsemanship. Alva Gimbel was an accomplished rider who showed her horses at the National Horse Show in New York City and frequently participated in hunts in England, Ireland, and on the European continent. She often rode and jumped sidesaddle and hunted with her daughters. The family kept up to twenty horses at Chieftans for both carriage use and equitation.

In addition to horses, the family owned ten or eleven cows. The milk was processed at Chieftans and was consumed by the family and staff. Extra dairy products and eggs from the nearly two thousand hens were given to High Point Hospital and the Sacred Heart Convent, both of which were nearby. The Gimbel children enjoyed being with all the animals. They rode and jumped in the rings, and they occasionally had milking contests as well as egg hunts.

A substantial staff kept Chieftans operating as a working farm from its inception through World War II. In addition to the dairy cows, Angus cattle raised for beef were butchered at the farm, and the hens also provided many a meal. Farmhands kept busy working in the orchards, tending the vegetable garden, and harvesting the various field crops.

Four grooms, three chauffeurs, ten gardeners, three pantry maids, and a cook and two helpers were employed, as well as personal maids for Alva Gimbel and each of her daughters. Housing for most of the staff was provided on the estate. A shingle-style superintendent's house was built near the service entrance, in addition to the apartments Church had built above the stables and in one section of the barn. A chauffeur's apartment was located above the three-car garage, and the household staff lived above the kitchen wing of the main house.

151

South facade of the main house. Gil Amiaga photo.

The dairy house. Gil Amiaga photo.

The carriage house and stable. Gil Amiaga photo.

Alva Gimbel, an accomplished gardener, supervised the planting of the borders and specimen trees. A large English border planted with bulbs, perennials, and seasonal flowers, extending along a roadway, could be seen from the front of the house. One of the superintendents recalls planting one thousand tulips a year! To the south of the perennial garden was an elaborate rock garden, and nearby was one of Alva Gimbel's favorite trees, a weeping spruce. In addition, she planted a water garden surrounded by a large, mature boxwood hedge. She often joined in the maintenance of the estate, not just choosing plants, but helping with the pruning. The gardens were well enough known to be opened by the family for charitable tours.

Chieftans's main house was a large rectangular structure built of fieldstone culled from the property. The building had a slate gambrel roof punctuated by dormer windows. Large wooden porches with white Doric columns accented both front and rear facades. Instead of a central front entry, however, the main entrance to Chieftans was under a porte-cochere cut through the first floor at the southern end of the house. The heavy wooden front doors with large decorative strap hinges were, therefore, protected by the roof of the porte-cochere. Across the drive from the front door was the entry to the library.

On entering Chieftans, one realizes that the house was designed for elegant entertaining. The thirty-five by sixty-five-foot living room with its tall ceiling features a curving staircase that curls down one corner of the room. The staircase lends itself to a grand entry for a formal reception or special occasion. A large, elaborately carved Italian stone fireplace purchased by the Gimbels balances the stairs. The original plans show a pair of fireplaces flanking the entry, though it is not certain whether they were ever installed. Heavy beams decorate the ceiling, and several pairs of tall French doors open the living room to both the front veranda and the rear veranda with its grass terrace beyond.

A long, high-ceilinged dining room, the setting for many grand parties, is adjacent to the living room. Its glorious black-slate fireplace surround, the first thing a visitor notices, is framed by the doorway from the living room. A large banquet table with seating for twenty or more guests was once centered in the room. Windows at each end of the room gave light and views.

Mrs. Alva Gimbel taking a jump sidesaddle in the 1930s.

The Gimbel family off for a Sunday drive in their coach-and-four.

Beyond the dining room lies the generous-sized butler's pantry with its silver vault, the commodious kitchen, and the servants' hall.

The separate library, across the porte-cochere from the living room, is lined with bookcases, and a fireplace is located opposite the entrance door. Hidden underneath an oak bench is the trapdoor leading to the secret staircase which leads to a large wine cellar below. A tunnel also connects the wine cellar with the storerooms under the rest of the house.

When Alfred Church built Chieftans, he planned a master suite for the second floor and four other hall bedrooms, each of which had a private bath. Sleeping porches for hot summer nights were located at either end of the house. The Gimbels rearranged the flow of the second floor in their 1926 renovations. They joined several of the bedrooms to form suites for the elder Gimbels, the Bernard Gimbels, and the children.

The architecture of the fieldstone estate house was echoed in all the dependencies. The three-car garage, located near the kitchen, is built of stone with a slate roof. The stable was clad with shingles and accented by a squat tower with a tall octagonal roof. In the tower were grooms' apartments. One side of the stable had a tall curved door for the carriages to pass through; the other side was divided into stalls made of yellow pine.

The cow barn was half fieldstone and half shingle with a tall slate roof that appeared to hug the building. A shingle silo with its conical roof lent a touch of fantasy to the building. The gables and proportions had a massive feel to them. Near the cow barn was the fieldstone dairy, a charming small building with the steeply pitched roof that gave it a solid feeling. The outbuildings were all located a few hundred yards from the main house, though they were well screened by landscaping. The two hundred acres of property were divided into pastures, riding rings, and fields with acres of woods beyond.

Toward the end of her life Alva Gimbel donated thirty-seven acres of the property to Greenwich Audubon Society's Land Trust and seventeen acres on the Byram River to the Byram River Gorge Committee. The rest of the estate, however, remains intact today.

Old Mill Farm

The approach to the Elizabethan magnificence of Old Mill Farm.

Principal Owner: George Lewis Ohrstrom
Architect: Lewis Bowman
Construction Date: 1928

EORGE LEWIS OHRSTROM (1894-1955) chose a brilliant architect to transform his tract of 137 acres in northern Greenwich into an estate for his family and a farm for his horses. Old Mill Farm, created from four parcels of land purchased in 1927, was developed into a spectacular English-style country house by architect Lewis Bowman.

A passionate horseman, George Ohrstrom hunted locally with the Fairfield and Westchester Hounds. He served in that organization as honorary whip and as master; in addition, he was governor of the Greenwich Riding Association. He was also a member of several other clubs, including Round Hill in Greenwich and Rookery, Hangar, Bond, and the University clubs in New York City where he worked.

A successful financier, Ohrstrom was one of Wall Street's better-known underwriters. After graduating from Michigan State University in 1918, he served as a pilot in World War I. He was credited with shooting down the last German fighters of that war. In 1920 he married Emma King Riggs. They had three children. At the time of his marriage, he was working in New York for the firm of P. W. Chapman and Company. In 1926 he formed his own investment banking firm, George L. Ohrstrom and Company, which, in the following few years, financed hundreds of millions of dollars' worth of public utilities properties. The firm became one of the nation's largest securities dealers in the utilities field. In syndication with other firms, George Ohrstrom also underwrote many large office buildings in New York. After World War II he became involved in the acquisition and operation of various industrial and oil companies, both in the United States and abroad.

The Ohrstroms divorced in the mid-1940s. George Ohrstrom remarried and moved to Virginia in 1949. As in Greenwich, he built a large country home there with stables, and he continued to participate in fox hunts as well as steeplechases and horse racing. Emma Ohrstrom retained Old Mill Farm and lived in Greenwich until her death in the early 1950s. During her lifetime she was actively involved in the Greenwich Women's Exchange, serving on its board for over ten years.

Well known in the Northeast for his country house designs, Lewis Bowman revived and popularized the Jacobean and Elizabethan architectural styles. Having earned both his bachelor's and master's degrees in architecture from Cornell University, he began his practice with the preeminent firm of McKim, Mead, and White before forming his own firm in 1923. Old Mill Farm was one of his outstanding achievements for which the Greenwich Board of Trade awarded him a medal in 1931. The house was exhibited at the Architectural League of New York in 1932 and was featured in several publications of that period.

The original estate buildings and sixty-three acres of property remain intact today in the heart of Greenwich's horse country. A curving drive leads to the open meadow on which the main house is sited. The outbuildings are located to the right of and beyond the main house and slightly downhill from it. They include the stables, also designed by Lewis Bowman, and a small farm group. The main house sits on a gently sloping site, hugging the earth. At the rear, where the land drops away, the house is more open with its full height and mass visible.

A tall stone wall, punctuated with a gate, lies to the left of the house. It visually directs the visitor to the stone-gabled entry, which is left of center in the facade. A massive stone-and-brick chimney stack to the left, and a second, taller, stone-faced gable to the right, work with the steep ludovici tile roof to form the major elements of the facade. The architectural effect is strikingly Elizabethan: massive, protective, asymmetrical, and monastic.

The rear facade of the main building.

The rear facade of Old Mill Farm is an encyclopedia of Elizabethan and Jacobean architectural details. Banks of leaded-glass windows lighten the stone walls of the lower story. The second floor is built of half-timber with brick fill, the color harmonizing with the soft red tiles of the roof. Asymmetrically arranged gables give a sculptural quality to the facade; the chimney stacks act as counterpoints. The various

Georgian woodwork is the feature of the library.

projections are juxtaposed against the shadows formed under archways and arcades. A raised terrace, faced with stone, forms the transition between the bulk of the house and the lawn that falls away from the building.

A visitor enters Old Mill Farm under the limestone Tudor arch of the entry gable and passes through a vestibule of cut stone with a slate floor and on into a magnificent stair hall. The Ohrstroms incorporated quantities of antique paneling in their home. The stair hall walls are clad in coffered paneling, and the ceiling is heavily beamed. The staircase is reputed to be Elizabethan: its large carved newel posts, spindles, and rails attest its authenticity. Under Lewis Bowman's skilled guidance, it appears that the staircase was designed specifically for the house.

The most notable room in the house is the Great Hall. Constructed of stone and timber, the walls rise two stories to meet the steeply pitched ceiling that continues upward to forty feet above the floor. Timber ribs create a regular pattern against the white plaster. The steep pitch is supported by four heavily pegged arches that brace king posts. Gothic arches, repeating the rhythms of the ceiling arches, are used in conjunction with the ceiling ribs.

A large stone-faced walk-in fireplace encased in oak paneling is centered on one wall. The paneling continues around the room and is capped at the second-floor height by a carved frieze resembling Gothic windows and Tudor rosettes. A minstrel gallery on the second floor looks down into the room, and the end wall is glazed with diamond-patterned windows at clerestory height. The windows contain stained-glass panels designed for the Ohrstroms and referring to events in their lives. There is, for example, the seal of the University of Michigan, Ohrstrom's alma mater.

Adjacent to the Great Hall is a small library. Three walls are fitted with bookcases over cabinets. The fourth wall, with its central fireplace, shows off glorious Georgian antique pine *boiserie* that matches the other woodwork. The doors are also antique, and they match the richly carved door frames and their horizontal pediments as well as the cornice molding and window framing. A bank of leaded-glass windows looks out over the property. The library also has a fine plaster ceiling with a central medallion and perimeter molding in high relief. An intimate room, the library is quietly elegant.

Also decorated with exquisite Georgian woodwork imported by the Ohrstroms is the dining room of Old Mill Farm. More richly carved than that of the library, the dining room paneling is honey-colored, and the panels are divided by fluted pilasters that support a large cornice molding. The fireplace is accented by a deeply and finely cut surround and topped by a large rectangle of molding designed to accept a painting. The dining room doors are capped with ornately carved triangular pediments. The ceiling in this large room is plaster with an Adam-style central medallion and an oval line of high-relief plaster that follows the perimeter of the room.

Also on the first floor is a spacious service wing located to the right of the entry. It includes the pantry, the kitchen, and a three-bedroom staff apartment.

The second floor of the Ohrstrom home includes the master bedroom suite of a bedroom, a dressing room, and a pair of baths. There are also seven other bedrooms and related baths divided into family rooms and guestrooms as well as a second staff apartment of four bedrooms, a kitchen, and a bathroom.

Of the outbuildings at Old Mill Farm the stable is the most striking. A long low building, the stable, at one end, is built of stone and holds a five-room apartment for the groom. Attached to it are the actual stables built of wood. In addition to the tackroom, which had a fireplace, are six box stalls. The stable section is punctuated by a series of heavy-timbered arches with a decidedly Elizabethan feeling. Between the arches the siding is vertical boarding with groups of small multiple-paned windows. A large peaked tile roof, accented by vents, makes the stable appear close to the ground and strongly reflects the vision of Lewis Bowman.

Another stone building on the property was designed to house the staff. Called the Community House, it was divided into four separate staff apartments.

The grounds of Old Mill Farm consist of open lawns around the house featuring specimen plantings, a walled garden to one side of the house, and meadows that recede into the woods. There is a pond and a stream that flows through the northern edge of the land. One can easily envision the family's horses grazing in the pastures and the sounds of excitement from elegant parties given in the main house. Old Mill Farm was a horseman's haven—and an exceedingly elegant one at that.

The Orchards

The impressive Greek Revival entrance of The Orchards.

Principal Owner: Tyler Longstreet Redfield
Architect: Frank Ashburton Moore
Construction Date: 1909-1919

THE GLORIOUS white Georgian-Colonial mansion that crowns a four-hundred-foot rise off Round Hill Road was known until recently as Seabury House. Between 1947 and 1983 the stately wood-framed residence was the conference center for the Protestant Episcopal Church and the home of its presiding bishop, the scene of countless meetings and endless activity. However, it was first conceived as a quiet country estate; it was a working farm in 1909 when Tyler Longstreet Redfield brought the 112 acres from Benjamin Fairchild. The rolling land contained extensive woods, a brook, a three-acre lake, and splendid apple orchards. Redfield aptly named his new property The Orchards.

Tyler Redfield (1865-1922) was born in Clifton Springs, a small town in northern New York State, forty miles below Lake Ontario. He took advantage of the opportunities offered by the long period of unusual peace and enormous economic growth that followed the Civil War and developed a career in printing and publishing. In 1881 he joined his brother, Judd, as a partner in the New York City printing firm of Redfield, Kendrick, and Odell. At the same time, he was vice-president of the Redfield Advertising Agency and publisher of *Newspaperdom*, a monthly trade paper for editors. His interests included civic responsibilities and sports; he was a director of the Putnam Bank in Greenwich and a vice-president of the Bank of Pinehurst in North Carolina, where he owned a large estate known as Box Court. He was also an incorporator of the Greenwich Hospital and a trustee of the Brunswick School. His club memberships included the Field Club of Greenwich and the Greenwich Country Club, the New York and the Indian Harbor yacht clubs, and the Apawamis Club in Rye. He married Lydia Wright Pearson, and although they had no children of their own, she had four sons from a previous marriage; the youngest, Oliver S. Pearson, changed his name to Redfield in a gracious gesture to his stepfather.

In July 1909 Redfield hired Frank A. Moore of New York City to be the architect of his thirty-two-room mansion. The approach is a broad, straight drive lined by birch trees whose white trunks echo the six great Doric columns supporting the Greek portico above the entrance. Two long wings reach out on either side, perfecting the harmony of understated magnificence. The slate roof is topped by seven tall brick chimneys; three dormers on each wing carry windows whose arches are defined by the delicate tracery of the fan motif used on top of the towering Palladian windows of the first floor. The fan motif appears many times: in the semicircular windows at the center of the main portico, above the French doors to the second-floor balcony, in four oval windows—two on each wing—and even in the arches over the gates in the stone wall bordering the property. On the southern face of the mansion there are fan windows in the porticoes of the two wings that jut out from the building at right angles to the flagstone terrace, and the design is repeated above each of the seven dormer windows in the roof. A white balustraded widow's walk nestles like a tiara above them all, Moore's fanciful digression from classicism. Although it is set deep in the lush countryside, The Orchards claims a spectacular view described by one of Redfield's friends as "delightful . . . up and down the Sound for twenty-five miles."

The spacious entrance hall, which includes a marble-faced fireplace, is centered by a three-story gallery reached by a divided staircase. The stairs meet on the second floor where the landing gives access to the balcony above the entrance. Off the reception hall is the sunken living room with an exquisite paneled fireplace, a molded ceiling, and gigantic Palladian windows. French doors open to the terrace, whose broad steps lead to the formal gardens. Handsome fireplaces

The central portion of the estate complex.

The Palladian windows and garland balustrade of the east wing.

The arbor.

and paneling also enhance the formal dining room, the library, and the music room, which once held an electric Aeolian pipe organ. Before it became Seabury House, The Orchards had a glass-enclosed breakfast room which looked onto a tiled porch covered by awnings.

There are six master bedrooms—one with two dressing rooms—and six baths on the second floor. Originally there were two sleeping porches as well. Another four bedrooms and two baths are on the third floor, and an entire wing was given to the service establishment. In all, the mansion contains more than 21,000 square feet of living space.

After Judd Redfield was married at The Orchards in 1911 to Emily Rockwood in a magnificent wedding that featured a breakfast catered by Delmonico's, he brought his bride home from their wedding trip to Pinehurst to live there. Although there was certainly sufficient space for the newlyweds in the great house, it is likely that they occupied the twelve-room colonial house on the estate known as Dover House, also designed by Moore and completed in 1910. A five-room cottage is attached to Dover House by a covered walk, built at the same time as the servants' quarters. The eight-room stone gate lodge was also finished in 1910. A six-room farmhouse and a two-room bungalow were on the property when Redfield bought it, as were the barn and the stables. Redfield added a garage, a greenhouse, and a tennis court.

The facade.

Unfortunately, Tyler Redfield enjoyed his Greenwich estate for a brief eleven years; he died suddenly in 1922 at the age of fifty-seven. His widow sold The Orchards to Herbert L. Satterlee in 1925 and moved to New York City. At her death in 1928, Lydia Pearson Redfield left an estate in excess of $1 million to be distributed among her family and various institutions, one of which was the First Church of Christ Scientist in Greenwich.

Herbert Satterlee, whose wife Louisa (1866-1946) was the oldest daughter of J. Pierpont Morgan, purchased 89 of the original 112 acres including the lake in its delightful rock-ledge setting, the gardens — both formal and vegetable — and the apple orchards. As they advanced in years, the Satterlees found that the great house required too much of their energy and moved into Dover House where Louisa Satterlee died in October 1946 at the age of eighty.

In May 1947 Satterlee, who was an ardent Episcopalian, sold 50.39 acres to the Protestant Episcopal Church of the United States of America at less than one-third of its assessed value. The sale included the main house, six additional residences, and the lake. Two months later, ill and despondent over the death of his wife, Herbert Satterlee committed suicide. The church gave 8.15 acres to the Greenwich Land Trust, subdivided 17 acres for building lots, and in 1983 sold the great house and 25 acres. The Orchards became a private residence once more.

Organ pipes, concealed at the left in the formal living room, as they appeared during the Redfield ownership.

Ream Château

Ream Château... Norman architecture in the back country of Greenwich. Gil Amiaga photo.

Principal Owner: Norman Putnam Ream
Architect: James W. O'Connor
Construction Date: 1924-1927

N 1924 Norman Putnam (1881-1964) and Mary Green Ream (1881-1975) began the construction of a French château in back-country Greenwich. The building would take three years to complete, involve dozens of men, and use tons of locally quarried stone in its attempt to reproduce several historic French landmarks within the intimate framework of a family residence. The Reams' desire to create such an unusual home reflects the legacy of culture and wealth left to them by their unusual fathers, Norman B. Ream and Adolphus W. Green.

The children of those remarkable fathers, Norman and Mary, were both born in Chicago in 1881. In the 1880s Chicago was a boom town, a huge marketplace for the commodities flooding in by rail from all over America. Men of ability were drawn to the challenges and the profits of that market. Norman B. Ream and Adolphus Green were two such men— though coming from markedly different backgrounds.

Norman B. Ream grew up on a farm in Pennsylvania, fought in the Civil War, became a clerk in a country store, and in 1871 went to Chicago as a grain commission merchant. He laid the foundation of his wealth as a broker for Armour in the famous 1879 pork-barrel "corner" and by 1883 became one of the "Big Four" sustaining the grain markets during the panic of that year. He invested his burgeoning fortune in real estate, railways, and public utilities and shifted his headquarters to New York around the turn of the century. He went on to become one of the organizers of the National Biscuit Company and of U.S. Steel Corporation and was a director of a score of other companies. Norman Ream's career was a remarkably successful and lucrative one.

Adolphus Green was born in Boston and graduated from Harvard in 1863. He worked as a high school principal and as a librarian before becoming a lawyer in 1869; his first practice was in Chicago as counsel to the Chicago Board of Trade. Corporate law became his primary focus and led to his involvement in the formation of the American Biscuit and Baking Company. In 1898, when the National Biscuit Company was formed in New York, Green was appointed general counsel and a director. In 1905 he was elected president. Although the corporate world increasingly became the focus of his interest and was to be responsible for the bulk of his fortune, at heart, Green remained a scholar.

The converging careers of these two men inevitably brought their children together. Norman and Mary, each one of six children, were in their late teens when both their families moved from Chicago to New York. The Reams lived at 903 Park Avenue; the Greens, at the Plaza Hotel. But the Greens had brought their carriage and horses by rail from Chicago to enable them to travel up to their Belle Haven weekend home in Greenwich.

During those prewar years before their marriage, Norman and Mary, like other wealthy, young New Yorkers, must have devoted a great deal of time to European travel. But for Mary, traveling with her family, the trips were a carefully designed education in history, literature, and culture. Adolphus Green was insistent that his children read extensively before their annual vacations. Once, having read Nathaniel Hawthorne's *The Marble Faun*, the children were dismayed to find the statue of the *Virgin with the Perpetual Light* removed from its original site in Rome. The Greens inquired of the Vatican librarian and in the course of having the statue replaced, became friends of the papal librarian. This love of literature and books inspired Mary to return to France to study the art of bookbinding. After their marriage Norman and Mary amassed an extensive collection of incunabula, or preprinting and early printed books, including a Gutenberg Bible, which has since been donated to Harvard University.

163

Rear courtyard tower replicates the Inn of William the Conqueror in Normandy.

The Great Hall off the entrance foyer features hand-carved beams.

In 1915 the senior Norman Ream died, leaving a sizable fortune; a few months later his son Norman bought a seat on the New York Stock Exchange to manage his investments. The next year Norman and Mary were married and lived with Norman's mother at 903 Park Avenue. However, they began to spend more time in the Greenwich area, near Mary's father's home, and in 1919 Norman sold his seat on the stock exchange. By 1923 the Reams had purchased seventy-eight acres of land in back-country Greenwich and retained architect James W. O'Connor to help them create a Norman château.

Christiano Builders undertook the massive three-year project. The stone for the walls was quarried on the site, and twelve Italian masons cut the stone and carved the reliefs; the Reams' nephew, Jack Carrott, was responsible for taking their tools to the blacksmith for sharpening each evening. The family was amazed at the ease with which the average Calabrian mason could create statues and plaques. The cobblestones in the courtyard came from New York City, torn up when the trolley lines were removed. Many of the tiles and mantels were imported from France and Spain.

The house which they built is approached by a long winding drive leading to a Belgian block courtyard. The main part of the house is symmetrical with double oak doors centered under a portcullis-styled overhang. Set between a pair of windows above the door is a bas-relief plaque of the Reams' daughter, Carolyn, seated on her pony.

The dependent wings, which are massed to the left of the main block and house the dining room, kitchen, and staff quarters, are asymmetrically grouped as though the house had expanded over a period of years. Squat towers add a solidity to the house and relieve the stark simplicity of the stone facade. For example, a tower to the right of the entry enlivens the face of the building. A second tower anchors the rear courtyard and provides a foil for the balcony and arcade. A third tower accents the rear facade. The roof of ludovici tile has a steep pitch, and the intersecting gables form visually interesting patterns. Dormers and massive chimney stacks add to the sculptural quality of the house.

The heavy oak front doors open into a marble foyer, beyond which is the spectacular Great Hall, which measures twelve by ninety-one feet. Hand-hewn beams run the length of the Great Hall and are supported by lintels carved with vine motifs. The wooden ceiling members set up a rhythm the length of the hall and contrast with the white-plaster ceiling and walls. A smooth stone-block floor adds to the medieval quality of the hall. The original decoration for the house, executed by the well-known interior design firm, McMillen, Inc., of New York, called for French Renaissance furniture to blend with the stone, beams, and wrought-iron gates and torchéres.

From the Great Hall, a visitor to the Ream estate would enter the most magnificent room in the house: an oak-paneled living room, measuring thirty-seven by nineteen feet, which featured a twenty-foot vaulted wooden ceiling. This library/living room was a copy of the top chapel at Mont-Saint-Michel. It was a room lined with shelves to house their special collection of books and featured a massive white stone fireplace as well as extraordinary carved panels, doors, and friezes between the bookshelves. Large arched windows, with leaded-glass and stained-glass insets, gave the room a venerable air. It was, however, comfortably furnished with overstuffed chairs, sofas, reading tables, and a grand piano. Antiques were interspersed among the other furnishings. A large wrought-iron chandelier hung from the center of the ceiling.

A pair of oak doors in the library led to the rear courtyard of the house, which was modeled after the Inn of William the Conqueror in Normandy. Above the door was another bas-relief—this of Norman, Jr., the Reams' son, fishing. A squat hexagonal tower, an overhanging balcony of stucco and timber, and flat arches set on sturdy wooden piers gave a look of solidity to the courtyard articulation. A central wellhead was placed at the intersection of garden paths in the medieval style.

The dining room of the château mirrors the style of the rest of the house. An elegant antique stone fireplace is set along one wall, and oak paneling rises to chair-rail height. Heavy ceiling beams add to the medieval feeling in the room. Original furnishings included a Jacobean table and chairs with a buffet in a complementary style. Adjacent to the dining room is a solarium with a tile floor and cut-stone walls.

The circular tower staircase from the Great Hall led to the master bedroom suite, consisting of a bedroom with a marble fireplace, a dressing room with a door to the balcony overlooking the courtyard, a bath with a fireplace, an oval sitting room with a fireplace, and an adjoining bath—truly a private retreat. Also on the second floor were three other double bedrooms, each of which had a fireplace and adjoining bath. Four smaller bedrooms and two hall baths completed the

Bas relief of son Norman Ream, Jr. embellishes the arch of the library door.

family quarters. Two maids' rooms and a four-room apartment were located over the service area of the house.

The house became the Reams' year-round home and the center of their active life in Greenwich. Elegant functions were held there to promote their volunteer interests in the Greenwich Garden Club, the YMCA, the Greenwich Boys Club, and the Red Cross. During World War II and gas rationing, Mary Ream rode the bus to town to devote her services to the Red Cross. Norman Ream was an avid sailor; one of his boats, a motor launch, exploded, and the rebuilt boat became the launch to Calf Island for fellow members of the Round Hill Club. Ream was also involved in financing the rebuilding of St. Mary's Church.

The Reams lived at the château for nearly thirty years before retiring to a more manageable home in Belle Haven. Norman Ream died in 1964; his wife, in 1975. Though neither of their fathers lived to see the château, in building a house of such proportions and detail the Reams paid just tribute to their legacy of wealth and culture.

Overlook Farm and Eastover

The facade of Overlook Farm, now the Convent of the Sacred Heart School. Gil Amiaga photo.

Overlook Farm
Principal Owner: Henry Steers
Original Architect and Construction Date: Unknown
Architect for Reconstruction (1908): Carrère and Hastings

Eastover
Principal Owner: Henry Steers
Architect: Unknown
Construction Date: 1916

ENRY STEERS (1868-1928) loved to race his trotters down King Street from his country home, Overlook Farm, to the Port Chester train station. From there he commuted to his New York City office at Battery Place. Steers purchased Overlook Farm in 1904 from New York banker John H. Schultz. It was a perfect blend of country house and self-sufficient farm with facilities for breeding horses. Unfortunately, but three years later, in February 1907, the house burned to the ground.

Carrère and Hastings, the well-known New York firm, designed an elegant new brick Georgian Revival house for Steers and his family. It was placed on the same site as the original house and was completed in 1908. The 1908 house was very similar, both stylistically and in size, to the house that Steers purchased from Schultz. Although he maintained a city residence on East Eighty-eighth Street, the family spent their summers, until 1916, at Overlook Farm.

Henry Steers was the older brother of James Rich Steers whose home, Faircroft, is a half mile north of Overlook Farm. The son of a banker, also named Henry, and the grandnephew of the designer of the yacht *America*, Steers was a yachting enthusiast. He was a member of the New York Yacht Club, listed as serving on the club's race committee, and the Indian Harbor Yacht Club.

Married to the former Adeline Coster, Steers was a successful construction engineer. His firm, Henry Steers, Inc., founded in 1904, was involved in large New York City construction contracts including bridge abutments and shipping piers along the Hudson River. During the 1920s he was also president of the Henry Steers Sand and Gravel Company, which sold almost all the sand-and-gravel mixtures used in New York City at that time. At his death in 1928, Henry Steers, Inc., was constructing a bridge over

Newark Bay for the Lehigh Valley and the Pennsylvania railroads.

Overlook Farm was entered from King Street. Stone walls surrounded the property and opened at a brick entryway fitted with wrought-iron gates. A long winding drive led uphill through mowed meadows defined by spruce trees, through an orchard, to the front entry. A drive partway up the hill led off to the stables, the barn, and other outbuildings, which were located downhill from the main house. The main drive ended in front of the stately portico which marked the entrance to the estate house.

The Carrère and Hastings house was a two-story rectangular brick building with matching wings. A large rectangular portico, composed of four tall fluted columns with Corinthian capitals supporting the molded entablature, marked the front entrance to the house. The paving was herringbone brick, and a balustrade defined a small front terrace on either side of the portico. The front door was flanked by attached brick pilasters and crowned with a semicircular white pediment. Windows illuminating the entry hall were on either side of the front door. Above were three bedroom windows.

On either side of the portico was a large French door/window combination which opened onto the brick terrace from the dining room and the front sitting room. The second-floor windows repeated the motif. At the top of the house, a large balustrade crowned the cornice.

The two wings on the house were enclosed sun porches. The porch to the left of the entry, off a sitting room, had a terra-cotta floor; the porch to the right, no longer extant, was similar.

A visitor to Overlook Farm passed through a very small marble vestibule into a large entry hall

167

Overlook Farm's elliptical portico as it appeared before the fire of 1907.

which originally had a domed ceiling. The formal staircase, supported by columns and pilasters, was at the rear of the room. A fireplace was centered on the right-hand wall. Its festooned mantel and surround were of plaster, decorated with cherubs holding garlands.

One could reach the dining room through pairs of walnut doors on either side of the hall fireplace. A large room, it had rectangular wooden paneling to the ceiling. A heavy bracket molding formed the cornice. The windows opened onto the front terrace and probably also onto the porch that was at the right of the facade. From there one could see across miles of Greenwich countryside to Long Island Sound.

To the left of the entry hall were two sitting rooms. The front sitting room opened onto the terrace as well as into the porch. It had a ceiling ribbed in a Gothic manner and a delicately carved marble fireplace.

The rear sitting room was elaborately paneled with coffered wainscoting and Venetian-style wall panels. Fluted pilasters bracketed the various doorways in the room and the fireplace. The cornice molding was decorated with clusters of grapes on a vine. The fireplace, in white-and-cream marble, was carved with garlands of flowers.

Upstairs were four large corner bedrooms, each of which had a fireplace and private bath. A fifth bedroom or sitting room was added over the entry hall when the domed ceiling was removed. Servants' quarters were at the rear of the house over the kitchen area.

Today the main house has been vastly altered. Later owners added a second floor over the porches, and a third floor was added over the central block of the house. The domed entry hall and the original staircase were also removed. In addition, the outbuildings, with the exception of a small barn and some sheds, are no longer extant. Today, Overlook Farm houses a school. The main building, however, retains much of its formal grace. Because many of the fields remain mowed, and some of the original apple trees are still visible, one can imagine the estate as it was in the days when the Steerses owned it.

Eastover from the Sound side. Gil Amiaga photo.

In 1916 Steers purchased six acres in the Byram Shore section of Greenwich. Apparently, with children grown and Steers's passion for horses on the wane, Overlook Farm was too much of a burden. He sold the estate to Alfred Jaretski, the attorney for E. C. Converse, owner of Conyers Manor, and built a shore-front home. Named Eastover, the house was set to take full advantage of its waterfront site. Eastover was a starkly simple masonry house shaped liked an angular U. The front entrance was at the base of the U with wings that projected forward on either side. The rear of the house featured a large raised terrace with paired staircases that led to the lawn, from which one could walk to the water's edge. Although not of the same scale or elegance as Overlook Farm, Eastover was a lovely shore home.

The front entrance of Eastover. Gil Amiaga photo.

Henry Steers died suddenly at Eastover in 1928. His widow, Adeline, inherited his considerable estate. She kept Eastover until 1944 but sold her husband's shares in Henry Steers, Inc., to Steers's brother, James Rich Steers, who renamed the firm and continued to run it until his death a decade later.

Sabine Farm

Principal Owner: Henry Johnson Fisher
Architect (1910): Hunt & Hunt, Architects
Architect for Farm Buildings (1915): Alfred Hopkins

ABINE FARM, one of the earliest homes built in back-country Greenwich by a New York businessman, was named for the original Sabine Farm located outside Tivoli, Italy. The Roman poet Horace mentioned this farm; its name alludes to the sweetness of rural life, an apt description of Greenwich back country during the early part of the century when this home was constructed.

Henry Johnson Fisher (1854-1965) and his wife, the former Alice Gifford Agnew (1879-1946), purchased approximately 210 acres and sited their home at the intersection of two stone walls amid rolling fields with a view to the west. These stones, as well as those from other nearby walls, were used to construct their home in 1910.

Vice-president of the Crowell Publishing Company at the time he built Sabine Farm, Henry Fisher later became chairman of the McCall Corporation, from which he retired in 1946. He was a lover of books and greatly admired Horace, hence his choice of the name for the estate.

The main entrance to Sabine Farm faces east. Located in a central three-story section, which protrudes slightly forward from the flanking two-story wings, the doorway is framed by a Tudor arch of limestone set under a flat stone lintel. On either corner is a small medallion carved with the letters SF. Under the corners of the doorway arch are two stone faces: one smiles to show happiness at a visitor's arrival; the other looks sad at his departure. These masks set the overall tone of the home: friendly, straightforward, and family-oriented. Above the doorway is a stone plaque, the house's cornerstone. It is inscribed "November 1910," the date of the house. A triplet of stone-framed, leaded-glass windows above the doorway gives light to a second-floor bedroom.

The right side of the entry is marked by a two-story bay with long windows which illuminate the stair landing. The doorway and adjacent bay jut out slightly from the main body of the house, clarifying the entry. As originally constructed, this section was capped by a wooden balustrade and the bay by a wooden tower facade. The balustrade served as a cornice or parapet and functioned as a balcony for an octagonal third-floor room affectionately called the tower room. The wood facing was changed to stone as part of the renovations made to the house in 1926.

One enters Sabine Farm through a small vestibule leading directly into an oak-paneled hall. In the first half of the hall one sees the staircase to the right and a corridor to the kitchen and service areas. The newel posts of the stair are topped by a pair of oak squirrels, animals the family enjoyed watching in the gardens. To the left is a book-lined library. The second part of the hall, distinguished by its oak framing, continues forward to a doorway opening onto a pergola-covered terrace. To the right is the door to the dining room; on the left, the door to the living room.

This entry hall is paneled with English oak stained a medium brown. The rectangular panels are articulated at doorjambs by finely carved fluted pilasters. A handsome deep molding defines the ceiling. The original flat plaster ceiling was remodeled during the 1926 renovations; medallions were added at that time, the designs copied from Haddon Hall, the great Elizabethan house in England. Chairs and settees of the Jacobean style were used to furnish the entry hall, and a tapestry hung on one wall lent it a decidedly English air.

One of the most remarkable rooms at Sabine Farm is the small library to the immediate left of the entry. This bookcase-lined room, with its Caen stone fireplace, looks out over the front drive and the gardens to the south. Above the stained bookcases is a remarkable cycle of painted panels executed by William A. Mackay. These panels were inspired by Sir Thomas Malory's *Le Morte d'Arthur* and illustrate nine events from the search for the Holy Grail. Vivid colors and

South view of the enclosed garden.

clear illustration in a style derived from the Pre-Raphaelites make the panels extraordinary. The story unfolds sequentially around the room: (1) Merlin Casts an Evil Spell; (2) Arthur Draws the King's Sword from the Anvil; (3) The Dolorous Stroke; (4) Vivian Binds Merlin in a Great Oak; (5) The Castle of the Maidens; (6) King Solomon Builds the Ship; (7) The Girdle of Fortitude; (8) The Grail Is Found; (9) End of the Quest. Combined with shelves of books and linen-fold carving on the small cupboards below the bookcases, the painted panels lend a truly remarkable air of romance to an exquisite study.

The large rectangular living room flanks the library to which it is connected by a movable panel/bookcase but is generally entered from the entry hall. A glorious view of the walled garden may be seen from the large bay window on the south side of the house. A second set of five windows faces west and is protected by a porch that forms part of the porch-pergola-porch articulation of the western side of the building. The living room ceiling is detailed with graceful plaster tracery patterns which were installed in 1926. Family lore tells of the "mistake" or "puzzle" in the ceiling; one rib does not fit the overall pattern. It was said to have been an intentional error to bring good luck.

The family dining area, with its large five-unit window, also has a view to the west. It, too, is protected by a porch which serves as the outdoor dining room. The room has a brick-faced fireplace with a simple pilastered surround on the north wall. The room is paneled to eight-foot wainscot height. Above, a line of molding finishes the room without making it overly formal.

Upstairs are five family bedrooms, three of which have fireplaces, and there is also a sewing room. The master bedroom is located over the living room and thus affords views to the west and of the garden. The tower room on the third floor was a single room until alterations were made in 1926, when two small bedrooms were added.

Staff quarters at Sabine Farm were located beyond and above the kitchen on the north side of the house. They included a servants' hall on the first floor and six staff bedrooms and a bath on the second floor.

As with many of the estates in Greenwich during the period before World War II, the grounds of Sabine Farm were used for crops and animals. The architect Alfred Hopkins designed a handsome complex of outbuildings for Henry Fisher about 1915. They are reminiscent of the shingle style, and architectural ornament was accomplished with tower forms, bell-shaped rooflines, and cupolas. The barns and outbuildings of stone and heavy timber with shingle roofs were sited to the south of the main house. The main group of buildings is U-shaped with the hay barn forming the base of the U. A cow barn with an adjacent dairy and a garage form the other flanks. Additional buildings include a horse barn, with stalls for hunters and farm horses, space for carriages and tack, and a paddock. Apartments for the help were above the barn.

The Fishers kept seven or eight cows and a bull. They had the requisite three or four riding horses, the most famous in the family having been named Playboy, whom only their daughter could ride. Chickens, squab, and pigs were kept for family consumption; vegetable gardens were also cultivated; and a greenhouse was maintained. Although the Fishers sold some of their dairy products in town, the bulk of the produce was consumed by the family.

The staff required by the estate lived either on the property or nearby. The chief gardener lived in Riversville and walked to work through the Ernest Thompson Seton property, once owned by the Boy Scouts.

As with many estates of this type, the period during and after World War II brought changes. It was no longer economical to maintain the animals, and they were finally sold. The use of the greenhouse and gardens diminished after Alice Fisher died. Although much of the land constituting the estate has been divided, the main house and several acres are still lovingly maintained.

Goldenrod, one of the Fishers' prize horses.

The stables in 1923.

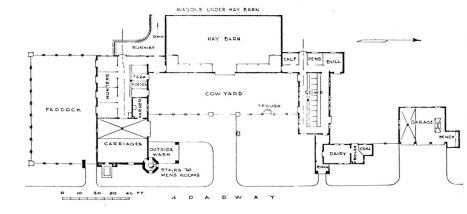

Sunridge Farm

The rear facade of Sunridge Farm's main building retains its original distinctive character despite major changes. C. Christopher Semmes photo.

Principal Owner: Clarence Woolley
Original Architect (1912): Unknown
Architect for Remodeling and Additions (1928): Henry E. Senft

INFORMALITY may be found among the Greenwich estates as evidenced by Sunridge Farm, once owned by Isabelle and Clarence Mott Woolley (1864-1956). This farmhouse is a realistic copy of the rustic *fattoria* of northern Italy, the farmhouses of the Veneto region. The site of this home affords long views to the south and west and provides a magnificent setting for the informal Italian villa-style house.

Clarence Woolley purchased his first parcel of 49 acres in Greenwich during 1915. Further acreage was added in succeeding years until his property totaled approximately 222 acres along Quaker Ridge in western Greenwich. The Woolleys and their three children lived at Sunridge Farm until 1944.

An imaginative and prominent industrialist, Clarence Woolley was credited with developing and promoting one of the basic necessities of twentieth-century living, indoor heating. He founded the American Radiator Company (now American Standard) and served as its president and then as its chairman for many years. In addition, he was vice-chairman of the War Trade Board during World War I, a class C director of the New York Reserve Bank, a trustee of Columbia and St. Lawrence universities, and a recipient of honorary L.L.D.'s from both institutions.

In 1928 the Woolleys extensively remodeled and enlarged the original house on their property, entrusting the work to architect Henry E. Senft. Today Sunridge Farm, in its mix of dressed fieldstone with stone quoins and cement stucco, paved courts, and barrel-tiled rooflines, evokes a pastoral feeling. The house is approached by a winding drive which passes through a pair of stone gateposts with wooden gates. Masses of pines, rhododendrons, azaleas, and laurels flank the drive as it leads to the slate-paved courtyard which once featured a central fountain. The main house is L-shaped and consists of two main blocks: the bedroom wing to the left and the main living area to the right, or north. Staff quarters extended farther to the north of the main living area.

The facade of the house is constructed primarily of stone. Heavy timber trusses support ludovici barrel-tiled roofs and emphasize the informality of the home. The second-floor windows feature plank shutters, and wrought-iron grilles were designed for each of the first-floor windows in keeping with Italian tradition. The main entry loggia is paved in black-and-white marble squares and leads directly to the large sitting area with its double-height ceiling and corner walk-in fireplace. The formal dining room is to the right, overlooking the gardens, the reflecting pool, and the view to the west. A loggia sun porch leads from the sitting room into the formal parterred gardens. A crenelated balcony above the sun porch provides a similar view from the bedroom area on the second floor. The gardens extend axially from the sun porch with an antique wellhead as the focal point at the end of an arbor vitae *allée*. Balustrades and retaining walls define the sloping view to the west and lead to the reflecting pool and then to the rustic garden house which was used for outdoor sunning.

A second entrance to the house leads from the entry courtyard to the master bedroom suites. The two main bedrooms of the house are connected by a vaulted and groined loggia-style corridor and are paved with imported terra-cotta tile. These are two of the most stunning rooms in the house.

As mentioned earlier, the bedroom wing added in 1928 was designed by Henry Senft. Clarence Woolley's bedroom, at the far left, measures approximately twenty by thirty feet and boasts impressive twelve-by-twelve-inch rough-hewn oak beams taken from the Pickhardt cigar factory building which once stood on the southern edge of the estate. The architect used the handsome beams to support a natural-wood-paneled ceiling. An antique carved wood fireplace in the Elizabethan style complements the room.

A longer view of the entire rear facade. C. Christopher Semmes photo.

The gazebo and reflecting pool in 1929.

A second major bedroom is adjacent but far more feminine with its Venetian-style wood panels and moldings. One would assume it to have been Isabelle Woolley's room. The ceiling is detailed with delicate filigree moldings; wood niches and doors are customized according to the architect's plans; and the fireplace has a black onyx surround.

Both of these rooms, as well as others throughout the house, feature numerous bronze casement windows of European style and manufacture. Custom-designed recessed radiators were installed below each window. Several of the paneled doors in the bedrooms, as well as other rooms, have floral paintings in the door panels. In addition, many of the windows were fitted with interior shutters also bearing floral and ribbon motifs.

In keeping with Woolley's commercial interests, several baths feature fine Art Deco tilework and fixtures from American Standard. One exceptional bathroom off a large bedroom on the second floor was designed in 1937, and many of the tiles hand-painted by Henry Varnum Poor. The design included wall tiles laid in a decorative manner, and a tile floor custom-painted in a large floral motif, signed and dated by the artist. A corner sink designed in an inverted

The entry courtyard. The original entrance was under the stone arch at the right. C. Christopher Semmes photo.

fluted cone shape incorporated the blue-and-green color scheme of the wall tiles and the floor. Soap dishes and accessory shelves were carefully integrated into the overall design.

The grounds, designed in 1932 by Armand R. Tibbitts, made extensive use of native landscape material. Large groups of Australian and Japanese black pines, clumps of birch, and rhododendrons, azaleas, and dogwoods were used. Existing specimen trees were carefully saved where possible. Lawn areas were edged with these native materials, and formal gardens were maintained to scale. A green garden, parallel to the arbor vitae *allée*, was designed to be seen and entered from the bedroom wing. Lawn and floral borders led in stepped terraces to the reflecting pool. In addition to vineyards and tobacco plantings, vegetables were grown in a separate walled garden behind the servants' wing. A greenhouse and a pumphouse completed the garden buildings adjacent to the main house.

The requisite outbuildings for the Sunridge Farm estate were located just north of the main house. A ten-car garage, with staff quarters above, was but a few hundred yards from the main house. Farther north still were the stables. Both Clarence Woolley and his son were avid polo players, and a portion of the estate grounds was maintained as polo fields. Additional houses for the staff were also built nearby, each of the outbuildings reflecting the main house in style and building materials. They were all built of stucco with matching tile roofs, creating a stylistic unity to the entire estate.

After the Woolley family disposed of Sunridge Farm, portions of the property were sold. The Bruce Memorial Golf Course was built on some of the property. Both the garage complex and the staff houses became residences. The main house was divided into two separately owned properties, one of which comprises the former staff quarters and kitchen. The second building now contains most of the public rooms and family bedrooms. Nonetheless, architectural details in the house have been saved where possible, and the gardens remain magnificent.

Knob Hill Farm

The imposing entrance of Knob Hill Farm, now the guest house of American Can Company. All Knob Hill photos by Gil Amiaga.

Principal Owner: Samuel Fuller
Original Architect (Circa 1916): Unknown
Architect for Rebuilt Estate (1929): Peabody, Wilson and Brown

*K*NOB HILL FARM was the Greenwich estate of Samuel L. Fuller (1875-1963), a successful New York stockbroker. Born in Middletown, Connecticut, where his father was a physician, he was educated at Phillips Andover, to which he donated a bell tower that bears his name, and at Harvard College. In 1899 he joined Jackson and Curtis in Boston, one of the original firms merged into Paine Webber, and he was made a partner in 1904. In 1906 he moved his wife, the former Constance Greenough, and his three children from Boston to New York. At that point in his career, Samuel Fuller joined Kissel Kinnuitt and Company, a firm which specialized in underwriting, usually in conjunction with J. P. Morgan and Company. He formed his own company, Fuller, Rodney and Company, in 1932, and after its merger with Merrill Lynch, Fuller remained there for the rest of his career, having become a general partner in 1941.

Samuel Fuller, a man of many interests, gave generously of his time. During World War I he served as an official of the Emergency Fleet Corporation. He was involved as both deputy director and director of Red Cross operations in Italy. Governor Franklin D. Roosevelt appointed him to the St. Lawrence Power Development Commission in 1930. He also served as trustee on the boards of the Massachusetts Hospital for the Insane and the Beekman Downtown Hospital in New York. In addition, he served on numerous corporate boards including those of Sinclair Oil; International Paper; Revere Copper and Brass; the New York, Chicago & St. Louis Railroad; and the Seaboard Air Line Railroad. Samuel Fuller died on November 19, 1963, on Martha's Vineyard where he had a home. He was eighty-eight.

The estate that the Fullers built in Greenwich was located on Upper King Street. Family diaries note that the family lived, or at least summered, there soon after 1916. They kept a town house on Park Avenue in New York as their winter residence.

Knob Hill Farm's main house was a large elegant stone building set amid gardens, orchards, and pastures. Unfortunately, at the end of March 1928 while the family was vacationing in Europe, the house burned to the ground. Local newspaper accounts put the loss at over $400,000. All of the contents were destroyed, according to the *Greenwich News and Graphic*, with "the exception of some furniture, books, valuable oil paintings and oriental rugs carried from the library by firemen."

Despite the loss, the Fullers rebuilt the house in 1929. They hired Elliott Brown of the New York firm Peabody, Wilson and Brown to prepare their plans. The second Fuller home follows the original foundation and was stylistically similar to the first. Minor changes evident in the rear facade were the raising of the roofline to a full second floor, thus eliminating second-floor dormer windows, and the adding of some third-floor rooms. Because the Fuller house is preserved today as a corporate guesthouse, it remains much as it was during the Fuller family's tenancy.

One entered Knob Hill Farm via a curving stone-walled driveway from Upper King Street. The drive split on approaching the house. To the right the road continued to the outbuildings, which were sited to the south and downhill from the main house. Large clapboard barns with shingle roofs were built to house the Fullers' horses and cows, and apartments were located there for the staff. The chicken coop was nearby; beyond lay a pond and acres of apple orchards.

The driveway to the main house turned north, past the brick walls of an enclosed garden, to an entry court. A smooth limestone portico accented the central block of the cut fieldstone house. Fieldstone wings flank both side of the entry. The double hung windows were framed with shutters bearing the monogram F. Four Doric columns supported a Greek

179

This view of the rear facade clearly shows the granite quoining and brick overwindow detail.

Looking across the terrace from the opposite angle.

Revival entablature and announced the simple but elegant front door. A finely detailed stone pediment and carved door frame added another elegant note to the entry.

A visitor to Knob Hill Farm passes through a rectangular entry hall paved in black-and-white marble, a corridor at the left leading to the pantry and the kitchen area. Across from the entry door, the visitor passes under the sweeping staircase into the gracious living room.

The large, high-ceilinged living room is decorated with smooth polished paneling and heavy polished beams. A stone fireplace to the left features carved lions' heads and a wrought-iron-hinged ash screen. Though the paneling is simple in design, the warm wood tones dominate the space and give a richness to the room. Long windows and French doors provide access to the slate-and-grass terrace which runs the length of the south side of the house. The view from the living room sweeps over the terrace to the formal perennial beds, the sunken garden, and the woods beyond. Along the north wall of the living room, the staircase ascends to the family living quarters. It blends into the wood of the paneling, yet is distinctive with its brass spindles and brass banister.

Adjacent to the living room fireplace is a tall pair of doors that leads to the elegant dining room. The dining room of Knob Hill was designed for entertaining. A large room, it too has doors opening onto the terrace and a fireplace to cheer winter evenings.

To the west of the living room a small tile-floored reading room serves as a corridor to the commodious paneled library. The library is gracious and inviting with its mellow-toned bookcases and smooth wall paneling. A large storage closet, concealed by a movable panel, is further secured by safe doors. In the floor of the storage room is the trapdoor leading to the wine cellar below. Two sets of doors flanking the library fireplace open onto the side veranda, a covered porch with views into the walled garden as well as over the terrace and the formal gardens to the south.

The second floor includes a master suite and sleeping porch over the library and hall bedrooms, most with fireplaces and private baths, for the children. Additional small guest bedrooms for the children's friends are located over the dining room and the pantry. The household staff is quartered above the kitchen and the servants' hall as well as in third-floor rooms.

As a retreat from New York, as a home designed for entertaining, and as a well-run estate, Knob Hill Farm is one of the most gracious of Greenwich's distinguished estates.

Semloh Farm

The approach to Semloh Farm's main estate building, now the Stanwich Club.

Principal Owners: Edwin T. Holmes / Jacob Hekma
Architect: Unknown
Construction Date: 1910

SEMLOH FARM might be referred to as a gentleman's farm-estate, since it embodied features of both. Certainly the large house with its multitude of rooms put it in the estate class, just as much as the large herds of cows, two thousand chickens, numerous pigs, farm and riding horses, and 320 acres qualified it as a farm. Located in the Stanwich section of Greenwich, this farm was formed in 1909-1910 when Edwin T. Holmes (1849-1920) and his wife purchased several parcels of land totaling 218 acres for approximately $110 an acre.

Edwin T. Holmes's father founded the Holmes Electric Protective Company, which manufactured and distributed burglar alarms. Working with Alexander Graham Bell, he invented the automatic cut-off switch for telephones. He was also involved in the early marketing of telephone systems in Boston and New York, as well as of various electric call systems. Edwin T. Holmes continued the successful leadership of the company.

The name given to the property and inscribed on the stone-and-timber entrance gate on North Street, was Semloh Farm, Holmes spelled backwards. A large fieldstone house was constructed in 1910. Shortly after the building was completed, the stone facade was stuccoed over at the request of Marion Holmes, as she did not care for its roughness. Today the stucco facade gives a smooth elegance to the house.

A central doorway, flanked by windows and a tall Palladian window grouping over the doorway, accentuates the front of the house. The slate hip roof appears to embrace the central portion of the house. Shutters are used to punctuate the regularly spaced double-hung windows. A service wing joined the central facade at the right side of the building.

The rear of the house underwent several changes made by the Holmeses as well as others made by later owners. Early photographs (1913) show a colonnaded porch on the rear facade. By the 1920s the colonnade had been removed, and an octagonal summer room was built on the left side of the house, balancing the service wing at the right. Along the back of the house, overlooking fields and gardens, a terrace was constructed so that the family might enjoy views of Long Island Sound to the left and the formal gardens to the right.

Much of the interior of the house reflected the decor and furnishings typical of a particular country or decorative style. Extensive later remodeling changed much of the interior layout. Remaining from the original construction, however, is the oak-paneled entry hall and the double staircase which flanks two walls of the entry hall. From the entry one passes directly into the living room, which features the original plaster-ribbed ceiling. The family dining room with its fireplace is to the right of the living room. A small sitting room with a fireplace, adjacent to the living room, remains, as does the octagonal summer room.

In addition to the main house, the Holmeses built the requisite outbuildings. There were barns for the seventy to eighty cattle, stables for both riding and farm horses, large chicken coops for several thousand hens, a piggery, and an eight-car garage. The Holmeses also built a greenhouse to supply flowers for use in the main house.

Housing for the staff included a two-story shingled superintendent's house and apartments within the outbuilding complex. All the outbuildings were constructed of wood in the shingle style popular at the turn of the century. A summerhouse was set on an island in one of the lakes.

In order to maintain Semloh Farm, a large staff was required. In the Holmeses' day, the staff included four or five gardeners for both the produce and the extensive floral gardens, which featured fifteen fountains; two poultrymen; three men for the cows; and one man for the pigs. The indoor staff included two butlers, a cook, a kitchen maid, and three other domestic servants to handle the family's needs.

183

Facade of Semloh Farm in 1913.

The rear facade and newly planted grounds.

Mildred Holmes and her prize-winning wolfhounds, 1916.

Off to an outing in the Holmes' coach-and-four, 1918.

Edwin T. Holmes.

The broad vista of the "little farm" with the main house in the distance.

After Edwin Holmes died in 1920, his widow and his son, Edwin T. Holmes, Jr., retained title to the property until 1926, when they sold it to a second owner. In 1929 the estate was purchased by Jacob Hekma (1879-1949), a Dutch immigrant who had been successful in the utilities field. When he died in 1949, Hekma was a director of the Commonwealth and Southern Corporation. One of the young men whom Hekma had brought into that company was Wendell Willkie, and for that reason, in 1940 Semloh Farm became the site of several Republican meetings and much political activity. Apparently, had Willkie defeated Roosevelt, Jacob Hekma might have been named secretary of the treasury.

Semloh Farm was unofficially renamed Boerderij, meaning "little farm" in Dutch. Greatly enlarging the farm, Hekma increased the acreage, bringing the total to approximately 320, and made numerous improvements to the land and the house. He extensively remodeled the interior of the house, combining many of the small rooms into a more manageable twenty-room home. A staff of eleven, nevertheless, was retained to maintain the interior of the house. Outdoors Hekma added many plantings; hired a landscape architect to mark out tree plantings along new bridle trails; and employed a crew of thirty groundskeepers to set and maintain the paths, plantings, and gardens. The estate continued to function as a gentleman's farm, with sixty cows supplying milk to Round Hill Dairy and approximately two thousand chickens whose eggs were sold locally. The Hekmas also kept six riding horses for family use.

Although a number of estates foundered during the Great Depression, Jacob Hekma set up an endowment of $1 million in government securities for his home. Thanks to the fund's income, he was able to guarantee employment for his staff of sixty throughout the depression and the years following it.

The Hekma family continued to occupy the house after Jacob Hekma's death and rented the fields to commercial farmers, thus ensuring that the pastures remained grazed and in good condition. In the 1960s the family sold the estate to a local corporation composed of Greenwich residents who transformed the grounds into a fine golf course. Semloh Farm continues to be appreciated today as the Stanwich Club.

The main entrance of Faircroft in 1985, then the corporate headquarters of Avco Corporation. Gil Amiaga photo.

Principal Owner: James Rich Steers
Architect: Carrère and Hastings
Construction Date: 1905; Rebuilt: 1925

HEN James Rich Steers (1869-1936) married, he wanted to present his wife, Mary Dolores Beales, with a pearl necklace, a customary gift at the time. His wife declined, requesting instead that he give her a trip to Europe every two years. During one of their trips to England and Scotland, Mary Steers saw a Georgian house that she adored. On their return she and her husband, a civil engineer by training, worked out all the plans for a Georgian house of masonry construction based on the English country home they had seen.

In 1904 they purchased a fifty-seven acre parcel of land in northwest Greenwich, then hired Theodore Blake of the firm of Carrère and Hastings to do the final drawings. The only item not fully specified by the Steerses was the staircase. "Well, we had to leave *something* for you to do!" Mrs. Steers told the architect. The family named their Greenwich home Faircroft, the name being derived from "fair," to describe the view from the site, and the Scottish word "croft," meaning "farm."

James Rich Steers owned a successful construction company in New York City in conjunction with his brother, Henry. The firm carried Henry Steers's name until his death in 1928 when James bought his brother's share and renamed the firm J. Rich Steers, Inc. The firm received many major New York construction contracts and, among other jobs, built Pennsylvania Station and several New York bridge abutments, including those for the Narrows Bridge and the Throgs Neck Bridge.

The Steers family spent their summers, from mid-May until early November, in Greenwich, leaving their New York City residence for winter use. During these summer months, Steers commuted to his New York office at Battery Place. The children, J. Rich, Jr., and Etta Mary, spent their summers playing tennis, riding horses, or making the day-long trip by carriage to the American Yacht Club in Rye for swim-

ming. Many of Mary Steers's friends summered in the Rye area, and J. Rich Steers, who was an avid sailor, also spent a great deal of time at the club.

He was also a member of the New York Yacht Club and had a special affection for that club. His great-uncle, George Steers, was the naval architect who designed and built *America*, the New York Yacht Club boat that won the America's Cup from the British. For generations afterward, the family maintained a strong interest in the America's Cup races.

While in Greenwich, Steers enjoyed his hobby of raising Morgan horses for which the estate was put to good use. He was instrumental in saving the breed, and he and a friend, Chauncy Stillman, established a society to preserve the breed. The Steerses kept ten or eleven horses and their colts at Faircroft, and the family rode and hunted, Etta Mary riding sidesaddle, through the countryside.

The Faircroft property originally had a farmhouse occupied by the former owner of the property, Fred Field. After selling to the Steerses, he continued to live on the property, working as superintendent and managing the farmlands. In order to clear the hilltop for fields and the site for his own house, Steers had the farmhouse relocated farther down the hill for the Field family.

Always an athletic person, J. Rich Steers died suddenly in 1936 at the age of sixty-seven while playing at the New York Racquet Club. A year after his death, the family sold Faircroft.

Faircroft's main facade was two stories high, symmetrical and approximately 180 feet long, at the center of which was a two-story portico. Four Doric columns carried a horizontal entablature crowned with a balustrade. The portico framed the pedimented front door. Long windows flanked the door and were repeated on the wings on either side of the entry. The second-story windows were slightly smaller but repeated the pattern established on the first floor. Shutters accented all the windows.

Faircroft as it originally appeared before the fire in 1924.

The original split staircase from the second floor.

Faircroft was probably the first house ever constructed of smooth poured concrete blocks laid like stone. The effect was that of limestone. The rear facade of the house featured a large covered porch that ran the length of the house and created a large outdoor room. The roof above was also supported by Doric columns. From the porch one looked out over a large grass terrace, defined by a stone balustrade, and down to the horse pastures. Mary Steers was an avid and knowledgeable gardener. She was a member of the Rye Garden Club and served a term as its president. Her perennial garden was to the left of the terrace, and her rose gardens, featuring a cherub fountain fashioned by Louise Yarnell, were to the right.

In 1924 the house was destroyed by fire. Only the exterior masonry walls were left standing. The tremendous heat generated by the fire caused the masonry blocks to expand nine inches. As a result, the house was declared a complete loss. Undaunted, Steers began its reconstruction, and by June 1925 the new building was complete.

In the rebuilding of Faircroft, Steers made several changes. He eliminated the third-floor bedrooms, which were originally guest quarters for Mary Steers's family. She was guardian for her younger sister and three brothers after the early death of her parents. As these children were grown by 1925, the third floor was no longer required and, therefore, was eliminated. Shortly after the fire, Mr. Steers also added a swimming pool.

A 1920 property description noted "two dwelling houses, one 80-foot × 180-foot [the main house], as well as 8 outbuildings, stables, a garage and a water tower." The stables and kennels were located to the northeast of the main house. The water tower, located to the south of the main house, was a well-known Greenwich landmark until it burned in the 1970s. The tower and its pump system provided all the water needed on the estate during the early years.

Fred Field's house was located to the southeast of the main house and was connected with the main house by a drive. Nearby were the other farm buildings and sheds, as the Steerses kept some cows for milk and had large vegetable gardens for produce.

Fortunately, a number of photographs taken prior to 1925 exist, so that the original interior of Faircroft is known. The front door, centered under the portico, led to a large rectangular entry hall. A fireplace enlivened the left wall near the door leading to the dining room. The music (or Adam) room was to the right of the entry. Opposite the front door was the staircase, which was set in an arcade of Doric pilasters paired with Doric columns. The wide stair rose a half flight, then split in opposite directions to finish its run to the second floor. Turned spindles supported a carved banister. The entry hall had a parquet floor and ceiling moldings and was decorated simply with floral wallpaper, oriental rugs, and antiques. A hand-painted scenic landscape ran along the foyer wall.

The dining room, which was across the entry hall from the music room, was also simple in its furnishing. Painted wainscot panels decorated the lower two-thirds of the room and framed the fireplace on one wall. A damask paper was used above the wainscot. The room was sparsely furnished with an antique Sheraton table, chairs, buffet, and secretary.

Steers's smoking room was situated behind the dining room overlooking the rose gardens. Decorated in a masculine style with grass-cloth walls, an oak-and-brick fireplace, stained woodwork, and Mission-style furniture, the room evoked a comfortable, relaxed mood. A trophy fish hung over the fireplace. Originally the room also held a model hull of the yacht *America*. Members of the family recall that women were not allowed in the room without Mr. Steers's permission.

To the right of the entry in the original house was the delightfully delicate music room decorated in the style of Robert Adam. Without question, the glory of the music room was the plaster-relief ceiling which featured a central medallion with delicate filigree spokes to an outer oval band, which followed the perimeter of the room. Medallions and filigree designs filled the corners. Below were bands of intricate cornices with carved brackets and rows of egg-and-dart molding. The wall panels were treated in a French manner with the panels framed in molding and the centers of the panels painted in a contrasting color. Long tie-back silk draperies, edged with fringe, hung at the windows. Antique Venetian wall sconces complemented the delicate design of the room, as did the marble fireplace surround set with a finely carved mantel, the English antiques, and the large oriental rug. An unusual feature was a harp which was occasionally played by a relative of the Steerses, though not by any member of the immediate family. After the fire the room was reconstructed but without the elaborate ceiling and cornices. By 1925 the Steerses could no longer find craftsmen capable of executing such detailed work.

To the right of the entry hall was the commodious living room, which had deep cove moldings, a fireplace, and two sets of French doors opening onto the rear veranda. Parquet floors, a large oriental rug, English antiques, and upholstered furniture made the room handsome, but gave it an unpretentious, country house feeling.

The second floor of Faircroft had a master bedroom suite over the living room, the son's bedroom over the music room, and there were also two guestrooms. The daughter slept over the entry from where she enjoyed peeking down on arriving guests. Over the smoking room was a large linen closet in which was stored a fine collection of monogrammed linens that Mrs. Steers had had embroidered by convent girls in Ireland. Beyond, over the pantry and kitchen, were quarters for the staff of eleven.

After Steers's death in 1936, the family sold Faircroft. A later owner, Claire Boothe Luce, removed the original staircase and replaced it with a glass-spindled circular stair. Mrs. Steers, described by her daughter as a Victorian type, apparently reflected on the change and remarked, "Wouldn't it be fun to be under that stairway when a woman came down!"

Today the interior of Faircroft, which houses business offices, bears no resemblance to its original design. The exterior of the main house, however, has been restored to simulate its 1925 condition. Office wings have been relatively discreetly tucked into the rear of the building. From the road Faircroft looks almost as inviting as it undoubtedly did when the Steers family enjoyed their summers in Greenwich.

The Nuckols Estate

The facade of the main house.

Principal Owner: Henry Wade Nuckols
Architect: Thompson and Churchill
Construction Date: 1927-1929

HENRY WADE NUCKOLS (1868-1958) and his wife, Florence Belding Nuckols (1870-1958), lived in Pelham Manor, New York, for seventeen years prior to building a home in Greenwich. In 1927 they purchased 182 acres of land on Tod's Hill from the brother of J. Kennedy Tod. Thompson and Churchill designed a large Georgian Revival house for the couple. The estate, completed in 1929, included a horse barn, a gatehouse, and a greenhouse.

Henry Nuckols was a native of Indiana and an 1893 graduate of Indiana University. His business career began with Armour and Company in Chicago, and then he entered the fledgling auto industry. Nuckols moved east to become president of the Columbia Motor Car Company in Hartford, Connecticut. Subsequently he served for fifteen years as vice-president of the Valvoline Oil Company. Florence Nuckols was also from the Midwest. Her father, Alvah Belding, was a pioneer in the silk industry, after whom the town of Belding, Michigan, was named.

The house the Nuckolses built was designed for entertaining and its location chosen for its proximity to the Greenwich riding trails. Both of them were active in the horsemen's association and enjoyed hosting hunt breakfasts.

The main house is set back on the original parcel of land. The drive passes a small gatehouse, a U-shaped barn, and a greenhouse before ending at the two-story colonnaded porte-cochere that framed the main entry. One enters the Nuckols house through a small marble-floored vestibule, then proceeds through double doors into the two-story stair hall. A hall to the left leads to the service wing. The stairway rises one half flight along the right-hand wall, joins a landing over the entry vestibule, and continues to rise along the left-hand wall to the second floor. The stair hall features paneling on the walls to the second-floor height, and turned

spindles support a graceful mahogany handrail. A two-story arcade of paired columns and fluted pilasters, in the Corinthian style below and in the Doric above, divides the stair hall from the major reception area of the house.

Guests were received in "The Hall," a thirty-seven-foot-long room that has a Vermont marble fireplace centered on the far wall so that it can be seen through the stair hall arcade on entering the house. On either side of the fireplace are glass-paned pairs of French doors leading out to a spacious brick terrace. Centered on the left-hand wall is a pair of doors that opens into the spacious dining room. On the right-hand wall opens a twelve-foot-wide corridor that runs twenty feet to the spacious living room at the southern end of the house. Since the house was designed for large-scale entertaining, the architects created an open feeling by placing the dining room, The Hall, the corridor to the living room, and the living room itself on an axis. One can throw open the doors in these rooms to create an open space one hundred feet long.

On either side of the passage between The Hall and the living room are more intimate rooms. On the eastern side, overlooking the terrace is a small library (about twelve by twenty feet) with bookcase and trim of stained wood, plaster ogee cornices, and oak floors. The library boasts a pair of windows looking to the east and a set of French doors that also open onto the brick terrace.

Across the corridor from the library is a bookcase-lined den measuring about twenty feet square. A black marble fireplace, set between Palladian-style bookcases, gives elegance to this simple room. A pair of windows overlooks the western lawns. The room has an adjoining hidden bar.

A longer view of the approach and facade in 1984.

The rear facade and terrace overlooking the Sound.

The large and gracious living room is at the southern end of the corridor. Windows face east and west; French doors flanking the fireplace open to a bluestone terrace at the southern end of the room. Despite its large size—twenty-eight feet eight inches by thirty-eight feet—the room is sunny and friendly. The moldings are simple but elegant as throughout the house, with dentils and decorative acanthus leaves at the ceiling. Simple pilasters flank the fireplace. The overall feeling is that of graciousness.

From The Hall, toward the northern side of the house, is the dining room. As with the other major rooms, the view from the dining room is to the east. The room's warmth comes from simple coffered paneling which rises to cornice height. A fireplace with an oak surround is centered across from the door to The Hall. The room measures approximately twenty feet by thirty feet. It, too, has access, via French doors, to the terrace.

A small and cheerful breakfast porch, next to the dining room, provides an informal environment for meals. Windows facing north and east admit abundant light to this small room—which measures fifteen feet four inches by twenty feet two inches. Soft colored Mexican tile was used on the floor and in the fireplace surround. The most detailed ceiling moldings in the house are found here.

The master suite, above the library and the living room, is separated by a door and a small foyer from the rest of the second floor rooms. Henry Nuckols's bedroom is above the library facing east. It features a fireplace, a wall of fitted closets, and a bath with marble floors and walls. A private hall leads to what was Florence Nuckols's room, which is above the living room. This part of the suite is far more commodious, with a twenty-one by thirty-foot bedroom, bay windows flanking the fireplace, a large dressing room with walk-in closets, and a substantial marble bath. In addition, a sewing room with ample closets is accessible from this room.

Since the Nuckolses had no children, the remainder of the second floor was divided into guestrooms, three of which open off the second-floor corridor. Each has a private bath, a fireplace, and is generously proportioned. One guestroom is located over the dining room, a second over The Hall, and the third over the den.

A portion of the walled garden.

In case more guest space was needed, the center portion of the third floor was finished to include two adjoining guestrooms with baths. Both rooms have eastern views of Long Island Sound. A large cedar-lined storage area completes the third floor.

The kitchen wing with its large butler's pantry and kitchen at the north end of the Nuckols house is extensive. The indoor staff of six shared two sets of back stairs, a rear porch, a servants' lavatory, several commodious closets, and a servants' hall on the ground floor. Above this area are four servants' bedrooms and hall bath, the housekeeper's room and bath, and a laundry or pressing room.

Basement facilities include furnace and coal rooms, six storage rooms, both warm and cold wine storage, a repair shop, a main laundry room, and a service lavatory.

Today the house stands much as it was constructed. Although the porte-cochere is missing, as are the original shutters, the interior structure and details have been well preserved. The property has been divided, but unobtrusively. Even the barn, now converted to a house, retains much of its character. A visitor can easily imagine the gaiety of a hunt breakfast or a garden party on the Nuckolses' terrace overlooking the Sound.

The east terrace from the walled garden.

Conyers Manor

The south facade of the manor house.

Principal Owner: Edmund C. Converse
Architect: Donn Barber
Construction Date: 1904

THE CONCEPT of a large country estate as the capstone to a successful business career was epitomized by Conyers Manor, built by Edmund Cogswell Converse (1849-1921). Converse named his estate Conyers Manor after the old English spelling of Converse. Not only did Conyers Manor overshadow the other grandly conceived homes in Greenwich, it was also one of the most profitable estates in the Northeast. The estate had tremendous economic impact on both Greenwich and nearby Banksville, New York. Tons of produce and dairy products were sold in both towns, and Conyers Manor employed a large number of townspeople.

After having spent several summers in the Belle Haven section of Greenwich, Edmund Converse hired a Greenwich realtor, William Smith, to acquire a parcel of 1,000 acres of land in the back country. Several pieces were put together by 1904, and construction of the main buildings began. By 1913 Converse owned 1,330 acres of farmland and woodland in northern Greenwich and southern North Castle, New York. It was a private domain unlike any other.

Edmund Converse was born in Boston, one of five children of Sarah Peabody Converse and James Cogswell Converse. The elder Converse, a Boston businessman, founded the National Tube Works and served as its president in the 1870s. Young Edmund was reared in Boston and graduated from Boston Latin School in 1869. According to later accounts, the family suffered some financial reverses at this time, so that young Converse was unable to attend Harvard College for which he had prepared. Instead, he went to work as an apprentice at National Tube Works, which was relocated from Boston to McKeesport, Pennsylvania, at about the same time. In 1882, he was granted a patent for his invention of lockjoints for water and gas tubing, a significant industrial development which, along with his other patents, brought millions of dollars' worth of orders to the company.

During this period Edmund Converse married Jessie MacDonough Green (d. 1912). Their happy marriage on January 2, 1879, produced three children: Antoinette MacDonough, Edmund Cogswell, Jr., and Katherine Peabody Converse.

By 1899 Converse had become a general manager in the corporation and subsequently was associated with William Nelson Cromwell in an attempt to combine the principal wrought-iron and steel-tube concerns in the country. Acting finally as agents for J. P. Morgan and Company, they brought about an amalgamation of about twenty such companies. In 1893 Converse was elected president of this enlarged firm, which was later incorporated into the U. S. Steel Corporation. For his contributions and participation, Converse became a large stockholder of U. S. Steel Corporation, as well as a vice-president and director.

Thus, by the age of fifty-two, Edmund C. Converse had had a notable impact on American business. His interest in manufacturing corporations must have waned during the period of U. S. Steel's formation for he retired from the firm in 1902. During the next fifteen years Converse was occupied with banking, serving simultaneously as president of three major New York banks: Liberty National, Astor Trust, and The Bankers Trust Company.

Converse had many interests other than business; certainly the formation of Conyers Manor was one of them. After having secured the first six hundred acres, he hired three people who were critical to the development of the estate. Donn Barber was chosen architect for this unique commission. George A. Drew was hired away from the Massachusetts Agricultural College in Amherst, Massachusetts, to be superintendent of the estate. He is credited with the early site planning and the farm layout, the orchards, and the water system. Henry Wild was fully employed for eight years designing and supervising the aesthetic plantings on the property.

The elegant salon of the manor house.

The clock tower and manor garage.

The projecting wings of the enormous dairy barn.

Donn Barber's designs for Conyers Manor were drawn from several sources. He was a proponent of the English country manor as the model for estate-sized summer homes, an inclination tempered by his training which included studies at Columbia University and the Ecole des Beaux-Arts in Paris. Barber formed his own practice in 1900. His commission from Converse, then, was critical to the early development of his career. It included the design of the so-called manor house as well as the gate house; the James Converse House; the Strong House; the eight greenhouses; the manor garage; the manor stables; the boathouse; the clock tower; the dairy barn; the poultry barn; the superintendent's house built for George and Rachel Drew; the farm garage; and the blacksmith's shop.

The vast extent of Conyers Manor is evident when one considers that, in addition to the buildings designed by Barber, all the original farmhouses on the property were retained and used as housing for the nearly two hundred employees. Additional buildings were added as needed and were constructed of similar materials. By 1913 there were over forty buildings on the property.

The estate was divided into several areas each with a particular function. The site chosen for the manor house was the crest of a hill at the southeast corner of the property from which there were views to Long Island Sound. Nearby were all of the buildings related to the manor house itself. The main farm buildings were located slightly to the west and south. The orchards and cold-storage barns were to the northeast, where the topography and microclimate were best suited for fruit culture. The northwestern part of the property was left in woods or planted with orchards, although certain support buildings were located there. The estate was unified by an internal road system.

One entered Conyers Manor from the southeast corner of the property. There, at the gate, was located the first building constructed. The gatehouse was built of stone quarried on the property, as were all the other buildings designed by Barber. This attractive, if modest, gatehouse was the home of the head gardener and his family. Its stone walls and its steeply pitched shake roof were in the style of the manor house. The area by the gate was planted with specimen spruces. Evergreens, rambler roses, and clematis were planted near the house itself.

Evergreen plantings lined sections of the drive to the manor house. The drive, along its one-mile route to the house, passed a small lake designed as a woodland and water garden. It featured Japanese-style bridges and woodland walks around the lake and over a spillway. Mallard and pintail ducks and greylag geese lived on the lake and nested on its small island. A larger lake, which supplied the estate's water, was located in the northern section of the property. Left wild but well stocked with game fish, it had a stone Adirondack-style boathouse in which a launch was kept. Children of the farm staff recall happy days fishing and swimming there. From this lake Converse gave water to the town of Greenwich during a winter of drought.

The drive continued up the side of the hill with woods to the right and hayfields visible to the left. It swung around to approach the manor from the north. The manor house was an imposing four-story stone building with a steeply pitched green-tile roof with triangular dormer windows and gables at either end. Wooden balconies projected from the second floor. Shutters accented the windows. The overall stylistic feeling was of a European country villa with elements borrowed from English, French, and German sources. The overall dimensions were approximately 188 by 88 feet. It was built of stone quarried at the farm, concrete, brick, and steel to make it fireproof.

On entering the manor house from the porte-cochere, a visitor passed through a marble-floored vestibule. To the right was Converse's office or den; across the vestibule was the salon. Directly in front of the visitor was the large, two-storied living hall which opened onto the terrace. Behind the living hall fireplace was a billiard room. Continuing forward through the living hall a visitor would find the library to the left, the dining room directly ahead, and a large butler's pantry to the right. None of the service facilities was on the main floor. A large portion of the basement was used for the kitchen, pantries, and storage. Supplies and food were brought up by a dumbwaiter.

The salon was one of the more elegant rooms in Conyers Manor. The walls were hung with silk, and the furniture was in the style of Louis XV. The paintings, however, were the main attraction. Best known was Sir Anthony van Dyck's portrait of *Mademoiselle de Gottignies*. Most of the two dozen other canvases were late nineteenth-century French works from the Barbizon and the Beaux-Arts schools. Charles

Daubigny's *The Oise near Anvers, 1873*, J. B. C. Corot's *Le View Pont, Nantes* and C. E. Jacque's *Forest of Fontainebleau* were highlights of this collection.

The living hall at the center of the house was the principal entertainment area. Its two-story height and intricate, if heavy, paneling made the room imposing. Above an Italian carved stone fireplace was the balcony which gave access to the second-floor bedrooms. A pipe organ was encased in the wall adjacent to the dining room. The organ console faced the fireplace and was located between doors leading to the terrace. In this room many examples of Converse's principal hobbies were displayed: he was a passionate collector of Oriental pottery and bronzes as well as snuffboxes, ancient glass, and Persian faience. The many display cabinets as well as potted palms and tapestry fabrics gave the room a Victorian air.

Converse's smoking room was a retreat from the rest of the house. It was his office for the estate but also contained a steam room and, just below, a bowling alley which was used by the manor bowling teams. The ceiling of the office featured plaster ogee tracery, and the walls were dressed in tooled and painted leather.

The library at Conyers Manor projected east from the central block of the house at the end of the living hall. Filled with books on a range of subjects, it was where the Converses hung their English portrait paintings including Thomas Gainsborough's *Portrait of Count Rumford*. The painting had special meaning for Converse as he was descended, through his mother, from this man. Nearby were two portraits by Henry Raeburn, Sir Thomas Lawrence's *Portrait of Lady Wheatley*, and a portrait by George Romney. The room was decorated in tapestry cloth with a changeable ground and mulberry plush edged with gold galloon trimming. The furnishings were oak with the side chairs upholstered in needlework.

Converse was fond of specimen game hunting and had a substantial gun collection. Hanging in the dining room were trophy heads: a moose, a caribou, a bison, two reindeer, and a stag. The dining room, paneled in dark wood, had heavy beams across the ceiling. Above the large, carved fireplace hung Benjamin Constant's painting, *Interior of a Harem*. The dining room furniture was Italianate in style; the chairs were upholstered in leather. On one sideboard Frederic Remington's bronze, *Coming Through the Rye*, was displayed.

The farm stand on North Street about 1940.

The "overflow" barn.

The second floor of the manor house consisted of bedrooms accessible from the balcony around the living hall. In addition to the master suite there were four large bedrooms, each with a fireplace, silk draperies, and a tiled bath with elaborate fixtures. The master suite was located over the salon, vestibule, and Converse's office. Mrs. Converse's sitting room was the same size as the salon below and featured a delicately carved fireplace. The large master bath measuring seventeen by eighteen feet, was placed between the sitting room and the Converses' bedroom.

Running the manor house fell to Converse's butler and valet named Walker. He was recalled by a family member as being an imposing figure "who was garbed in a cutaway during the daytime and full dress suit and white tie at night." His assistant was a handsome young Englishman, Ernest Kendall. They were in charge of the household staff of nineteen, most of whom lived in the third-floor servants' rooms.

Visitors to the manor could reach the terrace from the living hall and the dining room. It overlooked a long mirror pool planted with water lilies and sur-

rounded by landscaped gardens. The rose gardens were to the south, between the manor house and the greenhouse complex. From the eight greenhouses came both flowers and out-of-season fruits such as grapes, cantaloupes, oranges, lemons, and nectarines. A full-time staff of sixteen was employed to tend the delicate crops grown in the greenhouses.

Additional buildings related to the manor complex included the fully equipped six-bay manor garage where cars for the Converse family were kept. To the north of the main house were the manor stables which housed the family's horses and carriages. Its most notable features, according to former employees, were a central water fountain made of gray marble and the marble feed troughs in each stall.

Converse built two private residences on the estate for members of his family. The James Converse House was built for Converse's brother's widow, Louise Keinfelder Dunshee Converse. It was designed in the style of the other manor buildings and had its own carriagehouse and pool house. For his daughter Katherine and her husband, Benjamin Strong, Converse built a similar twenty-six-room house. It, too, had a separate carriagehouse with living quarters above. Both houses were of the same construction as the main house. They were, however, gabled in a more picturesque fashion than the manor house.

In the fall of 1912 Jessie Converse died at Conyers Manor; she was in her sixties. Two days after her death, Louise Converse, Mr. Converse's sister-in-law, died very suddenly. In less than a week the sixty-three-year-old banker lost two people who were very important to him.

One of the greatest surprises to Converse's friends and business associates was his remarriage on January 30, 1914, to Mary Edith Dunshee. Converse had known her for some time as she was Louise Converse's sister, and had lived for several years with Louise Converse at her home at Conyers Manor.

The fine reputation of Conyers Manor as a farm was created by George A. Drew. Drew, his wife Rachel, and their children lived near the center of the farming complex. He supervised a staff of nearly two hundred people. Drew began to clear and replant farmlands for fruit crops soon after Converse purchased his land. By 1910 the apple orchards were producing hundreds of bushels of fruit that were sold both locally and out of state. But apples were only a portion of the produce from Conyers Manor farm. An account in the *Greenwich Graphic* notes that "the peach crop is valued at between $30,000 and $40,000 a year . . . [and] hay valued at $30,000 is produced. A ton of asparagus a day is sent to the market in the season. Pears, plums, strawberries are grown in large quantities." George Drew also supervised the dairy herd that produced thousands of gallons of milk and cream for the manor and for sale. Butter, stamped "ECC," was made and packed in the dairy. The E-shaped dairy barn which housed the herd and had hay storage and apartments above, dwarfed all the other buildings. Like the manor house, it was built of stone with fanciful dormers and vents. Around 1911 Drew hired a poultryman. Shortly afterwards accounts show approximately 2,000 Rhode Island Reds and Leghorns were kept as well as smaller numbers of pheasant and quail. That venture was as successful as all others under Drew's supervision and made Conyers Manor self-sufficent except for red meat.

Edmund Converse died on April 4, 1921. Most of his estate went to his widow and to his children in spendthrift trusts. He made significant philanthropic gifts, and he remembered each of his employees in his will. None of the family, however, was able to maintain the vast property, or was especially interested in doing so. The second Mrs. Converse visited the estate occasionally but preferred to live in Europe. In 1927 she put Conyers Manor up for sale.

Frederick Sansome purchased the estate and immediately changed its name to Homewood. He had grandiose plans but fortune was against him. Because he had purchased the property with an $800,000 mortgage and had other business liabilities, he was unable, during the depression, to continue holding the estate. According to the terms of his mortgage and the trusts of Converse, Conyers Manor reverted to The Bankers Trust Company in 1931. The bank took over management of the estate, keeping the dairy and orchards producing under the supervision of a capable superintendent until the late 1930s.

Today the remains of the manor house have been torn down, and the property is being sensitively subdivided. Those original buildings which have not fallen prey to time and vandals are being reconstructed. Fields are being cleared, and the woods and landscaping are being restored where doing this is economically feasible. Though the era of Conyers Manor is over, glimpses of its glorious past can still be seen and appreciated.

Authorship

The author or authors of each estate section are listed below.

The Shore Estates	
Indian Harbor	Virginia G. Monroe
Quarry Farm	Renee F. Seblatnigg
The Frueauff Estate	Renee F. Seblatnigg
Whitney Castle	Renee F. Seblatnigg
Innis Arden	Virginia G. Monroe
Kincraig	Val P. Storms
Horse Island	Renee F. Seblatnigg
Walhall	Val P. Storms
Round Island	Renee F. Seblatnigg
Rocklyn	Kathy H. Richards
Glen Airlie	Renee F. Seblatnigg
The Pryory	Renee F. Seblatnigg
Miralta	Renee F. Seblatnigg
Milbank and The Towers	Renee F. Seblatnigg

The Mid-Country Estates	
Rambleside	Val P. Storms
The Castle	Val P. Storms
Grahampton	Val P. Storms
Northway	Virginia G. Monroe, Cynthia Petrow
The Rockefeller Estates	Val P. Storms
Beausite	Val P. Storms, Susan D. Elia
Three Oaks	Val P. Storms
Lochwold	Val P. Storms
Chelmsford	Val P. Storms
Northbrook Farm	Val P. Storms
Khakum Wood	Val P. Storms
Fort Hills Farm	Val P. Storms
The Johnston Estate	Virginia G. Monroe
Greyledge	Val P. Storms
Wyndygoul	Val P. Storms
Wildwood Farm	Val P. Storms
Hilltop	Val P. Storms

The Back-Country Estates	
Dunnellen Hall	Virginia G. Monroe
Chieftans	Susan D. Elia
Old Mill Farm	Susan D. Elia
The Orchards	Virginia G. Monroe
Ream Château	Susan D. Elia, Kathy H. Richards
Overlook Farm and Eastover	Susan D. Elia
Sabine Farm	Susan D. Elia
Sunridge Farm	Susan D. Elia
Knob Hill Farm	Susan D. Elia
Semloh Farm	Susan D. Elia
Faircroft	Susan D. Elia
The Nuckols Estate	Susan D. Elia
Conyers Manor	Susan D. Elia

Sources

Information about many of these great estates is fragmentary especially from the earlier years. Data pertaining to estate families and their properties has been gathered from both primary and secondary sources. These sources include interviews, probate court records, deeds, plans, maps, school and town reports, as well as newspapers, periodicals, city directories and oral histories.

The most valuable help came from interviews with past or present estate owners and their families, in addition to present and past employees and their families, whose cooperation and encouragement contributed materially to the completeness of the text. The next most important information source was the various newspapers which have been published in Greenwich over the years and appeared under several mastheads.

Finally, in a few instances research turned up a limited number of books, articles, miscellaneous publications, and oral histories, the most important of which are listed below.

Books

American Can Company, *History of the Guest House Located on the Site of American Can Company's Corporate Headquarters, Greenwich, Conn.* Greenwich, American Can Company, 1981.

Avco Corporation, *1275 King Street.* Greenwich, Avco Corporation, 1975.

Baker, John Cordis, Ed., *American Country Homes and Their Gardens.* Philadelphia, John C. Winston Co., 1906.

Biographical Dictionary of American Business. Westport, Conn., Greenwood Press, 1983.

Bonham, Valeria Langeloth, *Utopia in the Hills.* New York, R. M. McBride, 1948.

Bott, Penny, *Music in Greenwich, 1950s and 1960s.* Friends of Greenwich Library Oral History Project, No. 814.

Chapman, Josephine L., *Personalities in Greenwich.* Friends of Greenwich Library Oral History Project, No. 248.

The Encyclopedia of World Art. New York, McGraw-Hill Book Co., 1961.

Feree, Barr, *American Estates and Gardens.* New York, Munn & Co., 1904.

Finch, Louise, Ed., *A Driving Tour of Historic Greenwich.* Fairview Printers, 1982.

Hering, Oswald C., *Concrete and Stucco Houses.* New York, McBride, Nast and Company, 1912.

Lewis, Arnold, *American Country Houses of the Gilded Age.* New York, Dover Publications, 1982.

Lloyd's Register of American Yachts. London, Lloyd's Registry of Shipping, 1910-1930.

Manning's Yacht Register. New York, Manning's Registry, 1895-1903.

Metropolitan Museum of Art, H. O. Havemeyer Collection Catalogue. New York, Metropolitan Museum of Art.

The National Cyclopedia of American Biography. New York, James T. White & Co., 1896-1907.

New York Yacht Club Book. New York, 1880-1930.

Notable American Women, 1607-1950. Cambridge, Harvard University Press, 1971.

Pearson, Henry Greenleaf, *A Business Man in Uniform.* New York, Duffield & Company, 1923.

Pryor, Sam, *All God's Creatures.* New York, Vantage Press, 1982.

Saarinen, Aline B., *The Proud Possessors.* New York, Random House, 1958.

Silver, Nathan, *Lost New York.* New York, Houghton Mifflin Company, 1967.

Stein, Jean, *Edie, An American Biography.* New York, Alfred Knopf, Inc., 1982.

Wahl, Theodore, *The Fairfield-Westchester Hunt.* Friends of Greenwich Library Oral History Project, No. 586.

Wall, Bennett S., and George S. Gibb, *Teagle of Jersey Standard.* New Orleans, Tulane University Press, 1974.

White, Norval, and Elliot Willensky, *AIA Guide to New York City.* New York, The Macmillan Company, 1967.

Who's Who in America. Chicago, A. N. Marquis & Co., biannual.

Wild, Henry, *The Making of a Country Estate.* Greenwich, Conn. and New York (private publication, undated).

Withey, Henry and Elsie, *Biographical Dictionary of American Architects Deceased.* Los Angeles, Hennessey & Ingalls, Inc., 1970.

Newspapers

Daily News-Graphic
Greenwich Graphic
Greenwich News
Greenwich News and Graphic
Greenwich Observer
Greenwich Press
Greenwich Time
New York Times
Portchester Daily Item

Periodicals

American Architect
The Architect
The Architectural Record
Arts and Decoration
The Bolling Field Beam
Country Life in America
Creative Art, A Magazine of Fine and Applied Art
The Nutmegger
Scribner's Magazine
The Spur

Archival and Research Sources

American Can Company
American Institute of Architects
Avco Corporation
The Greenwich Library
Town of Greenwich, Public Records
Library of Congress
New York Public Library
Port Chester Public Library

Illustrations and Credits

In the following, all illustrations appearing in *The Great Estates*, including uncaptioned margin embellishment, are listed in the order in which they appear in the volume. The abbreviated caption or brief description of each is followed by the photographer's or delineator's name where known, the source, and the number of the page on which the illustration appears. In these credits the Greenwich Historical Society is abbreviated GHS and the Friends of the Greenwich Library Oral History Project FGL.

Index